THE FREEDMEN'S BUREAU

Reconstructing the American South after the Civil War

Paul A. Cimbala

AN ANVIL ORIGINAL
Under the general editorship of
Hans L. Trefousse

KRIEGER PUBLISHING COMPANY
MALABAR, FLORIDA
2005

Original Edition 2005

Printed and Published by
KRIEGER PUBLISHING COMPANY
KRIEGER DRIVE
MALABAR, FLORIDA 32950

FROM A DECLARATION OF PRINCIPLES JOINTLY ADOPTED BY A COMMITTEE OF THE AMERICAN BAR ASSOCIATION AND A COMMITTEE OF PUBLISHERS:
This publication is designed to provide accurate and authoritative information in regard to the subject matter covered. It is sold with the understanding that the publisher is not engaged in rendering legal, accounting, or other professional service. If legal advice or other expert assistance is required, the services of a competent professional person should be sought.

Library of Congress Cataloging-in-Publication Data

Cimbala, Paul A. (Paul Alan), 1951–
   The Freedmen's Bureau : reconstructing the American South after the Civil War /
Paul A. Cimbala. — Original ed.
      p. cm. — (Anvil series)
   Includes bibliographical references (p.) and index.
   ISBN 1-57524-094-7 (pbk. : alk. paper)
      1. United States. Bureau of Refugees, Freedmen, and Abandoned Lands.
   2. Reconstruction. 3. African Americans—Southern States—History—
   19th century. 4. Southern States—History—1865–1877. 5. Southern States—
   Race relations. 6. Southern States—Social conditions—1865–1945. I. Title.
   II. Anvil series (Huntington, N.Y.)

E185.2.C56   2005
975'.00496073—dc22   2004040821

10 9 8 7 6 5 4 3 2

 **THE ANVIL SERIES**

Anvil paperbacks give an original analysis of a major field of history or a problem area, drawing upon the most recent research. They present a concise treatment and can act as supplementary material for college history courses. Written by many of the outstanding historians in the United States, the format is one-half narrative text, one-half supporting documents, often from hard to find sources.

For Peter, Who is Turning into a Fine Young Man

CONTENTS

PREFACE

On March 3, 1865 the federal government created the Bureau of Refugees, Freedmen and Abandoned Lands. The legislated name of the new agency suggested the broad scope of its charge. Contemporaries, however, commonly referred to it as the Freedmen's Bureau, thus revealing the widespread understanding that the agency was the government's answer to one of the most pressing questions of the day: what should be done with the ex-slaves?

In answering this question, Congress provided the freedpeople with guardians who, through this extraordinary agency, would have authority to control "all subjects relating to refugees and freedmen from the rebel states." In doing so, it also created an opportunity for those officers and agents in the field to become involved in an exceptional range of activities that had previously been well beyond the purview of the central government. Even a moderate interpretation of this first Bureau law and the later ones that augmented it would suggest that labor, relief, education, civil rights, and politics fell within the boundaries of the Freedmen's Bureau's charge to help the South adjust to the consequences of emancipation.

The Bureau was in some ways a radical break with past practices, but still a creature of compromise and limitations that were unique to the circumstances of the period. One should neither confuse it with an agency created by a 1930s New Deal Congress nor compare it to organizations propelled to action by a national atmosphere charged with the ideals of the Civil Rights movement of a later century. It will fall short by both measures. The Bureau was a creation of the nineteenth-century mind, shaped by war and its consequences, but also by ideas that survived in spite of—or because of—those immediate circumstances.

Ideological concerns exercised a cautious brake on how far the government and its Bureau would go to oversee this transition from the old order to the new. From the outset, for example, Congress restricted the authority of this Reconstruction police, regulatory and welfare agency by limiting the resources it placed at its disposal. Congress also weakened what power the agency claimed by alerting all individuals subject to the Bureau's supervision that the agency would only be around to protect their interests or challenge their authority for a relatively short period of time. In the end, federalism and Northern ideas about the importance of individual initiative remained potent concerns that restricted how far the government was willing to go in shaping a new South. So, too, were the varying degrees of prejudice towards the ex-slaves that permeated the North and the Bureau. All of these limitations conspired to turn the efforts of the short-lived agency into more of a promise of what could come than into a reality on which to build the future. However, they did not necessarily preclude a degree of success for the Bureau.

The ideological parameters of the agency, while limiting its vision of the future and the action it could take to implement it, did embrace such powerful ideas as the rule of law and the enforcement of legitimate federal authority in the erstwhile Confederacy as well as economic, civil and political rights for the freedpeople. The possibilities presented by these ideas, despite all of the Bureau's limitations, could have left the freedpeople and the South in a very different condition but for the resistance the agency encountered from white Southerners at every turn. In the end, the Bureau was a failure and failed enterprises do not provide the happiest subjects for historical study. Nevertheless, they still offer useful lessons. Indeed, they still demand our understanding on their own terms if we are to have a full appreciation of the past. So we study the Freedmen's Bureau and the men who expected a much different outcome than the one they left behind in the Reconstruction South.

To come to grips with Reconstruction, arguably, one must start with the Freedmen's Bureau. Paul S. Peirce's *The Freedmen's Bureau: A Chapter in the History of Reconstruction* (1904), the first serious study of the agency, remains useful for its details, but there has not been a new general survey of this federal organization since the publication in 1955 of George R. Bentley's *A History of the Freedmen's Bureau*. This is unfortunate because even as Bentley's book remains the modern foundation for understanding the workings of the Bureau, his interpretation of the agency is dated. For Bentley, the Bureau tried to do too much for the freedpeople, but for the wrong reasons: to give the radical wing of the Republican party an opportunity to exploit economically and politically the erstwhile Confederacy.

Since Bentley's day, the larger corpus of Reconstruction historiography has undergone significant change, asking increasingly sophisticated questions of the documents and further distancing our perceptions of the era from what Bentley tells his readers about one of its central players. Modern scholars may not necessarily treat the Bureau more kindly than Bentley, but they approach the era in which the agency functioned with an understanding that things were much more complex than they appeared a couple of generations ago. While historians continue to pose fresh questions about Reconstruction, they cannot escape the fact that the Freedmen's Bureau remains at the center of much of the discussion about how Republicans tried to translate Union victory and emancipation in war into a new order in peace. After all, the Bureau, a personification of the victorious North, stood as the principal expression of federal authority in the defeated South. Consequently, few scholars fail to recognize the Freedmen's Bureau's significance in post-Civil War America.

Even a short book places the author in the debt of many people. All of the historians noted in the bibliography of this volume—and especially those who have researched the Bureau—have helped shape my ideas and provided me with information that no scholar in one lifetime could have gathered. Their scholarship provided much of the basic information about the Bureau that was critical for the production of this volume. Brooks Simpson, Hans L. Trefousse, Michael W. Fitzgerald, the late Michael L. Lanza, Randy Finley, E. Allen Richardson, Caryn Cossé Bell, Mary J. Farmer, John C. Rodrigue, James D. Schmidt, the late Barry A. Crouch, and Richard Paul Fuke contributed essays to the collection *The Freedmen's Bureau and Reconstruction: Reconsiderations* edited by Randall M. Miller and myself. They influenced my thinking about the Bureau in important ways, but I am in special debt to Barry Crouch and Dick Fuke, who, along with Donald G. Nieman, over the course of many years generously shared their knowledge about the Bureau with me. Michael Musick of the National Archives and Records Service has shaped our understanding of the Bureau as much as any author because of his extensive knowledge of the agency's records and the gracious assistance that he offers to all of us who sojourn at the old National Archives Building; I remain in his debt for his help with this project. John David Smith set a scholarly example hard to follow, while showing how one could still maintain a sense of humor in the process. Randall Miller, my former teacher at Saint Joseph's College (now University) and still my friend after being my co-editor for several volumes of essays on the Civil War and Reconstruction, encouraged me to press on. Dan T. Carter, who taught me about "when the war was over" in graduate school at Emory University, continued to inspire. Once again, Elly and Peter saved me from taking myself too seriously.

West Hartford, Connecticut   PAUL A. CIMBALA

PART I

THE FREEMEN'S BUREAU

CHAPTER 1

ESTABLISHING THE FREEDMEN'S BUREAU

Wartime Developments. At the commencement of America's Civil War, there was no apparent need for an organization designed to deal with emancipated slaves because most Northerners assumed there would be no emancipated slaves. The initial general belief among Northerners was that the conflict would be short and the nation would be made whole with little disruption to the *status quo ante bellum.* During the spring of 1861, Union generals offered to assist border state officials in quelling slave rebellions. President Abraham Lincoln, always concerned about the commitment of the border slave states and always hopeful of luring the rebellious states back into the Union, publicly avoided the subject of emancipation. And in July 1861, Congress confirmed the nation's conservative stance when it accepted the Crittenden Resolution, which assured Americans that the war upon which the nation now embarked was a war to preserve the Union; the federal government had no designs on the "established institutions" of the Southern states. In September 1861, General John C. Frémont proclaimed the end of slavery in Missouri, and in May 1862, General David Hunter issued his own emancipation proclamation for Union controlled territory in South Carolina, Georgia and Florida; both found themselves rebuked by the president, their proclamations revoked.

Wartime circumstances would change the minds of Northerners who came to look upon slaves as an untapped source of military manpower and of politicians who saw emancipation as a means of weakening a determined and often victorious foe. Indeed, Lincoln's revocation of Hunter's proclamation indicated that if it became necessary to free slaves to maintain the national government, he reserved the right to do so. Laws passed by Congress on August 6, 1861 and July 17, 1862, that authorized the confiscation of certain rebel property including slaves, fell short of emancipation. At the same time, they turned advancing Union troops into armies of liberation, certainly imperfect ones, but armies of liberation just the same. The future direction of the government's policy glimmered in these and other acts, including one that prohibited Union officers from returning runaway slaves. By the time Lincoln issued his Preliminary Emancipation Proclamation on September

22, 1862 and the final document on January 1, 1863, he and many other Northerners saw a different future for their reunited nation.

Critics of Lincoln's Emancipation Proclamation rightly pointed out its limitations. The document freed slaves behind Confederate lines where the president had no real power to do so while it failed to free slaves in the border states where he might have acted with some authority. Indeed, the Union border states of Maryland and Missouri did not abolish slavery until January 1865, while Kentucky and Delaware tenaciously clung to the institution until the Thirteenth Amendment, the emancipation amendment, became part of the Constitution on December 18, 1865. But Lincoln's proclamation went beyond his realistic assessment of the political circumstances and set the war on a new tack, one shifting the nation onto a course that could not avoid black freedom with all of its implications.

Policy decisions made in Washington were critical for defining the future status of the Confederacy's slaves, but politicians alone did not plot this new course. Slaves, too, had some say in their own future. For example, on May 23, 1861, three slaves made their way to the Union lines at Fortress Monroe on the Virginia peninsula where the James River spills into the Chesapeake Bay. General Benjamin Butler, a savvy, opportunistic Democratic politician from Massachusetts, sensed the direction of the political winds in his native state and refused to return these slaves who had been working on Confederate fortifications. Without exactly proclaiming them free, he confiscated them as "contraband of war," that is, property being used by the enemy to the military disadvantage of the United States. The name, an ironic turn on the Southern argument that slaves were property, took hold; other "contrabands" followed these trailblazers into Union lines even as Union lines advanced to absorb those slaves who were more cautiously waiting to see how the war developed.

Regardless of how they came under the protection of the nation, contrabands—over a half a million by the end of the war—created the circumstances that forced the nation to think about how to deal with their future. There was no general federal policy for handling these former slaves. Army officers, such as those in the Mississippi River valley, might have been more concerned with an efficient use of the manpower contrabands provided or with maintaining order and profit on plantations within their jurisdictions than with the future elevation of the race. Their policies reflected their specific wartime concerns and black workers found themselves in situations that were little better than they had experienced before their liberation. On the southern coast of South Carolina centered at Port Royal, an area under Union control since November 1861, about 10,000 abandoned slaves competed with military men, capitalists, government agents, and philanthropists in their efforts to give meaning to freedom. Idealistic teachers offered educational opportunities to these former slaves, an early indication of the importance attached to schooling by many Northerners in setting freedpeople on the right path. Some ex-slaves were able to purchase land, a step they saw as equally important if not more so for giving substance to their own expectations. Most of them, however, continued to work for whites.

General William Tecumseh Sherman's Special Field Order No. 15, issued on January 16, 1865 after his successful march across Georgia, further complicated matters by offering an alternative that was misinterpreted by the freedpeople who fleetingly benefited from it. The general, no philanthropist or reformer, was primarily concerned with pursuing Confederates into South Carolina. He needed to rid his army of the thousands of slaves who had marched along in its train. To do so, he created a black reservation along the Atlantic coast south from Charleston, South Carolina, down into Florida along the St. Johns River as well as along the nearby rivers and on the coastal islands as a refuge for those former slaves. At the same time, he left the consequences of the temporary "possessory" titles that the freedpeople received for Congress to handle at a later date. By June 1865, General Rufus Saxton, who had been the superintendent of this reservation and who became a Freedmen's Bureau officer, had supervised the settlement of over 40,000 freedpeople and the distribution of temporary plots of land totaling some 400,000 acres. Sherman's order raised the hopes of former slaves that freedom would actually mean more than the right to earn a living and that they would be able to lay claim to the land that they perceived to be their Civil War inheritance.

Philanthropic concerns were not a high priority among military men preoccupied with winning a war. However, as soon as Northerners learned about the plight of the contrabands, they began to try to alleviate their immediate suffering and plan for their future. Lecturers and editorialists made Northerners aware of the ex-slaves' circumstances and their audiences responded enthusiastically, giving funds to tend to the needs not only of the ex-slaves but also of white refugees. Philanthropy channeled through such organizations as the American Freedman's Aid

Commission, the Ladies' Aid Society of Philadelphia, and the American Missionary Association would remain an important part of the North's efforts to cope with the wide-ranging problems of the postwar South. In the meantime, Northerners were not unaware of the fact that by providing aid they would help to keep both white refugees and the freedpeople in the South, where they would have to develop an economy based on Northern principles of free labor. The exact role of the federal government in this scheme of reshaping the postwar South was the subject of much discussion before the Freedmen's Bureau finally came into existence in early 1865.

Establishing the Freedmen's Bureau. In January 1862, Frederick Douglass rhetorically asked what the nation should do with freed African Americans. His answer was simple: "[D]o nothing with them; mind your own business, and let them mind theirs." After all, he argued, "Your *doing* with them is their greatest misfortune." He advised the nation that "the best way to help them is just let them help themselves." Douglass, the runaway slave who with some help from white friends and a large amount of personal fortitude had become a famous writer, editor and orator, feared that any government intrusion into the transitional phase from slavery to freedom would end up limiting, not expanding, the scope of the ex-slaves' liberty. For different reasons, racist Northerners and constitutional conservatives agreed that the government had no business interfering in an area that at best should be left to state authority. Other editorialists and politicians disagreed. In the December 26, 1863 issue of *Harper's Weekly*, George William Curtis editorialized, "It is idle to say that no particular class of our population demand a peculiar care, but they must all take their chance." Common sense should dictate policy, he argued, and pointed to the Bureau of Indian Affairs and the Department of Agriculture as examples of tending to the specific needs of particular segments of society.

The shape and duration of such an agency prompted debate even among supporters of federal action. Some politicians and philanthropists argued that a permanent agency should oversee the freedpeople's affairs, while others argued that a temporary agency should guide the ex-slaves to freedom. Still other reformers contended that the distribution of property to the ex-slaves would not only guarantee the freedom of Southern blacks but also remake the South. Many more believed that such an extreme measure was not necessary and would have readily agreed with an editorialist for the Auburn, New York, *Daily Advertiser and Union*. In the January 18, 1864 issue of that paper, he argued that the freedpeople would be able to support themselves and add to the wealth of the nation when "the country is settled and the system of a 'fair day's work' takes the place of force and cruelty." As is generally the case with the creations of politicians, the Freedmen's Bureau was shaped by compromise, becoming something more than Douglass had hoped for and something less than the most radical of Republicans had desired. The War Department's American Freedmen's Inquiry Commission, however, had much to do with the final form that the agency would take.

In March 1863, Secretary of War Edwin Stanton instructed his appointees to the Commission to investigate the conditions of black refugees who had come within the actual jurisdiction of the federal government. The Commission's preliminary and final reports supported the notion that the government had a responsibility to establish a special bureau to oversee the nation's transition from slavery to freedom. The June 30, 1863 preliminary report recommended a specific organization, with a commissioner supported by state and local subordinates. The Commission's proposed agency would offer medical assistance, oversee labor, assist with education, and administer justice where needed. The final report of May 15, 1864, however, revealed how uncomfortable most Northerners were with such extraordinary governmental involvement in the lives of the ex-slaves. "[T]here is as much danger in doing too much as in doing too little," the commissioners advised. "The risk is serious that, under the guise of guardianship, slavery, in a modified form, may be practically restored." Nevertheless, they recognized a pressing need for the government to offer some assistance, "not because these people are negroes, only because they are men who have been, for generations, despoiled of their rights." Temporary assistance, then, was what the government should cautiously offer to the freedpeople. At the same time, the Commission suggested a radical step forward within the context of nineteenth-century practices: "If, like whites, they are to be self-supporting, then, like whites, they ought to have those rights, civil and political, without which they are but laboring as a man labors with hands bound."

The Commission's work was important for shaping the Bureau, but Congress and the president still had to give its views legal standing. The political process leading to the passage of the first Freedmen's Bureau bill was a complicated one encompassing a range of ideological concerns, priorities and proposals. On March 1, 1864, the House passed a bill introduced by Representative Thomas D. Elliot of Massachusetts. In June 1864, Massachusetts Senator Charles Sumner made a revealing case for a freedmen's bureau (*See Document No. 1*) and the Senate passed its own version of the bill. Finally, a compromise bill that incorporated the care of white refugees, an aspect included to suggest a policy of no discrimination based on color, became law, passing both houses and receiving the president's approval on March 3, 1865.

The Duties and Authority of the New Bureau. The law establishing the Bureau of Refugees, Freedmen, and Abandoned Lands was not very specific in explaining what Congress expected of the new agency. (*See Document No. 2.*) Some things, however, were clear. The Bureau would be a temporary agency within the War Department and exist for one year following the end of the rebellion. Also, the Bureau would be the branch of the federal government charged with managing abandoned property, while exercising control over all things pertaining to white refugees and freedpeople from the erstwhile Confederacy. The agency's control of abandoned property would provide it with some funds, as Congress had not given it an appropriation to hire personnel. More importantly, placing confiscated and abandoned property under the Bureau's authority intimately linked it with one of the freedpeople's greatest hopes and disappointments. Congress authorized it to set aside "not more than forty acres" of land for loyal refugees and freedpeople to rent for three years, with the prospect of purchasing that property, thus reinforcing the myth that continues to this day that the government had promised the ex-slaves "forty acres and a mule." Congress also authorized the War Department to use its supplies of food, clothing and fuel to help the destitute, but provided little else in the way of resources to help the agency do its job. Beyond these few things, Congress did not bother to list the various legitimate duties of the Bureau that would devolve from its broad charge. The lack of specificity meant the Bureau's job would be as big as the problems its men encountered in the war-ravaged South.

The agency's unprecedented task began during what is best described as the uncertain summer of 1865, a time when Bureau organization was weak, federal policies fluid, and both black and white Southerners unsure of what to expect from the national government. Congress technically provided the agency with the power of armed force when it placed the Bureau within the War Department. In reality, the agency was at the mercy of military commanders throughout the South who were authorized to detail officers to serve in the agency. Those detailed officers continued to depend upon the good will of the military commanders for any soldiers that they might need to enforce their decisions. Also, as the Georgia assistant commissioner Davis Tillson noted in December 1865, the Bureau could not take for granted the cooperation of the Army commanders because of the different purposes of each organization; he warned that these military men "may know how to make war, but they may not know how to make peace." Thus, doing the job assigned to the Bureau by Congress would require tactful officials who could deal with the jurisdictional egos and different priorities of the military men who had the wherewithal to give teeth to Bureau decisions.

Also, by limiting the duration of its creation, Congress from the outset alerted all those white Southerners who opposed the Bureau that sooner or later they would be rid of the agency. That situation would make it necessary for the Bureau's men to convince whites as well as blacks of the benevolence of Northern intentions in such a way that the lessons learned would outlast the agency. This aspect of the Bureau's charge made it all the more essential to find men of ability and diplomacy to staff the agency from the state level down through departments to the local level of authority to make a lasting impression on former masters and slaves.

Even the geographic boundaries of the Bureau's authority were somewhat elastic and could provoke controversy. The law did not require the Bureau to deal with ex-slaves and refugees *in* the former Confederacy but "from the rebel states, or from any district of country [*sic*] within the territory embraced on the operations of the army." Thus Kentucky, a loyal slave state, would have a Bureau presence resented by many of its white citizens who had supported the Union cause. Later in February 1866, that state's governor protested the Bureau's activities in Kentucky and argued that the agency could have no authority in a state that had a government "in harmony" with Washington.

Also, caring for people, not places, meant that the agency could stretch its jurisdiction and follow its charges beyond the boundaries of the slave states. The Missouri assistant commissioner, for example, appointed officers to deal with freedmen's affairs in parts of Illinois. And Samuel Craig, who would spend most of his Bureau service in Texas, served as a Bureau officer in southern Indiana from September until sometime in November 1865 in order to tend to the needs of the large number of freedmen who had crossed over the Ohio River from Kentucky.

Freedpeople, who tested the boundaries of their new status in numerous ways, had wide-ranging notions of what they could expect from their new lives. An officer familiar with affairs in South Carolina, Georgia and Florida complained in July 1865 that the ex-slaves "take advantage of their freedom to cease work, to travel around to see the cities and towns and their 'kin folks'." Their ex-masters, disturbed by the postwar disorder resulting from black experimentation with independence, had a difficult time adjusting to the reality of emancipation. White Georgians, for example, wrote to President Andrew Johnson, who succeeded the assassinated Lincoln on April 15, 1865, asking him to modify or postpone the Emancipation Proclamation. Some of these former masters wondered if such a wartime measure could reach into peace and asked Johnson if the government was serious about enforcing it. Ex-masters in other states held similar views. In parts of Tennessee, freedpeople feared the return of bondage as their former masters appeared to assume that slavery was not quite dead. In the Houston, Texas, area planters gave evidence that they expected slavery to return "flattering themselves the Supreme Court will sometime revoke the Proclamation," and throughout the state there was the assumption that gradual emancipation would be most appropriate for Texas. Even after emancipation became part of the United States Constitution in December 1865, some Southerners resisted the change. Kentuckians—according to one Bureau man "some of the *meanest unsubjugated* and *unreconstructed, rascally rebellious revolutionists* . . . that curse the soil of the country"— argued that the Thirteenth Amendment had no force until Congress passed laws to put it into effect. At best, many of these white Southerners initially perceived the new Bureau to be their ally in reasserting control over an undisciplined labor force. (*See Document No. 3.*) All of this confusion meant that one of the Bureau's first jobs—and one certainly not specified by Congress—would be to educate black and white Southerners in the meaning of the Union victory. The task of organizing the agency to cope with this duty and all other matters relating to the freedpeople fell to a veteran soldier well known for his Christian ideals and the bravery proven by his empty right sleeve, but with little experience with ex-slaves, Major General Oliver Otis Howard.

CHAPTER 2

ORGANIZING THE BUREAU

Howard Takes Command. Major General Oliver Otis Howard was a 34-year-old Maine native, a West Point graduate, a veteran of eastern battles and western campaigns, and the commander of the Army of the Tennessee during Sherman's marches through Georgia and the Carolinas. He was an experienced officer who had learned from his mistakes on the battlefield, including the disastrous May 2, 1863, performance of his XI Corps at Chancellorsville. Nothing in his past, however, had suggested that he understood the needs of black Americans or had prepared him for the problems of Reconstruction when he accepted the job on May 12, 1865. He formally announced his assumption of command of his new Bureau on May 19, 1865 with no more assistance than his own staff and a few War Department clerks could provide. What he did have was a warning from his former commanding officer, William T. Sherman, who cautioned "it is not in your power to fulfill one tenth part of the expectation of those who formed the Bureau."

Howard, appropriately headquartered in the abandoned Washington house of a senator who had given his allegiance to the Confederacy, quickly appointed staff officers and immediately issued circulars establishing the broad principles of his administration. The ex-slaves must be secure in their freedom, he proclaimed, but "on no account, if able to work, should [they] harbor the thought that the Government will support [them] in idleness." His men would introduce "practicable systems of compensated labor" while removing "the prejudices" of the white landowners who were "unwilling to employ their former servants." As far as relief and education were concerned, his Bureau would act as a coordinator of the efforts of the various benevolent associations. On May 30, Howard issued a circular clarifying what he expected from his assistant commissioners, whose jurisdictions generally coincided with one state and sometimes another or parts thereof. (*See Document No. 4.*) In various letters to these and other officers written throughout the summer of 1865 he made it clear that "Equality before the law is what we must aim at." In June, he urged his assistant commissioners to avoid "ill-advised schemes" and to perform their duty "wisely, faithfully, conscientiously fearlessly," while reminding them that "the less

11

government, consistent with assured security of life and liberty and property, the better." Nevertheless, he remained reluctant to be too specific as to how his subordinates were to carry out the general principles he had set forth. Consequently, while Howard's presence set the tone of the Bureau and provided the agency with an important degree of continuity throughout its existence, much of what the Bureau did or did not accomplish would depend on who his assistant commissioners were, how they perceived their duty, and who they appointed as their own subordinates.

Assistant Commissioners. Howard immediately began to expand the reach of his Bureau when in the spring of 1865 he appointed nine assistant commissioners. By the end of the summer, Howard's interpretation of the Bureau law justified the appointment of three more assistant commissioners, although the Georgia assistant commissioner was formally titled "acting" technically under the supervision of the South Carolina assistant commissioner. In making these appointments, Howard favored men who had served with him or men he had come to know by their reputation, although Secretary of War Stanton guided Howard's hand in some of his selections. By the time the Bureau terminated its operations, 55 individuals had held appointments as assistant commissioners at one time or another.

The wide-ranging experiences and diverse backgrounds of Howard's assistant commissioners certainly had prepared them for positions of authority. Importantly, their wartime service indicated a commitment to the Union cause. Clinton B. Fisk, the first assistant commissioner for the Kentucky and Tennessee, was a teetotaling New York native, an abolitionist, a successful merchant, and a failed banker who bounced back to work in insurance; he was a veteran of the war's western theater. Alabama Assistant Commissioner Wager Swayne, the Ohio-born son of United States Supreme Court Justice Noah Haynes Swayne, had a Yale education, a law degree, and experience practicing with his father before fighting in the western theater, where a battle wound forced the amputation of his right leg. Rufus Saxton of Massachusetts was a professional soldier, having graduated from West Point in 1849; he had gained much practical experience working with the contrabands on the South Carolina coast during the war. Elipahlet Whittlesey had been a minister and professor at Bowdoin College in Maine, Howard's alma mater, and had served as Howard's wartime judge advocate. During the war, Davis Tillson, a civil engineer and an active antebellum Republican politician from Rockland, Maine, had served in several responsible command positions and had recruited black troops for the heavy artillery; immediately after the war he had supervised the Bureau's Memphis, Tennessee, subdistrict.

The list of impressive backgrounds goes on, but most of these men, even if they had worked with contrabands during the war, had no real idea of what they were about to tackle when they accepted their assistant commissioners' appointments. Most of them had to learn about freedpeople, intransigent white employers, labor relations, educational requirements, civil rights, and Reconstruction while on the job. Furthermore, a commitment to the Union cause did not mean that all assistant commissioners would share Howard's genuine Christian concern for the ex-slaves. And impressive backgrounds were no guarantees of successful Bureau service.

Despite such caveats, Howard's assistant commissioners held to views that could indeed prompt them to make the Bureau into an agency of change. Assistant commissioners were representatives of a government that had to reassert its authority in states that had only recently been up in arms against it and circumstances throughout the South constantly reminded them of this situation. At the least, they expected freedpeople and ex-masters alike to accept their new responsibilities while respecting the rights of each other; that concept in and of itself was an important shift away from old antebellum relationships. Assistant commissioners could readily accept Howard's early outline of his views of the Bureau's purpose concerning relief, work, and especially his injunction that they should secure for the freedpeople equality before the law, even if they were wary about the ex-slaves' ability to cope with their new status. Arkansas Assistant Commissioner John W. Sprague, for example, feared for the future of a race weakened by slavery, but insisted that "No rules or regulations can be made for the government and control of freedmen that do not legally apply also to whites." Sprague's statement is not so remarkable by modern standards, but within the context of the postwar South it was a significant challenge to the way white Southerners viewed their relationships with black Southerners.

A "Radical" Bureau. Howard's first round of appointees gave the Bureau a decidedly progressive tone, one that would earn the wrath of the president and shape the criticism of the agency in Washington and elsewhere for some time to come. Almost from the outset, reports from his supporters in the South convinced the president that Howard's agency was aligning itself with those politicians who held radical views of the purpose of Reconstruction. Later on, an investigation of the Bureau initiated by President Johnson in April 1866 apparently con firmed that the Bureau was developing into a radical agency. Two officers, Howard's former Bureau adjutant general Colonel Joseph S. Fullerton and the former postwar commander the military district of Georgia General James B. Steedman conducted the politically motivated inspection, which ended in mid-July. Along the way, on June 26, 1866 Steedman mailed a personal report to the president that aggravated Johnson's fears about the Bureau. "Our investigations have developed in my mind, clearly, that the Bureau officers, with a very few exceptions constitute a Radical close corporation, devoted to the defeat of the policy of your Administration," Steedman informed the president. "In Virginia, they were all Radicals. In North Carolina, all we met but one . . . were of the same stripe—South Carolina the same as the other two States." Alabama's assistant commissioner, Wager Swayne, "is a good officer and a man of ability," Steedman allowed, "but he is as fierce a radical as Thad. Stevens himself." He also alleged that there was a conspiratorial alliance between Bureau men and radical Republicans to undermine Johnson, with the Bureau men corresponding with radical politicians and newspapers in northern states. Hardly any of these men, he informed the president, even subscribed to a newspaper that supported Johnson's administration!

Such reports from Steedman and Fullerton only confirmed what the president had already concluded about Howard's Bureau. Johnson, after all, had begun to try to reshape the Bureau long before he had sent his two supporters on their Southern tour. Historian George Bentley notes, for example, that two personnel changes made during the fall of 1865 were important in changing the face of the Bureau, even if later ones were to become more routine in nature. In Louisiana in October Howard replaced Thomas Conway first with an interim assistant commissioner, the conservative Fullerton, who within a month unsurprisingly reversed much of Conway's freedmen-friendly policies before relinquishing the agency to the more moderate General Absalom Baird in November. Also, in September he appointed Davis Tillson as acting assistant commissioner in Georgia, effectively removing Rufus Saxton's influence from that state, while placing the agency's energy in the state behind a contract labor system to get the freedpeople back to work.

The replacement process continued into the next year, certainly changing the face of the Bureau at the state level. In January 1866, Saxton lost his hold on the South Carolina Bureau, superceded by Robert K. Scott. Scott, in ways similar to his Georgia neighbor, followed policy decisions made in Washington and restored property to white land-owners, while enforcing a free-labor system. Later in April 1866, Mississippi's Samuel Thomas, an officer that Thomas Conway placed in the same category as Rufus Saxton as being "true to liberty," "could not stand" in the face of the president's conservative onslaught. In April, Texas Assistant Commissioner Gregory's administration gave way to that of General J. B. Kiddoo, who also committed the Bureau to enforcing a contract labor system in the hopes that the freedpeople would produce a fine cotton crop, a sure sign of the correctness of the government's emancipation policy. In May 1866, General Thomas Ruger replaced Assistant Commissioner Whittlesey, whom Steedman and Fullerton had accused of wrongdoing and the president had placed under arrest.

By the summer of 1866, all things appeared to point to the development of a Bureau more concerned with labor discipline than anything else, and the emphasis on labor discipline suggested a Bureau sympathetic to the needs of white Southerners at the expense of the expectations of the freedpeople. Certainly, the Bureau assigned a great deal of importance to productive labor, but it is too easy if not simplistic to characterize its policy changes in some strict chronological fashion, with the agency moving from a youthful radical vigor to a more conservative maturity with Johnson guiding Howard's hand. After all, John Randolph Lewis, a man committed to the advancement of the freedpeople, succeeded Clinton B. Fisk in Tennessee in September 1866, exerted great influence in Georgia under Assistant Commissioner Caleb Sibley whom he eventually replaced, and continued to serve with the agency into 1869. Absalom Baird tactfully reversed Fullerton's policies and remained in command for almost a year, prompting Howard to write later that he was too close to the state's carpetbaggers. Even Davis Tillson was not as warm a supporter of the president's policies as Steedman led Johnson to believe. He was just tactful in voicing his opposition in private correspondence to Howard, realistic in the understanding of the scope of his power, and well aware that Johnson was his commander-in-chief. Also, Swayne, whom Howard appointed at the same time as Tillson, remained with the Alabama Bureau until January 1868. Perhaps he endured because of his father's political weight or perhaps he was not as radical as Steedman made him out to be. He was, however, competent and fair, which may have immunized him from the harshest of white criticism. Regardless, Swayne's ability to endure suggests that Johnson could not have his way all of the time, that competent individuals such as Swayne and Baird could survive criticism, and that the progression of personnel through the various assistant commissioners' offices followed no neat and rigid ideological shift guided from the White House.

Complicating efforts to categorize assistant commissioners or other Bureau officials with facile political labels was the fact that they might have been "conservative" on some measures and "progressive" on others, while many of them simply might have been pragmatic in still other aspects of policy. In Mississippi during the summer of 1865, Assistant Commissioner Samuel Thomas, for example, made no effort to lease small plots of land to the freedpeople because he believed that such an act would "meet with strong opposition from all parties." Taking a realistic assessment of that opposition, he concluded that such a distribution would "require a hero to execute it, and a military force to protect the Freedmen during the term of their lease." At the same time, he feared the consequences of a resurgence of white control of the freed population. A reestablishment of the state militia without the moderating presence of federal troops, he warned Howard in September 1865, would lead to the re-enslavement of black workers. Indeed, he worried, "It seems to me that any attempt to assume charge of the welfare of the Freedmen by the State authorities, with all their prejudices, and independent of national control, will result in a failure to secure for the black man what he has a right to expect by the Emancipation proclamation and the acts of Congress." Thus, Thomas held ambivalent feelings about the Bureau. He was part of an agency that was, he believed, not expressly sanctioned by the federal constitution and that must eventually pass from existence. At the same time, he understood the Bureau to be an agency that Mississippi needed because of the untrustworthiness of the white population.

Any assistant commissioner might have held apparently contradictory views about their duties at any point in time, but many officers also did not approach their service in a static way. Many of them simply did not hold unyieldingly to initial assumptions as they learned more about black and white Southerners and Reconstruction. Alabama experienced fairly constant Bureau leadership in the person of Wager Swayne, who served for about two-and-a-half years in the state. Administrative stability, however, did not mean that Swayne assumed a static position in his approach to dealing with black and white Alabamans. As historian Michael Fitzgerald argues, Swayne's initial labor guidelines emphasized the contract system, with the understanding that the freedpeople had to come to accept "the binding force" of their agreements. Because he soon found the system working to the disadvantage of the freedpeople, he concluded that it would be best abandoned; the market demand for labor would better tend to the freedpeople's economic advancement.

Indeed, white resistance to what Bureau assistant commissioners considered the agency's reasonable and fair policies often led to a shift of focus. Davis Tillson first assumed that the greatest challenge to the new order would come from the freedpeople, but before long he had changed his mind as white resistance to the Bureau became more apparent to him. In December 1865, he proposed a plan for military Reconstruction for Georgia and the rest of the erstwhile Confederacy to teach whites "some regard for the law . . . otherwise loyal men to say nothing of negroes, would find it extremely unpleasant living South." Also, as historian Robert Engs notes, Virginia assistant commissioner Orlando Brown in 1865 held to the Bureau's expressed policy of being an impartial referee for disputes between whites and blacks, but by the end of 1867 was unabashedly an advocate of the Bureau as the guardian of the freedpeople.

Ideological Boundaries. Even the best of these assistant commissioners held nineteenth-century ideas that may appear regressive to modern Americans, but at the time had the potential for promoting positive action in favor of the freedpeople's cause. For example, almost all Bureau men from the assistant commissioners down to the local agents held to a paternalistic view of their relationships with the ex-slaves. Even progressive individuals such as Rufus Saxton, Eliphalet Whittlesey and Clinton B. Fisk assumed that they had to set the freedpeople on the right path and carefully guide them along the way. Through their circulars, Saxton and Whittlesey, for example, lectured the freedpeople on their responsibilities, especially their need to obey the law, work hard, honor the sanctity of marriage, and support and care for their families. (*See Document No. 5.*) Fisk went one step better than both of his colleagues and produced a lengthy pamphlet containing his advice to the freedpeople on such subjects as temperance, courtship, marriage, and thrift.

Paternalism of this sort, shared by most Yankee Bureau men, could frustrate freedpeople who expected the respect and equality that came with freedom. But the Bureau's paternalism had another side to it, one that prompted officers and agents to take seriously their role as guardians. It was in that capacity that Bureau men sought justice for the ex-slaves. For Whittlesey and others who shared his views, the Bureau was "the appointed instrument for redeeming the solemn pledge of the nation . . . to secure the rights of the freedmen."

To be sure, as assistant commissioners shifted into and out of Howard's Bureau, they brought different approaches to their jobs and set their agendas in accordance with their own perceptions of the most efficacious means of bringing Reconstruction to a favorable resolution. These inclinations, however, should not obscure what these men shared in common, aside from the limitations that the federal government placed on the agency. Bureau chiefs generally accepted a multifaceted approach to securing the future of the freedpeople, using whatever tools they had at their disposal to further the ultimate goal of Reconstruction. Furthermore, if one must apply labels, it is wrong to assume that only the most obviously "radical" individuals had any desire to make the freedpeople's lives safe and secure in their future prospects. Ideas about labor, charity, education, civil rights, and law more often united Howard's subordinates than divided them.

In the end, it may be that the Bureau personnel changes had less to do with the agency's apparent metamorphosis into a more conservative organization than events it could no longer control. Limited from the outset by Congress, the Bureau's power diminished almost as soon as its assistant commissioners established it on a firm footing, and it became all the more difficult for the men of the agency to influence the course of freedom. By 1866, for example, because state legislatures were passing new laws that technically defined the civil rights of freedpeople, the Bureau was returning judicial authority to civilian courts, reacting to rather than preventing injustice. And all the while, white Southerners were reasserting themselves with a confidence that would contribute mightily to Reconstruction's failure.

Staffing the State Bureaus. The assistant commissioners had a fairly free hand in organizing their states but necessarily followed Howard's overall organizational structure for the Bureau. Thus, they appointed adjutants general, quartermasters, medical chiefs, education superintendents, and inspectors general to deal with the various aspects of their agency. In the process, they became painfully aware of the limited resources at their disposal that always seemed to have them stretching their organizations to its limits. Nowhere was this problem more obvious than in the assistant commissioners' efforts to expand their authority into the towns and hinterlands of their states.

State assistant commissioners depended on military men, who were commonly referred to as superintendents, subcommissioners or subassistant commissioners, to supervise the larger divisions or districts of the state organization and the local agents who were available to service them. During the summer of 1865, assistant commissioners first turned to the military commanders of their states to secure officers for their agencies with mixed results. In Georgia, the vigorous if imprudent efforts of Saxton's officer, Brigadier General Edward A. Wild, to confiscate state and private property to use to support black education alienated General James B. Steedman, the military commander of the state. In Virginia, however, Assistant Commissioner Orlando Brown received willing assistance from Fortress Monroe's commanding officer, General Nelson A. Miles.

Complicating such arrangements was the fact that many Army officers stationed in the South during the summer of 1865 had no inclination to serve in Howard's Bureau. Furthermore, the pool of officers shrank as the Army mustered out its volunteer regiments in an effort to return to peacetime footing, a situation that troubled Texas Bureau Assistant Commissioner Edgar Gregory into 1866 with "Great delays and difficulties in obtaining officers from the Army and in keeping them." Wager Swayne had the cooperation of military commanders, but he, too, found it difficult to hold onto officers as the Army reduced its personnel. In July 1865, he informed Howard that he was "practically alone owing to the muster-out order." But even at best, Swayne pointed out, relying on military commanders to detail officers to the Bureau or to allow them to assume Bureau duties along with their normal military duties was haphazard.

Consequently, during the summer of 1865, the Bureau was hardly a

major presence in the South at a time when it might have had an impact
on the early direction of Reconstruction. Arkansas was among the more
fortunate jurisdictions with men staffing 11 agencies at various times
during the summer months; east Texas freedpeople had to look for assistance in Louisiana until Gregory arrived in the state in September.
In early August 1865, there was no Bureau organization on the mainland
of Georgia beyond Augusta and Savannah and in September Clinton B.
Fisk proposed to annex Atlanta to his jurisdiction because it lacked a
Bureau presence. Earlier in July 1865, Colonel Joseph S. Fullerton, then
on an inspection tour for Howard, reported that Saxton, who was temporarily in charge of Florida, had appointed only three agents there,
concluding "almost nothing has been done for the freedmen in said
state by agents of the Bureau." And as late as the end of 1865, Saxton's
Florida successor, Colonel Thomas W. Osborn, who relied first for a
brief period on the part-time assistance of military post commanders
and then on civilian officials for his subordinates, had not done very
much better in expanding his agency's authority in the state. The Bureau, however, soon turned to a group of individuals who had a significant stake in securing the fruits of Union victory to flesh out its ranks:
officers of the United States Army's Veteran Reserve Corps.

The VRC, a national organization on par with the Regular Army, was
originally established in 1863 as the Invalid Corps for wounded and
camp-sick soldiers who could still perform light duty. During the summer of 1865, it was not subjected to the muster-out schedule of the state
volunteer regiments, which made it an appealing alternative as a source
of officers compared to what was available through local commanders.
In January 1866, Wager Swayne, for example, welcomed the VRC in Alabama for the stability that it would bring to his organization.

As the Bureau matured, the presence of VRC men increased. In Mississippi during the summer and fall of 1865 through March 12, 1866,
there were 25 field officers, all commissioned officers in the United
States Colored Troops. After a March 1866 reorganization, all of the 15
field officers who were on duty were members of a VRC regiment. In
North Carolina in June 1867, of the 29 men on duty, 24 were Army
officers and 5 were civilians; 20 of those army men were VRC officers.
In Florida by November 1866 of the thirteen military men on duty in
the Bureau as subassistant commissioners, 10 were VCR officers. In
Georgia, by September 1, 1867, all of the Bureau's 13 subassistant or
assistant subassistant commissioners were or had been connected with

the VRC. Indeed, by the end of the Bureau's existence, the majority of the agency's field personnel had had some connection with the VRC.

One of the advantages of turning to the military for personnel was that detached officers still claimed their Army pay. If assistant commissioners turned to civilians, they would need to rely for the most part on the revenues generated by confiscated and abandoned property, a source less than generous as President Johnson rapidly pardoned ex-Confederates who then reclaimed their property. The alternatives were a fee system for services rendered by agents or payment for agents drawn from fines collected. Still, Osborne and other assistant commissioners throughout the South on occasion turned to local whites to act as Bureau agents.

No assistant commissioner relied so heavily on white native civilian agents as did Davis Tillson in Georgia and Wager Swayne in Alabama. Both Tillson and Swayne used native civilians to staff their Bureaus at the outset of Reconstruction, which might have appeared to be an indication of their commitment to stability and the old order. Their approach to staffing, however, was more than an effort to deal with their inadequate resources or an indication that they would favor whites over blacks in their policies. Rather, their intention was to embark on a pragmatic effort to change attitudes among whites in the South, thus contributing to a "self-Reconstruction" that would take hold and last long after the Bureau was gone from the region. Swayne saw this approach as "an educator of public sentiment," while Tillson believed that his actions would "test the spirit of the civil officers." Indeed, Swayne, in explaining his use of local magistrates as Bureau agents, noted that "The colored people must at some period be left to the civil courts, and it is better they come into them under the auspices of this Bureau than after they have come to be regarded as the protegéés [*sic*] of a hostile jurisdiction and the Bureau is no longer present to defend them."

Once the context of their actions becomes clear—a context shaped by the realization that the Bureau would soon be gone and that any lasting success depended on changing the minds of those white men opposed to freedom—it becomes less plausible to charge these officers with being disciplinary appendages of the planter class. That said, the unfavorable consequences of using local civilians, unanticipated as they might have been, resulted in granting initial trust and "forbearance" to individuals who had been members of the local antebellum and Confederate elite and who were less likely to gain the confidence of the ex-slaves.

Soon both Swayne and Tillson found themselves under attack for their decision to use local white officials. Tillson readily replaced inadequate agents on an individual basis, but did not completely abandon the system. By April 1866, Swayne realized that his conciliatory policy was a failure, finding fault in the system; he began to rely on Union officers. His successor Julius Hayden continued to make certain that the Bureau was a loyal one, promising to avoid using anyone "who has shown in any way a disposition to fraternize with those whose walk and conversation shows [sic] that they are enemies to peace." He, too, relied on military men, as did Tillson's successor who eventually replaced Georgia's civilian appointees with officers, Union veterans, or loyal local civilians. At the same time, assistant commissioners rarely looked to the loyal black population to fill their agencies, either because of their own prejudices or their fear that such appointments would render whites reluctant to cooperate with the agency. (*See Document No. 6.*) Eventually, the second Bureau law of July 16, 1866 made this reorganization easier to accomplish; it authorized Howard to pay civilian agents an annual salary ranging between $500 and $1,200 depending on their duties, with hiring preferences given to veterans of the United States Army.

Historian John A. Carpenter has estimated that 2,441 officers and agents served in the Bureau in the South between 1865 and 1870. That is an impressive figure, but in reality there never was a sufficient number of men on duty at any one time to handle all of the problems facing the region and the agency. In May 1867, for example, there were only 68 Bureau agents spread though the expanses of east Texas. In 1867, South Carolina, a state with a significant population of freedpeople, only had 40 agents and officers in the field. In Arkansas, a state with 57 counties, there were 29 local agents in the field for most of that year with 22 on duty during the latter part of 1868. In Georgia, another state with a large black population as well as the largest land area east of the Mississippi River, there were 45 officers and agents in the field during the latter part of 1868. At the end of 1868, there were 901 men on the Bureau's rolls, but of those, historian George Bentley points out, 348 were clerical personnel, leaving a hardly adequate number in the field to give any meaning to a forceful Yankee occupation.

Continuing the Bureau. The vicissitudes of the fledgling Freedmen's Bureau suggested to its supporters that Howard and his men would need more time and more resources to remake the old slave states in the image of the free-labor North. The first Bureau law required the agency to terminate its activities a year after the end of the war and by Howard's reckoning that meant that the Bureau would need to wrap up its activities by June 30, 1866. Howard and many other Bureau men as well as Republican politicians believed that there was sufficient evidence showing that white Southerners had yet to come to grips with the requirements of the new order of things. Reports from the South indicated that they resented the interference of the Bureau in their affairs and they had become sufficiently confident to ignore or actively oppose the agency's activities. Furthermore, Howard rightly believed that President Johnson's lenient Reconstruction policies and his outright opposition to the Freedmen's Bureau were hindering him in his efforts to carry out the charge given him by the first Bureau law.

The effort to give the Bureau more power as well as time took shape in a bill introduced to the Senate on January 5, 1866 by Lyman Trumbull, an Illinois legislator who had taken the time to consult with Howard about the needs of the agency. The bill would have expanded the Bureau's power and activities, including its efforts to settle freedpeople on land. Congress passed the bill in February, but President Johnson's veto prevented it from becoming law. Congress then set to work preparing another bill that would garner sufficient support to override the expected presidential veto. In the meantime, Howard cautiously proceeded with his work and Johnson continued to do his best to discredit the Bureau, something that his veto had gone a long way to accomplish.

Whites throughout the South believed that Johnson's veto was the death knell for the Freedmen's Bureau. In late February, one Virginia Bureau officer complained that whites now assumed that Johnson's policies "will restore them '*as they were*' and 'leave them to manage the nigger', instead of us, who 'don't understand him'." Another Virginia Bureau man reported that the veto encouraged whites to believe "that slavery was to be reestablished." Assistant Commissioner Fisk informed Howard that Johnson's veto had convinced Kentuckians that the president opposed the agency "in any shape or form." "Stumping politicians and the pro-slavery press announced that the 'furniture was smashed'," he explained. It took a letter from Howard to reassure his assistant commissioners that the president, despite his evident opposition to the agency, believed that the Bureau would continue for some time.

Two additional events combined to reinforce the presidential veto's negative message about the Bureau despite Howard's reassurances. On

April 2, Johnson proclaimed the end of the rebellion throughout the South but for Texas and directly attacked military authority in the region. On April 3, the Supreme Court's Milligan decision confirmed the right of citizens to be tried by civilian courts where they were functioning instead of military tribunals. Both the president and the Supreme Court appeared to confirm the conviction of white Southerners that the Bureau lacked legal authority to interfere with their affairs and they acted accordingly.

Shortly thereafter, Johnson launched his investigation of the Bureau, which Howard believed was designed to ruin him. Reporters from the *New York Herald* accompanied Steedman and Fullerton, virtually guaranteeing a steady stream of bad press for the Bureau. Johnson's officers concluded in their final report that the Bureau had done "more harm than good."

The information provided by these men and publicized in the Northern press presented an unflattering portrait—expensive, radical and corrupt—of Howard's agency, but not a fatal one. On July 16, 1866, Congress overrode another presidential veto to pass a new if not as wideranging Bureau law that extended the agency's life for another two years. Importantly, Congress provided the Bureau with its first independent source of funds, now allowing it the resources to extend its relief and educational efforts, including renting and repairing schoolhouses, through an Army appropriations law.

Earlier in April 1866, Congress had passed a Civil Rights Act, which extended equal rights to the freedpeople, and in June 1866 Congress had passed a Southern Homestead Act, which opened government land for settlement initially to freedmen and loyal refugees. Also, beginning in the spring of 1866, the Bureau became more closely tied to the military establishment as the positions of assistant commissioner and district commander merged into one, which presumably would make it easier for assistant commissioners to use soldiers in enforcing their orders. In addition, on July 6, General Ulysses S. Grant had issued General Order No. 44. Grant authorized military commanders and thus through them Bureau officials to arrest individuals "charged with the commission of crimes and offenses against officers, agents, citizens and inhabitants of the United States, irrespective of color" who had escaped justice because of the neglect or inability of civil authorities. It also allowed the Army to detain these individuals "in military confinement until such time as a proper judicial tribunal may be ready and willing to try them."

These laws and Grant's order provided the Bureau with more time, power, and resources to renew its efforts. On the surface, the inauguration of Military Reconstruction in March 1867, which divided the former Confederacy excluding Tennessee into military districts, did the same. However, the close relationship of the Bureau with the military was a mixed blessing, at times actually limiting the scope of the Bureau's power to protect the freedpeople. In June 1866, South Carolina's Assistant Commissioner Robert K. Scott assumed command of the military forces in the state, but later reported that his "command of the military was only nominal" and that he was "merely the medium for the transmittal of orders." In fact, military interference with civil authorities was more often than not considered a measure of last resort by higher military authorities, further hurting the Bureau's ability to take aggressive action before civil officials had done some harm to the freedpeople. Thus, despite military orders and congressional laws, much still depended on the skill and commitment of Bureau men to negotiate the shoals of the South's unsettled postwar conditions.

CHAPTER 3

BUREAU MEN FACE RECONSTRUCTION

Bureau Men and the Wards of the Nation. The assistant commissioners struggled to make the South more like the North. They did their best to interpret Howard's guidelines for labor and the Bureau's other duties while doing much to set the tone of the agency in their various states. All of their efforts, however, still required that their own subordinates turn the assistant commissioners' statements about just wages, equal rights, and other Bureau concerns into real action. (*See Document No. 7.*) These subordinates, the regional officers and the local agents, became the men on the front lines of Reconstruction.

The men who served the Bureau at the state and local level held a range of views about the freedpeople and about their duties. Their motives for accepting Bureau appointments were as diverse as their abilities to do the job. Some of the earliest appointees on the southeastern coast, for example, were fairly radical in their approaches to Reconstruction and saw their appointments as opportunities for reform. In Georgia, the Reverends William F. Eaton, William H. Tiffany, and Tunis G. Campbell, one of the Bureau's few black agents, all actively worked for the benefit of the ex-slaves. Tending to spiritual and temporal needs, their activities ranged from conducting marriages and starting schools to helping freedpeople settle on grants of land, form local governments, organize militias, and establish an independence that would be hard to alter when federal land policy shifted in favor of the ex-slaveholders of the region. Farther up the coast on the Virginia peninsula, Bureau assistant subcommissioner C. B. Wilder had been tending to the needs of the contraband there since 1862. In his study of the Hampton black community during this period, historian Robert Francis Engs refers to Wilder and other Bureau men who served in the region during the early days of the agency's existence as being "more nearly missionaries in uniform than officers assigned to the not always welcomed duty of Bureau agent." But even at this early stage of the Bureau's existence, officers and agents of all backgrounds reminded the freedpeople of the obligations that attended to their rights as free people.

The Reverend Charles W. Buckley, who would become first a Bureau district inspector and then the chief education officer in Alabama and later a Republican congressman from the state, brought a hopeful message to the freedpeople in the Montgomery during the early days of Reconstruction. But he also developed a theme that would be a constant one throughout the Bureau's existence in Alabama and elsewhere. On Sunday, May 27, 1865, speaking to three different groups of freedpeople, he "told them plainly that they were free and that the government would maintain their freedom." Furthermore, he explained that freedom in terms the freedpeople could have appreciated, assuring them that "No abuse, no personal violence, no selling, no buying, no breaking up families by force would be allowed." However, he also reminded them that "*They* were not *free* to be insolent, to be idle, to pilfer, to steal or do anything contrary to good order." In other words, "They *were free* to come under *the restraints of law*, free to toil and claim the fruits of their own industry." Even the most sympathetic of agents and officers would demand responsible action of the freedpeople, which might at times mean supporting white complaints again freedmen.

The appointment of civilian agents by Davis Tillson, Wager Swayne, and other Bureau assistant commissioners during late 1865 into 1866 brought a different kind of agent into the Bureau's service. One may safely assume that a Southern antebellum background that included as an article of faith the inferiority of black slaves imposed limitations even on the most conscientious and loyal individuals who came to work for the Bureau. Some of them did not necessarily find it improbable to seek simple justice for whites and blacks, but because so many of them had connections with the antebellum establishment, anything more was rare.

These civilians accepted their positions for a variety of reasons. A small minority of these agents had been Unionists or were transplanted Yankees who had come South before the war; such individuals accepted the postwar situation and their agencies looking towards the new future, hoping to make some difference in how their states adjusted to defeat, emancipation, and a reunited country. Some Southern civilians believed that they could make a few dollars from the fees they could charge. Others expected to use their positions to control the events of Reconstruction and especially impose some sort of discipline on black labor, as Clinton Fisk accused Alabama civilian agents of doing. Most of these men probably thought that cooperation with the Bureau would have the added benefit of speeding the Reconstruction process. As Wilkes County, Georgia, agent Brien Maguire explained, he accepted his appointment because he hoped "to render a public service," but also because "we want to get the management of affairs in our own hands, and we want to be rid of U.S. Soldiers."

Some of the Army officers and veterans who eventually became the backbone of the Bureau were not much better than were their Southern neighbors in their dealings with the ex-slaves. They shared in varying degrees the racist views of their Yankee contemporaries, which could limit their expectations for the freedpeople's future. However, as was the case with a number of their assistant commissioners, their conception of black inferiority did not necessarily tie that inferiority directly to race but rather to the freedpeople's previous condition of servitude. Accepting that slavery had been a damaging experience—one that could break the spirit as well as the body and one that stunted the intellectual and moral growth of the enslaved—they assumed that the freedpeople had yet to reach a level of understanding and competence that matched those of white Yankees. In early 1868, Samuel C. Armstrong, Bureau officer for the Hampton, Virginia, area, the son of missionaries and a former officer of black troops who would become the founder and first principal of Hampton Institute, was having difficulty raising money among the freedpeople for schools. In explaining his problems, he concluded, "All is summed up in *ignorance*. And for that they [the freedpeople] are not responsible."

If the freedpeople were victims of a destructive system, however, they could overcome its consequences once freed from its physical, emotional, and intellectual chains. Men such as Armstrong assumed that with hard work, education, sobriety, and frugality, the freedpeople would have good prospects for overcoming the debilitating mark left by slavery. At the same time, they placed a heavy burden on the freedpeople to prove themselves. Brevet Major I. Wickersham, the Wilmington, North Carolina, Bureau superintendent, made this clear. In December 1865, he informed the freedpeople in his jurisdiction that "You are at liberty to seek your own happiness," and "whatever privileges or property you acquire in the future, you must labor for and earn." Furthermore, "the order, prosperity and happiness of the country is, in a great measure, in your hands. Be patient, industrious, virtuous and pious, and satisfy the Government and your friends, North and South, that you are worthy of the freedom which has been given you."

Augusta, Georgia, agent, Captain John Emory Bryant, also told a meeting of freedmen in January 1866, that "a great work is before you."

But both Wickersham and Bryant reassured their audiences that they would not stand before these challenges alone. Wickersham informed them that the federal government was the "*guardian* of [their] liberties," while Bryant pledged to assist them in their efforts to make something of their freedom "so far as I am able." Other Yankee Bureau men would agree with these officers. Their shared sense of paternalism, commitment to securing the fruits of victory, and notions of simple justice encouraged them to help the freedpeople shoulder their new responsibilities.

There was a very good chance that the freedpeople would find Bureau men who were committed to justice and to their safety when they came upon Veteran Reserve Corps officers, individuals with a degree of professionalism that at least motivated them to perform their duty well. Handicapped VRC men viewed the Bureau as a means for extending their stay in the military at a time when prospects for them back home were not all that abundant. Many of them, desirous of an Army career, worked to advance themselves in the service; a few VRC men came to the war committed to the cause of the slave; and still more officers believed that their war work was not finished until the national government had secured the fruits of victory, including basic rights for the ex-slaves. In March 1867, Lieutenant Douglas Risley, a former officer of black troops before a wound in his right arm caused its partial amputation and made him fit only for the VRC, accepted his appointment as a Bureau officer on the Georgia coast already committed to the blacks' cause. In 1862, he had come to the war an abolitionist and at one point had explained to his family that "Had I a thousand lives, & laying them down would release a thousand slaves, I would give them." Erastus Everson, another VRC man and a South Carolina Bureau officer, might not have shared Risley's deep feelings for freedpeople, but he was equally eloquent in expressing his commitment to Union and securing the fruits of victory. In 1868, when he learned that he would be mustered out of the service, he offered to stay on with the Bureau as a civilian if the agency still needed him. He would do so, he explained, "that I might as far as possible be an instrument of perpetuating the principles which caused me to leave my home in 1861 & which in part have been my guide and support under the trials and hardships since endured." Even if some of Everson's colleagues lacked reformer's sympathy for the freedpeople, their desire to protect the fruits of their victory and the Union for which they had already sacrificed so much would leave them open to grappling with the legitimate needs of the ex-slaves.

Flawed Performances. By and large, Yankee Bureau men of all backgrounds could agree with the Virginian Bureau's Lieutenant Massey, who expected to prepare the freed slave "to place himself in a position, where he will be able to maintain himself, after the Bureau shall cease to exist." But Bureau men of all backgrounds had varying degrees of success in reaching that goal. Scholars such as Joe M. Richardson, who studied Reconstruction in Florida, Stephen V. Ash, who traced the transformation of Middle Tennessee during the 1860's, and Randy Finley, who studied the Arkansas Bureau, give mixed reviews to the officers and agents that they had encountered in their research. Historian Richard Paul Fuke, who studied Reconstruction in Maryland, judges Bureau men to have "had what they perceived to be blacks' best interests at heart," but that attitude in and of itself did not necessarily guarantee a smooth relationship with freedpeople who might have had very different notions as to what their own best interests were.

No matter how committed the Bureau as a whole was to the goals expressed by Howard and his subordinates, throughout its existence in the South there were individuals who for one reason or another failed to carry their weight or simply did not care about the future of the freedpeople. Historian Finley points to the irony of the Arkansas Bureau relying on a former Virginia plantation overseer named Thomas Hunnicutt, who for seven months supervised a district heavily populated with freedpeople while doing significant damage to the agency's reputation. Not only did he force freedpeople into labor arrangements, he demanded sexual favors from freedwomen who came to him for help.

Even military men at times fell short. In 1866 in Virginia Assistant Commissioner Orlando Brown had to deal with several officers who had shamed the agency. Lieutenant Louis Ahrens, a German-speaking soldier who could barely understand English, relied heavily on white Virginians for counsel, much to the detriment of the Bureau's agenda. Another veteran, Lieutenant Hite, apparently lacked the dignity the office required. On several occasions, people observed Hite "cutting up badly," dancing with and hugging black women. Furthermore, one Bureau officer reported, he "drinks like an old sucker, gets crowds of negroes at his office nights and with fiddlers & wine get up a shameful 'Hullabaloo' till long after decent hours." Captain Jeffries, another Virginia officer, also "drinks hard," but he apparently refrained from carrying on in Hite's manner. Such displays led the reporting officer to conclude that "I wish these Veteran [Reserve] Corps officers all where they came from, not to say worse." Indeed, enough Bureau men shared the vices of these officers to lend some credence to the complaints about a surfeit of drunken VRC men. Often plagued by poorly healed wounds and abscessing amputations and frequently ostracized by a hostile white population, a noticeable number of VRC officers turned to alcohol as a way to medicate their pain or cope with their loneliness. But these men were far from making up the majority of their ranks.

When freedpeople encountered unsatisfactory Bureau men, they complained and expected to be heard. At times, these complaints were unfair, resulting from Bureau men rightly deciding against a freedman's case or from whites refusing to abide by a Bureau decision. On other occasions Bureau men failed to meet the freedpeople's expectations because they simply could not handle the volume of complaints made by the ex-slaves in as prompt a manner as would please the complainants. In August 1867, freedpeople from Calhoun, Georgia wrote to the assistant commissioner because the agent, a former officer in a black regiment, had neglected their rights. The agent, however, was not ignorant of their needs; he simply could not cope with the amount of work the freedpeople brought to his attention. Such overwork, along with the Bureau's limited resources, authority and power and stubborn white resistance all contributed more than drink or indifference to Bureau's inability to do better for the ex-slaves.

A Difficult Service. From the Bureau's early days until its termination, conscientious officers and agents often fell short of the expectations of the freedpeople because of the enormity of the task confronting them. Initially, officers and agents had to deal with the confusion normally concomitant with the establishment of a new organization. These men, for example, lacked proper forms for conducting business —the Freedmen's Bureau, after all, was a bureaucracy—and adequate funds for establishing comfortable or even suitable offices. In the fall of 1865, the Talledega, Alabama, assistant superintendent delayed the opening of his office because the local Army Quartermaster "refused to furnish a solitary item or article—not even a sheet of paper for the use of the Bureau."

When Bureau men could open their office doors, they became overburdened with business required by whites and blacks as well as the paperwork required by their demanding superiors. In an article first published in the November 1868 issue of *Harper's New Monthly Maga-*

zine, John William De Forest went into great detail to explain the red tape (a reference to bureaucratic procedure drawn from the flat red cotton string or "tape" used to bundle trifolded official documents) that he encountered as a South Carolina Bureau officer. He recited a litany of the various types of paperwork he had to master, including the reports detailing complaints, educational progress, and the amounts of food and clothing issued to freedpeople and refugees and the shelf-full of copybooks into which he entered a complete history of his actions. His conclusion that "the system of army bookkeeping is a laborious and complicated perfection" was almost an understatement. Furthermore, he explained, "a Bureau officer is an official jack-of-all-trades," for not only did he have to maintain his paperwork, but also understand Army regulations and civil law, know how to lead troops, act as a commissioner of the poor, and be a statistician. And if he mastered "all this multifarious knowledge," the Bureau officer still had to be "a man of quick common sense with a special faculty for deciding what not to do."

At times, there were quiet months for agents and officers when it appeared that freedpeople and employers were reaching some sort of accommodation, but busier times often overshadowed the memories of those periods. De Forest might have managed to master the intricacies of Bureau work in such a way that he was able to handle his duties in the course of no more than five hours a day. Other Bureau men responsible for the needs of large black and white populations had to spend more time at their work. In September 1865, Colonel George D. Robinson assumed command of the Mobile, Alabama, district as an assistant superintendent and discovered "that the amount of business crowding upon the office renders it imperatively necessary that I should have an assistant." In November 1867, South Carolina's Erastus Everson complained, "I have been harassed so with complaints of freedmen, that I am perplexed beyond measure and nearly crazy." In December 1867, Christian Raushenberg, a southwest Georgia agent who did double duty as a Bureau surgeon, found himself overwhelmed with paperwork and pleaded for help. And later in 1868, Florida agent George B. Carse, found it necessary to keep office hours late into the night, noting that he had never been so busy in his life.

Registers of complaints further attest to the full days of Bureau men and the diverse problems they were expected to resolve even down through the last months of the agency's existence. Freedpeople bought to the attention of agents and officers cases of spousal infidelity and abandonment, incidents of seduction, threats of violence from whites, claims for wages and Army bounties, charges of the theft of personal property by other freedpeople, and child support issues. White employers added to the caseload with the usual complaints of unfaithful labor as well as the unusual but growing problem near Fernandina, Florida, of cattle shooting. Needless to say, Bureau men were at their busiest at the commencement of the planting season when they tried to supervise fair work arrangements for the freedpeople and at harvest time when they tried to mediate disputes over the freedpeople's pay claims.

The need to travel frequently and over significant distances compounded the work load problems of officers and agents. During the summer and fall of 1865, Bureau officers talked themselves hoarse as they tried to explain the purpose of the agency to whites and blacks. The Reverend Thomas Smith, a Mississippi Bureau official, for example, traveled to 25 locations, giving at least that many speeches, between the time he assumed his duties in mid-August 1865 and when he reported his activities on November 3 of that year. Other men reported giving talks wherever or whenever they could gather a group of whites and blacks to spread the message of the new order. While the need for such an intensive round of lecturing diminished as the Bureau matured, the need for extensive travel did not. In March 1866, Texas officer Samuel Craig road 15 miles to deliver lecture to some freedpeople who appeared to be failing in their contractual obligations. In May 1866, John Riggs spent almost all of his time traveling through his Kentucky jurisdiction making speeches to freedpeople and whites about their obligations. And even as the Georgia Bureau began to wind down during the late months of 1868, its Rome assistant commissioner, Carlos de la Mesa busily traveled through his jurisdiction to deal with the needs of the freedpeople.

The poor infrastructure of the postwar South as well as the elements often conspired to make communication and travel at best problematical. During 1865, for example, Georgia Bureau agents complained about interrupted mail service, while in another 1868 article for *Harper's* De Forest described how his official correspondence had to "meander its way about the country" in a "leisurely fashion," delaying communication with the farther reaches of his jurisdiction "from a fortnight to a month." In Arkansas, poor roads and flooded rivers added hardship to agents traveling about to tend to their business, while in South Carolina, spring rains turned the roads into quagmires making De Forest's work all the more vexing. Indeed, the very fact that Bureau jurisdictions tended to be quite large, frequently covering several counties and, as De Forest did not hesitate to point out, thousands of square miles, often led to less than satisfactory service for the freedpeople. In Florida, during the summer of 1866, the officer in charge of Branford County found "it almost impossible to attend to the affairs of that county, being [head-quartered] almost one hundred miles away from it." Consequently, freed-people took their complaints to Lieutenant F. E. Grossman, the subassistant commissioner in the neighboring jurisdiction, who unfortunately for those freedpeople felt he had no authority to deal with them.

By the latter part of 1868, Bureau men realized that they were fighting a losing battle in their efforts to convince white Southerners that the agency's message was one that would benefit all who came to accept it. The agency, always known as a temporary expression of federal author-ity, was coming to the end of its days and had no authority to make much more of an impact on Reconstruction. Mounting frustration burdened conscientious individuals. Agents and officers complained that they could do little more for the freedpeople unless given a renewed source of power that simply was no longer available to them. While they pleaded for power, they faced the ridicule of white Southerners who happily awaited the demise of the Bureau. In late October 1868, De Witt C. Brown, the subassistant commissioner stationed at Paris, Texas, made this plain to his superior. "The only means that will ever render the Bu-reau more efficient in this community," he advised, "is the presence of a sufficient number of troops to command respect." As matters stood, he continued, "The Bureau is and will be held in absolute contempt un-less there is power behind it." But not only did white Texans ignore Brown, they made attempts on his life, continued to threaten him, and tried to intimidate him. His courage alone, however, was insufficient to make the agency work for the freedpeople. "Although he has stood at his post in the face of all these things," Brown explained writing of himself in the third person, "he has found it impossible to enforce his authority through the Civil Officers." What he had learned, and what other Bureau men discovered on their own, was that white "Public opin-ion is too corrupt . . . to see any good" in the Bureau. The work fac-ing Bureau officials would have been taxing under the best of circum-stances, but white Southerners did their best to render a difficult job more so.

Southern Inhospitality. It was not uncommon for freedpeople to become disappointed with their Bureau men when those officers of the federal government rendered decisions concerning their complaints in favor of white employers or former owners. However, it was the white population, as Assistant Commissioner Orlando Brown well understood, that made the lives of these men uncomfortable and even dangerous. Bureau men arrived at their positions expecting to be able to reason with whites in order to gain their cooperation in establishing a new system of work and law that would benefit both races. Despite any effort of the Bureau at being even handed, however, white reluctance to accept the new order of things forced them to be more and more helpful to the freedpeople. Such action only further aggravated the resentment whites directed towards Bureau, characterized in 1868 by the Athens, Georgia, *Southern Banner* as "This agency of oppression, fraud and mischief." In November 1865, Mississippi Assistant Commissioner Thomas observed, "The simple truth is, that the Bureau is antagonistic to what the white people believe to be their interest." Consequently, "The people of the South are determined to get rid of it, and are not particular as to the means adopted to gain their end."

Bureau men soon learned that being associated with the agency attracted all manner of abuse from white Southerners. In 1866 students from Virginia Military Institute and from Washington College followed the officer at Lexington, Virginia, down the street hurling insults at him, a common practice elsewhere in the South. Captain D. H. Williams encountered "much bitter feeling towards the Bureau, the Northern people and the National government" in his travels from eastern Arkansas to Columbus, Kentucky during the spring of 1866. He also remarked on being subjected to numerous insults while at a hotel in Memphis, Tennessee, "which revealed their utter contempt for the United States Govt and for its representatives." Some Bureau men found it difficult to secure lodgings, as whites would boycott landlords who accommodated Yankees. Officers in Georgia and Alabama had United States flags torn down from their flagpoles, while meetings and public events across the old Confederacy became occasions for denouncing the Bureau and insulting its agents and their families. No wonder Lieutenant Hiram Willis concluded, "the majority [of Arkansas whites] seem to have no respect for God, man, or devil, and the most utter contempt" for the Bureau.

Throughout the South, Bureau men found themselves ostracized by white society because of the government and agency they served. In 1866, Captain Samuel Craig found himself isolated in Brenham, Texas, and Lieutenant Eldridge, stationed at Aberdeen, Mississippi, reported in September 1867 that whites ignored him even at church services, where women would leave the building rather than sit near him. In March 1868, the Reverend H. A. Hunter, a subassistant commissioner at Russellville, Kentucky, reported that he had "been strangely received here, having been bred in this place." While he was known to many white residents and had enjoyed a degree of respect "as a *man* & *minister*," he found himself condemned and excluded from preaching at local churches all because of his Bureau association.

At times, conscientious Bureau men found their best efforts stymied by civilians who treated their authority with contempt and local officials who ignored them, refused to work with them, or cooperated with whites who tried to hobble the agency with embarrassment or legal harassment. In May 1869, for example, J. H. Wager, the agent stationed at Hunstville, Alabama, complained that postmasters throughout his jurisdiction failed to turn over letters he had mailed to freedpeople who "call time and time for them." Earlier during the spring of 1866, the county clerk and the county sheriff at Gordonsville, Virginia, did not "openly oppose" the Bureau, but went "around secretly, and growl about the U.S. Government, get up false rumors and reports about the Officers of the Government; misrepresent the action of the Government" and dissuade employers from signing contracts with the freedpeople. Fortunately for Lieutenant A. B. Sweeny, the Bureau assistant superintendent at that town, there was sufficient cooperation from other whites to prevent him from either abandoning his position or calling for troops. Other local officials took more direct and successful approaches.

In October 1867, W. F. Henderson, the agent at Lexington, North Carolina, found himself charged with stealing a mule, which injured his reputation and his ability to do his job; he had "every whelp of a cur, mongrel, and the very excrescence of Society taunting & jeering me and my innocent family." Civilian magistrates charged other officers and agents with theft when they confiscated crops to secure freedpeople's wages and at least one district attorney threatened to present the Bureau to a grand jury as a "public nuisance." Indeed, in the fall of 1866, Bureau officer Captain Samuel Craig spent time in a small, vermin-infested jail cell in Seguin, Texas, for doing his duty until a troop of cavalry arrived from San Antonio to free him.

A Dangerous Service. Insults and threats of violence too often led to physical attacks, gunfights and assassinations, making a difficult job a very dangerous one as well. Officers and agents frequently reported that they felt unsafe without Army detachments close at hand. Other Bureau men admitted that they felt as if they were taking their lives in their own hands when they confronted whites over some offense. Some Bureau men resigned when troops withdrew from their towns, leaving them exposed to the wrath of the white population. During the summer of 1868, whites repeatedly threatened the agent at Washington, North Carolina. In July 1868, J. K. Nelson, the Murfreesboro, Tennessee, agent, went to bed armed to the teeth for fear of being attacked in his sleep by the Ku Klux Klan. And in August 1868, L. Lieberman, agent in Hawkinsville, Georgia, who had lived "in continued fear," became weary of the abuse he suffered at the hands of his white neighbors who tried to provoke him to violence. At least the Georgia Bureau knew what happened to Lieberman; earlier in 1867 a terrified, intimidated T. J. Herbert left his Carnesville, Georgia, agency without a word.

Other officers and agents were made of sterner stuff and instead of flinching defended themselves. Some men, when confronted by raging individuals or crowds, stood their ground, threatened retaliation, or frightened their antagonists with promises of stationing black troops in their neighborhoods. During the fall of 1868, De Witt C. Brown, the subassistant commissioner stationed at Paris, Texas, refused to allow "repeated attempts" of assassination or a general effort of whites "to frighten him with their Ku Klux disguise and their formidable array of arms" to deter him from his duties. However, he well understood that he was of little use to the Bureau or the freedpeople in the face of such strong opposition.

During the spring of 1866, J. D. Black, acting as an agent in Todd County, Kentucky, was the victim of an attempted assassination by outraged white men whom he had reported for refusing to turn over a black girl to her mother. Arrested but then released, these men returned to Black's headquarters town of Elkton. "Swearing they would have revenge for the wrong as they considered," Black reported, they "fired away at me and I gave them the best fight I could there being 4 against me." Black escaped injury, but his assailants continued to threaten him and what positive good he had accomplished as an agent evaporated in the heat of white resentment.

Elsewhere, agents and officers had similar experiences with hotheaded

Southerners. In March 1867, Arkansas officer Lieutenant Hiram F. Willis was at the center of a gunfight backed up by detachment of troops when a white employer refused to accept his judgment in a contract dispute. Major John J. Knox engaged in gunfights in 1866 in Meridian, Mississippi, and in 1868 in Athens, Georgia. Both survived for the time being. Knox might have been lynched, but for the intervention of Clark County freedpeople; he decided not to give his white enemies another chance and resigned after the troops sent to protect him left Athens. Hiram Willis eventually ended up a murder victim.

Neither Jabez Blanding nor William G. Kirkman were as lucky as Knox had been. Assigned to the Grenada, Mississippi agency in March 1866, Lieutenant Blanding ended his Bureau service "foully assassinated," shot in the back as he was taking an evening stroll on April 30, 1866 for the crime, his brother believed, of wearing a blue uniform. On October 7, 1868, Kirkman, a Union veteran, was gunned down in the town of Boston, Texas. An Arkansas agent, in addition to Hiram Willis, and a Kentucky officer came to this fate, but every man who associated himself with the Freedmen's Bureau shared the risk. (*See Document No. 8.*) It was a dangerous job that required more motivation than what a modest salary could provide.

CHAPTER 4

THE LIMITS OF PHILANTHROPY

The Need for Relief. As Bureau men began to organize their offices and survey their jurisdictions, they did so in the midst of the devastated economic and social landscape left in the wake of the war. Bad agricultural decisions on the part of planters as well as the vicissitudes of war, including the impressment of supplies by the Confederate government, contributed to food shortages and widespread destitution. The loss of livestock, farm equipment, and railroad capacity combined with the consequences of a population adjusting to the death of some 260,000 Confederate soldiers and the permanent scars of additional thousands rendered the southern landscape all the more depressing, making poverty a common denominator throughout the region. Clearly, Bureau men faced an extraordinary situation, but a situation that they believed had only one sound, lasting solution: the transplantation of a productive Yankee-style system of labor that would put the South back on its feet marching towards a prosperous future, one that blacks and whites would share.

Turning the Bureau into an eleemosynary organization to deal with postwar destitution was not what Commissioner Howard or his subordinates had in mind when they embarked on their duties during the spring and summer of 1865. Howard initially expected at most to act as a coordinator of the efforts of northern relief agencies. Certainly, Howard understood that Congress had made his organization responsible for addressing the immediate needs of hungry, naked and sick freedpeople and white refugees. In June 1865, with limited resources of his own, the Commissioner appealed to the Army's Commissary Department, which agreed to provide the Bureau with provisions to distribute to needy freedpeople and refugees. These rations (a military measure of supplies designed for a Union soldier that referred to an issuance of various combinations of meat, corn meal or flour and other things) became the saving margin for many a destitute Southerner, black and white. Assistant commissioners also obtained clothing from the Quartermaster Department, captured Confederate stores, and northern relief organizations that they distributed to needy individuals adding to the help the agency provided to a slowly recovering South.

By August 1865, the Bureau was feeding 148,120 individuals a day, about what the War Department had been assisting in May 1865. Howard, however, understood from the outset that his agency's relief efforts were to be limited and temporary. On May 31, 1865, the Commissioner informed his subordinates that they should discontinue their relief activities as soon as possible and in June he restricted an individual's access to Bureau relief for a maximum of seven days. By September 1865, the agency, Howard later reported, "by a rigid examination of every applicant, by the rejection of all who could support themselves by labor, and by the process of finding work for the willing" reduced the number of individuals helped by Bureau largess to 74,951. "[A]nd from that time on," the Commissioner noted with some exaggeration, "there was a constant reduction."

Relief and Character. Commissioner Howard's desire to end the Bureau's relief efforts almost as soon as he had organized his agency was not the result of a lack of concern for the sufferings of black and white Southerners; rather he believed that direct relief was unnatural and even dangerous for those who received it. As Howard later noted in his autobiography, the Bureau's relief work was "abnormal to our system of government." Furthermore, Howard believed that it was a kindness to those who requested such help to make them rely on their own initiative. "[I]t was in every way most desirable to do away with crutches as soon as the patient was able to walk alone," Howard explained.

Howard's subordinates had no difficulty accepting his views about relief. Assistant commissioners and their subordinates throughout the South scrutinized all applications for relief. They dispersed the large bodies of freedpeople who had congregated in contraband camps and in cities, put some to work on government-sponsored farms to earn their own support, and provided transportation to freedpeople from areas with surplus labor to areas with labor shortages. They made it very clear that, as Clinton B. Fisk explained in May 1866, "the Government's [corn] crib was not an easy thing to get into."

Bureau men aggressively pushed to reduce their relief rolls because they feared that, human nature being weak, both black and white Southerners would cheat the government in their attempts, as Wager Swayne acknowledged, to "claim any good that is gratuitous." As Mississippi assistant commissioner Samuel Thomas warned in April 1866, the "the utmost vigilance" had to be used "to protect the Governt. from imposition." During the summer of 1865, Clinton B. Fisk believed that he had found ample evidence of dishonest behavior on the part of blacks and whites. He was certain "that the Government is being immensely *swindled* by many of the recipients of its bounty." In certain sections of Alabama and Georgia, some families, he reported, "*claim it as a right* and alas too many think it no wrong to resort to any mean trick to more than duplicate the quantity they would be entitled to if found worthy." A Bureau blind to such attempts to cheat the government, argued Fisk, would only make matters worse by "fostering institutions for the promotion of idleness, vagrancy, pauperism and crime."

There was, as Fisk and other Bureau men feared, serious danger in the wholesale distribution of relief especially to black Southerners who had yet to develop a full appreciation of their new status. Slavery, they assumed, had been a destructive institution that had failed to teach black men and women habits of economy, habits that the freedpeople would certainly not learn while on relief. Indeed, in the minds of Yankee Bureau men continued black dependency was just another form of servitude, something that diminished the meaning of emancipation, and, thus, something that mocked the meaning of their own hard-won victory. Orlando Brown argued that "neither laws nor proclamations" could make the ex-slaves free until "they place themselves in a position, where their dependence on the Government or charity for support shall cease." Furthermore, relief challenged their notions of a good society and their interpretation of what kind of nation they had fought to save. In October 1865, for example, Rufus Saxton explained that "Idleness and vagrancy are discouraged in all well-regulated communities."

John Eaton, Jr. described what he believed would happen if the Bureau did not discourage these lingering vices of a past era. He wrote in December 1865, "Governments, as they approximate to the tyrannical may, to save themselves from violence of the mob, temporarily nurse multitudes into beggary." Such would not do for the United States. "[R]epublics, dependent on the labor, integrity, and intelligence of the individual," Eaton warned, "cannot for a moment afford to empty their treasuries, or degrade the self-respect of any of their individual members, by any such disbursement of supplies as will encourage beggary, or foster idleness, or other crime."

To prevent all of the negative consequences of relief, Bureau officers engaged in tough practices, cutting off rations for those who refused to work, assuming that such actions would cause only short-term distress as they circumvented the pernicious long-term consequences of the dole. In August 1865, Clinton B. Fisk told Tennesseans "without distinction of color" to "go to work." Troubled by "destitute shiftless refugees," he "cut off their supplies and made the rule 'work or starve'." "In a few cases my action may cause temporary suffering," he admitted, "but better *that* than to continue governmental institutes for the diffusion of ignorance and the promotion of idleness and crime."

This was an attitude that outlasted the early months of Reconstruction. In July 1866, North Carolina Assistant Commissioner John C. Robinson ordered his officers and agents to inspect the homes of freedpeople living in or near camps controlled by the Bureau. They were to register the names of those freedpeople who might become a "charge for the Government" during the next winter and find them work. If these freedpeople refused employment, the Bureau men were to do their best to change their minds, but also to inform them that "under no circumstances will further assistance be given them by the Government and in case of persistent refusal they will be removed from the camp." In the spring of 1868, Georgia Assistant Commissioner Caleb C. Sibley continued to hold to the belief that stopping the distribution of rations produced good results, "forcing many to successful exertions to obtain support, who (under other circumstances) would have lingered on in idleness as long as there was a chance to subsist on the bounty of the Government." Sometimes, as Orlando Brown noted, the "spur of necessity" was the only thing that could move freedpeople to become "self reliant, industrious and provident."

Ironically, even as northern conservatives and white Southerners complained about how Bureau rations kept the freedpeople lazy and unwilling to tend their fields, significant numbers of hungry whites laid claim to the agency's assistance. In September 1865, one Alabama Bureau officer reported from the northwestern part of the state that "not a single negro has been in my Office to beg, while white people come by the score each day." In late 1865, 95 Alabama whites, residents of Calhoun, Randolph and Talladega Counties in the eastern part of the state petitioned the Bureau to establish a depot in Oxford for the relief of small farmers. The state's assistant commissioner, Wager Swayne, reported that for the period from November 1865 through September 1866 his monthly totals of white men, women, and children receiving rations from the Bureau added up to 166,589. During the same period, the monthly totals for freedpeople came to 72,115.

Thus, many white Southerners were not too proud to take advantage of the government's largess, even though, as some North Carolina whites did in September 1868, they might "turn away with a load of corn given them by the Gov't, cursing that Gov't, and railing bitterly against it." There is more irony here in that the relief statistics for white indigents provided northern politicians with additional ammunition for their arguments to continue the agency by allowing them to describe it as being a benefit to whites as well as blacks. In March 1868, Congressman Thomas Eliot in part made his case for extending the Bureau's life by informing his colleagues in the House that white Southerners had received 5,234,779 rations out of a total of 18,319,522 issued by the agency.

Relief for the Deserving Poor. Efforts to get freedpeople back to work helped reduce the Bureau's involvement in charity. Nevertheless, there would always be some individuals and some circumstances that required the intervention of the agency to alleviate suffering. There would always be classes of "deserving poor" whose circumstances played on the Christian consciences of Bureau men. Officers and agents were generally more sympathetic towards women, children, the elderly, and the sick when it came to providing rations, but even here there were limits to what the agency would tolerate. As historian Mary J. Farmer has shown in her study of freedwomen's relationships with the Bureau, the agency was less likely to turn away black women who were facing hard times than able-bodied black men. Her statistics support this generalization. In Alabama 84 percent of more than 72,000 freedpeople and in Virginia 85 percent of more than 80,000 freedpeople receiving rations from November 1865 to September 1866 were women and children. However, she also notes that those indigent women who could not support their children risked having agents and officers apprentice the youngsters to white employers who could feed them without expense to the Bureau.

Consequently, even when agents and officers recognized a need for relief, they looked for alternatives to Bureau handouts. (*See Document No. 9.*) They tried to convince ex-masters to accept the responsibility of feeding their elderly former slaves in the immediate aftermath of the war. They insisted that estranged husbands and fathers to pay some amount of alimony and child support, which would alleviate the need for Bureau relief for indigent women and children. They did not hesitate to lecture the black community on the need to care for their own. They apprenticed the children of indigent parents. All the while, they held to the belief that local and state governments should bear the cost of public relief, not northern taxpayers.

Even as the agency strove to extricate itself from the "ration business," it found itself drawn back into relief work by major crises that it could not ignore. Throughout the South, the early plantings of Reconstruction did not lead to abundant harvests. In Texas, as J. B. Kiddo explained in June 1866, "The providential interference with the crops has been a source of deep regret." Severe flooding limited the potential for a decent 1866 harvest in Louisiana; in 1867, that state experienced yet another flood. During the spring of 1866 and again in 1867, the Georgia Bureau learned of extraordinary want throughout the state. In 1867 there were crop failures in Virginia. Even as the South Carolina Bureau worked to reduce the number of rations it issued, it had to confront the consequences of the poor harvests of 1866 and 1867. Other states experienced similar problems.

In periods of crisis, state and local governments pleaded poverty or simply refused to help black indigents, rationalizing that emancipation had freed whites of their obligations to their former slaves. In July 1866 in the Lake City, Florida area, for example, the civil authorities had an empty treasury "for great difficulties are being found to collect taxes." In Alabama, the state government tried to cope with destitution by issuing bonds, the proceeds of which would allow it to purchase food for the hungry. The bond issue was a failure and in May 1866 the governor informed Wager Swayne that the state would need federal assistance to handle the problem of destitution. And when in early 1866 the Bureau officer at Stafford Court House, Virginia, asked the local board of overseers if it would tend to the indigent freedpeople, the president of that board simply refused, replying, "Not a damn bite will I give them; I would choose hell first." Even when state law required comparable treatment of freedpeople and whites, as a Tennessee statute of May 1866 did, it could not force local officials to act with vigor in tending to the needs of the ex-slaves. There remained a need for the Bureau to step into the breach, despite all of its efforts to avoid doing so.

During 1866, the Bureau did what it could to alleviate the consequences of bad harvests and the lingering devastation of war. In April, Howard established a Special Relief Commission in the nation's capital thanks to a $25,000 congressional appropriation, which oversaw relief

efforts in Washington. Absalom Baird sent rations to the Louisiana parishes suffering from the effects of the flood. Davis Tillson hired special
agents to deal exclusively with the distribution of relief and at the end
of the year reported that the Georgia agency had distributed a total of
505,264 rations to freedpeople and 177,942 rations to whites. Wager
Swayne and civil authorities cooperated in the distribution of rations,
establishing eight depots throughout Alabama for this purpose. Other
officers did what they could for their states, even as Howard set an October 1, 1866 deadline to end rations. But the following year, the South's
continuing agricultural crisis prompted congressional action, which
gave the agency access to substantial funds for alleviating the widespread destitution of that year.

On March 30, 1867, Congress, ever reluctant to give more money to
the agency, gave Howard the authority to use funds from other budget
lines to purchase food for destitute Southerners, black and white, including whites who were not refugees. Shortly after Congress's joint
resolution, on April 3, the Commissioner set aside $500,000 for the pur-
pose of coping with renewed problems of hunger and destitution. The
next day Howard placed the Bureau's inspector general, Eliphalet Whittlesey, in charge of this renewed relief effort, while assistant commissioners appointed officers to oversee the distribution of this relief within
their states. In Georgia, the Bureau repeated its 1866 procedures for
distributing relief and used the funds on hand to assist 14,754 whites
and 8,574 blacks during May and as many as 22,376 whites and 19,318
freedpeople in July.

When the immediate crisis passed, however, so too did the Bureau's
concerns for helping the destitute. With better harvests in the offing,
the Bureau discontinued the general distribution of relief in August
1867 after Whittlesey had expended $445,993.36. By the end of the
winter of 1867, the Bureau had issued a total of 18,319,522 rations, with
5,234,779 distributed to white Southerners. Combined with the relief
the agency helped to distribute from northern organizations such as the
Boston Fund, the New York Southern Famine Relief Commission, and
the Philadelphia Famine Relief Commission, the Bureau was responsible for helping a significant number of hungry black and white Southerners. After the 1867 crisis, while the agency continued to provide rations for hospitalized and institutionalized individuals, its relief to
able-bodied poor was incidental, at times taking the form of loans with
the Bureau placing a lien on the borrowers' crops.

Health Care. The Bureau's efforts to provide health care for indigent, sick, orphaned and elderly freedpeople as well as white refugees, presented the agency with the same dilemma that it confronted in its efforts to feed and clothe deserving hardship cases. Providing hospital beds, dispensing medicines and treating diseases required the Bureau to balance Christian charity with economy, human kindness with the tough demands for independence, and temporary actions with real, pressing needs in the postwar South. The Bureau would best deal with the health problems of black and white Southerners by first helping alleviate immediate suffering, by working to prevent future problems, and by reminding civil officials and the black community that they had to accept responsibility for their sick. Finally, the Bureau believed that by establishing a good free-labor economy, it would provide the financial circumstances for maintaining good health along with the means for caring for less fortunate individuals long after the agency had disbanded.

The Bureau's Washington headquarters had a chief medical officer who supervised the state agencies' surgeons-in-chief. These men in turn supervised various numbers of civilian and military doctors tending to freedpeople and refugees in hospitals and dispensaries spread thinly across their jurisdictions. Bureau doctors provided medical attention for about half a million recorded cases and, according to the chief medical officer's 1869 report, probably another half million unrecorded cases. Their efforts fell short of the health requirements of the freedpeople and the Reconstruction South, but given the temporary nature of the agency, they relieved much suffering that might have gone unnoticed if the Bureau had not been on duty and significantly reducing the mortality rate of freedpeople and refugees.

From their arrival at their various state jurisdictions, Bureau medical men faced public health crises that flourished in the devastated postwar South. The Bureau obviously preferred to prevent rather than treat small pox, cholera and yellow fever, the diseases that either spread rapidly in close quarters of freedpeople's communities or flourished in the filth that was the consequence of the poor sanitary facilities therein. (*See Document No. 10.*) Bureau medical officers, therefore, went on inspection tours of their jurisdictions to become familiar with the health needs of their charges and to identify problem areas in need of attention.

The Bureau's desire to prevent sickness in part explains the agency's efforts to move freedpeople out of the towns and cities in which they congregated after the war. Preventive measures also extended to encouraging the freedpeople who remained in cities to clean up their urban neighborhoods and whitewash their houses. In Mississippi, the Bureau imposed sanitary regulations on the ex-slaves and in Tennessee in the face of the cholera outbreak of 1866, Assistant Commissioner Fisk ordered his superintendents to supervise the freedpeople in carrying out rigorous sanitation measures.

Another positive if limited approach to prevention was the Bureau's effort to encourage smallpox vaccination. In March 1866, when that disease threatened North Carolina, the Bureau required that teachers should have their pupils vaccinated; any students who refused would not be allowed to remain in school. By the end of 1867, Bureau had vaccinated some 49,631 individuals, not much more than a start and hardly sufficient to stop the spread of the small pox. When such good intentions failed, the Bureau established special smallpox hospitals or assisted civil authorities in their efforts to deal with the disease, although poverty or at times plain reluctance prevented the Bureau from obtaining help from the local officials or the black population.

Beyond dealing with public health crises, the Bureau expected to play a limited role in providing healthcare for ex-slaves. It presumed that employed freedpeople could look after their own health needs, preferably by negotiating labor contracts that contained provisions for medical care. But if there were deserving poor who could coax rations out of the agency, so, too, were there ill, indigent freedpeople and refugees who could convince the agency to the assist them. The Bureau established hospitals and dispensaries to care for these impoverished, sick freedpeople and refugees.

By November 1865, there were 42 hospitals with a capacity of 4,500 beds and at one point in 1866, there were 56 Bureau-sponsored hospitals as well as 47 dispensaries containing beds for 4,559 indigent patients. J. W. Lawton, the Georgia Bureau's medical officer, believed that medical facilities were best sited at central locations; other medical officers apparently agreed with Lawton's pragmatic philosophy, one made sensible by the limited resources at their disposal. In Alabama, Wager Swayne reported in October 1866 that the Bureau had established centrally located "colonies" in areas with large black populations, which he described as "a sort of infirmary, consisting of a hospital for the sick, and a number of cabins for orphans and helpless persons."

Hospitals, however, gave the appearance of a permanent Bureau presence, even if they were understaffed ramshackle affairs, and it appears that medical officers preferred relying on an outpatient dispensary system. They were more practical, the Bureau's chief medical officer reported in November 1867, while "causing [their] beneficiaries to be more provident for themselves." In 1866 when the Tennessee Bureau realized that civilian officials were stubborn in their reluctance to assume the costs of caring for sick indigent freedpeople, the agency established dispensaries in four locations. Keeping with Fisk's philosophy, surgeons were instructed to charge all but the destitute freedpeople for services provided, a way to encourage the ex-slaves to witness their own economic progress and self-sufficiency. In September 1867, the Bureau's chief medical officer told his state surgeons-in-chief to rely on dispensaries instead of hospitals in order to reduce the costs of the medical department. Georgia's Lawton and his successors favored such a system as the most economical means for dispensing medical care beyond population centers, but the Georgia Bureau established only a handful of them throughout the state, with only three still functioning in October 1867.

There probably were never enough of these establishments or the physicians to staff them in the other southern states, leaving the handfuls of doctors the Bureau had on its state rosters as busy as their nonmedical counterparts. George Dalton, a military surgeon who operated a Bureau dispensary in southwest Georgia, remarked as much. "I believe, Doctor, you might send a man into each of the several neighboring counties," he advised the Georgia Bureau's chief medical officer in April 1867, "& if he did simply his duty, attending to the *deserving* cases he would wear himself out as soon as well established, become completely used up, if he would allow it." Dalton's Albany dispensary was the sole Bureau medical establishment for 31,000 freedpeople in eight surrounding counties.

Many more Bureau physicians could have made the same recommendation and some did. During June 1868, the Covington, Kentucky, physician reported to the Bureau that he had tended to the needs of 432 individuals, while the Louisville dispensary averaged 750 freedpeople a month. No wonder Wager Swayne reported that he believed that the $100 monthly salary was an "insufficient return for the labor and professional skill" that such demanding situations required of the Bureau's civilian contract surgeons. But the need for an expanded network of well-paid physicians could not outweigh the belief that the agency's medical work should be only a limited foray into social services.

As with other forms of relief, the Bureau expected to close down its medical operations as soon as possible. In 1865, for example, Clinton Fisk prematurely ordered the hospitals within his jurisdiction closed and in the spring of 1866, after the Tennessee legislature passed a law requiring local officials to tend to poverty-stricken freedpeople, he ordered the Bureau's dispensaries closed. By 1868, Bureau officials were being especially careful about allowing their hospital populations to increase. By July 1 of that year, the Bureau operated only 21 hospitals and 48 dispensaries, with the expectation that state and local governments were now able to care for their own sick. The closings and the transfers of facilities to civilian authorities continued until by 1869, there were only hospitals in Washington and in Richmond hospitals with six dispensaries left open and in February 1970, the Bureau turned over to civil authorities the Richmond hospital. Earlier in May 1867, Georgia Bureau medical chief J. V. De Hanne made it clear that such a contraction of medical facilities was necessary to encourage state and local governments to assume their legitimate responsibilities; any continued Bureau activity would discourage them from doing so.

Getting the civil governments to cooperate in resuming their responsibilities to indigent sick as well as the aged, disabled, bind and insane, especially among their black populations, was a vexing tax for the various Bureau jurisdictions. To encourage local cooperation, Bureau officials often provided municipalities with funds, rations and other assistance if they would tend to the needs of the indigent sick freedpeople. Fisk, for example, gave officials at Memphis and some other Tennessee towns money to encourage them to care for freedpeople, which apparently worked.

There remained, however, a general sense among whites that emancipation had relieved them of their responsibilities to their former slaves, which dampened any eagerness to tax themselves to provide healthcare for blacks. Also, many Southerners exhibited a reluctance to work with the Bureau, which hindered the kind of positive partnership that Fisk and other Bureau officials hoped to develop in the area of healthcare. In January 1868, for example, the Bureau officer at Paducah, Kentucky, reported that the town's mayor and its physician, a former Confederate Army medical man, expressed a desire to help the "sick pauper freedpeople." However, while they were willing to accept medicine from Bureau to further that end, they refused to make any reports to the agency "or in any way to connect themselves with this Bureau." The officer recommended that the Bureau not give the town any assistance and the chief medical officer for Kentucky agreed. During the period of Military Reconstruction commencing in the spring of 1867, Bureau officials could appeal to military commanders to have the uncooperative officials removed, a process that only rarely produced desirable results. The more common occurrence was the consolidation and eventual closing of Bureau medical facilities with nothing left behind to fill the vacuum.

Such a limited, temporary, centralized system that assumed reasonable white officials would take up their civic responsibilities almost guaranteed that freedpeople would fall through the cracks. In March 1867, F. S. Town, the Kentucky surgeon-in-chief, noted that most of the state's freedpeople were beyond the reach of a Bureau-supported medical facility. Indigent freedpeople who did not reside near Bureau hospitals or dispensaries often found that local physicians would not treat ex-slaves either because of racism, fear of retaliation from their white neighbors, or the freedpeople's inability to pay for the care. At times, supervision of the freedpeople's health fell to officers and agents of the Bureau, not medical men, such as those Arkansas agents who coped with epidemics on their own by relocating freedpeople to healthier environs.

Even in the best of circumstances, agency requirements often caused delays and hardships. In January 1866, agent Brien Maguire found himself stymied by regulations, prejudice and stubbornness when he attempted to help freedpeople in Wilkes County, Georgia. Local authorities refused to respond to his request for assistance with smallpox cases among the freedpeople, arguing that the ex-slaves were the Bureau's responsibility. The state Bureau office instructed him to confront the local officials again before the agency would take any action, but those officials once again refused to act, claiming they had no funds for such cases. In the meantime, Maguire went to the aid of two ailing freedpeople only to witness their deaths for want of timely attention.

As the Bureau prepared to terminate most of its operations in the South, it continued to encounter reluctance on the part of local authorities to shoulder the burden of healthcare for poor freedpeople. The general policy was to transfer hospitals as well as their patients to the civil authorities, but there were times when the local officials balked at accepting such responsibilities. In December 1868, Sidney Burbank,

Kentucky's assistant commissioner, reported that his efforts to prepare for the Bureau's closing ran aground on the reluctance of the mayor and city council of Louisville to assume responsibility for the local Bureau hospital; he had written to the officials in October and had since visited them three times and still they refused to act. Howard eventually transferred the remaining patients from the Louisville hospital to a Washington facility, "repeated appeals having been made in vain" to state and local authorities to take over the place.

Local officials also refused to accept responsibility for hospitals in New Orleans, Vicksburg, Richmond, and Washington. By the fall of 1869, the Bureau had closed all but the Richmond and the Washington hospitals. After it turned over the Richmond hospital to the state of Virginia on February 1, 1870, it continued to supervise only the Washington, D.C., hospital, which remained under federal control for some time.

The Bureau's relief policies at best helped to budge the South out of its postwar rejection of the paternalist tradition of the past to a limited acceptance of its civic responsibility towards its unfortunate indigent black citizens. The agency's activities reduced mortality rates among ex-slave and relieved the suffering of a substantial number of black and white Southerners, but because of its temporary nature and limited resources could do little more than to deal with the immediate postwar crises. The Bureau's work fell short of the needs of the freedpeople because Congress never expected or encouraged the agency to do much more. Furthermore, the Bureau's relief activities were never designed to do anything more than act as a stop-gap in services that civilian governments would provide once the South's economy stabilized. Bureau men generally believed that the real changes in the South, including better healthcare, would come when the freedpeople could afford to take care of themselves. However, Bureau officials did insist that civil authorities care for their indigents with no distinction made according to race, a radical concept at the time even if it failed to take hold.

CHAPTER 5

THE BUREAU AND THE FREEDPEOPLE'S DESIRE FOR LAND

Bureau Land Policy. At the outset of Reconstruction, from Virginia down through South Carolina and Florida out to Texas, a noticeable number of freedpeople challenged the Bureau notion of their place in the economy as hired laborers because they expected the government to grant them their Civil War inheritance—land. During 1865, Bureau assistant commissioners were quite willing to follow the charge of Congress and distribute land according to the guidelines promulgated by the first Bureau law and by the Commissioner. Beyond doing their jobs, some Bureau men were aware of the justice in such work. In his first circular, Rufus Saxton reiterated his earlier views concerning the efficacy of land distribution for the freedpeople "where by faithful industry they can achieve independence." They deserved as much, he wrote to Howard in August 1865, because "They have been loyal to the Union cause" and the nation owed them something for "two hundred years of unrequited toil." He expected to continue to locate abandoned property within his jurisdiction upon which he could settle freedpeople.

At the same time, however, the Bureau tried to disabuse the freedpeople of the notion that the government would implement a general confiscation and redistribution of rebel property. Under orders from O. O. Howard, assistant commissioners advised their subordinates to counter the rumors involving land redistribution across the South at Christmastime or the New Year. In doing so, Wager Swayne hit upon one of the concerns of most Northerners when it came to the notion of property redistribution. His comments also illustrate the balancing act in which Bureau men engaged in their acceptance of the fact that even ex-rebels had constitutional rights worth recognizing. "Such expectations are fruitful of idleness, disappointment and mischief, and of no good whatever," he wrote to his men on September 7, 1865. "Every effort should be made to show to Freedmen the absurdity of supposing that a government which is simply vindicating their natural rights as one class of its citizens, will for their benefit invade the equal rights and property of another class." Property rights, even for most erstwhile Confederates, were sacred.

Other Bureau men made two additional important observations in reporting their concerns of the freedpeople's ambitions, which help to illustrate the complicated situation in which they found themselves. The freedpeople would not work for their ex-masters not so much because they believed they did not need to work, but, as J. S. Fullerton observed in Louisiana, because they expected to put their efforts into their own agricultural enterprises. Furthermore, the ex-slaves had some reason to expect that they would be able to carry out this vision of freedom: they hoped to receive land from the government by the end of 1865.

In January 1866, Eliphalet Whittlesey reminded Bureau headquarters that wartime federal confiscation acts as well as the words about Yankee schemes to destroy the South through land redistribution promulgated by "rebel politicians in their efforts 'to fire the southern heart'" had alerted the slaves and contrabands that something might be afoot to support such a notion as free land. Swayne also noted that the freedpeople "had heard" of federal confiscation of planters' lands "for years." Freedpeople were wrong in assuming wide-ranging plans for land redistribution, but by the end of the war there were examples that hinted that it was a possibility.

The war had left thousands of slaves cultivating land in the Mississippi Valley and on the southeastern coast. Reinforcing impressions from wartime events was the first Bureau law. Through this piece of legislation, Congress authorized the agency to lease up to 40 acres of confiscated and abandoned land to freedpeople and refugees, with the understanding that those individuals who resided on and cultivated such property for three years would have the option to purchase the land they diligently farmed.

In July 1865, Commissioner Howard issued without presidential preview or approval his Circular No. 13, which ordered his assistant commissioners to "select and set apart such confiscated and abandoned lands and property as may be deemed necessary for the immediate use of refugees and freedmen." At this point Howard believed that the presidential amnesty proclamation of May 29, 1865 and presidential pardons did not influence the general Bureau land policy. Relying on the United States Attorney General's positive interpretation of the Bureau's authority to distribute abandoned or confiscated property, Howard assured

his men that they could make use of the property they had at their disposal to help freedpeople and refugees knowing that "The pardon of the
President will not be understood to extend to the surrender of abandoned or confiscated property."

His subordinates acted under that assumption, too. During 1865,
freedpeople in Arkansas, Tennessee, Louisiana and elsewhere rented
abandoned and confiscated land under the Bureau's direction. In June,
Orlando Brown reported that he had settled freedpeople on 58 of Virginia's plantations. By that date, Rufus Saxton, who had supervised the
freedpeople's efforts on the South Carolina coast since July 1862, had
settled a total of 40,000 ex-slaves on 400,000 acres of land in the Sherman Reservation.

Unfortunately for the freedpeople's ambitions, Circular No. 13, as
Howard later reported with fine understatement, "did not please President Johnson." In September 1865, Johnson reversed Howard's plans
with a revised Circular No. 15 that he wrote for the Commissioner to
issue, having been "dissatisfied" with an earlier version from Howard.
"[W]ith masterly adroitness," by incorporating in the circular a very
limited definition of confiscated property, Howard concluded, the president "effectually defeated the *intention*" of the Bureau's purpose with
regard to land.

Claude F. Oubre, the historian of Bureau land policy, notes that the
Bureau could not do much but comply with the wishes of the commander-
in-chief and begin to restore the over 850,000 acres of land it held at
the beginning of Reconstruction. By January 31, 1866, it had restored
393,000 acres to planters who proved ownership and produced presidential pardons. By April 21, 1866, the total of restored acres had reached
430,104. The Bureau still held on to 427,000 acres at that time. Furthermore, by the end of 1867, Howard reported that "a large part of the
land" held by the agency was "unimproved lands, for which no claim
has been presented," suggesting that the Bureau controlled a good bit
of property that was not very desirable. The Bureau continued to return
land and in August 1868 near the end of its active life, it retained only
139,543 acres. Eric Foner in his survey of Reconstruction reminds us
that this restoration had personal consequences: in southeastern Virginia,
almost 20,000 freedpeople lost their hold on confiscated and abandoned
property, as did other ex-slaves elsewhere in the South. For these individuals, restoration was nothing less than betrayal.

As Commissioner Howard explained in his autobiography, even under more congenial circumstances, the agency could have only gone so far in helping the freedpeople to achieve their great goal. "Only about one five-hundredth . . . of the entire amount of land in the States seceding was available [to the Bureau]," Howard admitted; "it was all that had ever been held by the United States as abandoned." While the Bureau could have helped some black families become independent farmers if Johnson had not intervened—certainly a significant alteration of the traditional southern landscape—it still would have left the majority of them working for white employers. If freedpeople expected to achieve the ultimate goal of becoming landowning farmers, they would have to work, save, and purchase property according to the Bureau's free-labor formula.

Restoring Lands in the Sherman Reservation. It was one thing to inform hopeful freedpeople in Alabama or North Carolina that the government would not give them land. It was quite a different story for freedpeople who already had begun to work what they thought would be their land to learn that the government planned to remove them to favor the claims of erstwhile rebels. Nowhere was the disappointment so obvious as on the lands of the Sherman Reservation. Not only had the freedpeople in the reservation been cultivating property under Bureau supervision, but also under the guidance of sympathetic local Bureau agents they had established governments and militias of their own. In November 1866, South Carolina's assistant commissioner Robert K. Scott realized that the reservation freedpeople had come to assume the land was their "permanent inheritance." The task of removing them, Scott noted, "was the more difficult from their having occupied the islands under such positive assurance from men whose high official position would seem to justify the claimant in resisting any encroachments upon his supposed privileges."

Commissioner Howard learned something of this black commitment to the land when he, on orders from the president, journeyed to South Carolina to carry the government's restoration policy into the reservation. White landowners were clamoring for the same consideration enjoyed by their pardoned cousins beyond the reservation's boundaries and Johnson now expected the Bureau to comply with their wishes. On October 19, 1865, the Commissioner informed a meeting of freedpeople on Edisto Island that they would have to give up their land grants in an address, he remembered, that "met with no apparent favor." "Why,

General Howard, why do you take away our lands?" a freedman asked him. "You take them from us who are true, always true to the Government! You give them to our all-time enemies! That is not right!" Later that month Howard reported to Secretary of War Stanton that "the disappointment is very great on the part of the negroes." Howard tried to convince the Edisto freedpeople that their former masters would not oppress them because it would not be in the best interest of employers to do so, but that bit of reassurance was far from what the ex-slaves wished to hear from their Bureau.

The Freedmen's Bureau commissioner could do no more than to guarantee to the Edisto and other reservation freedpeople his support in their keeping what they had raised and in their efforts to secure fair contracts, but that was all he could do. When Howard arrived in Savannah, Georgia, to inform Georgia freedpeople of Johnson's policy, he found that word of his South Carolina activities had outpaced him. The freedpeople, according to plantation mistress Elizabeth Stiles, were in despair because the white claimants were to have their land.

Howard placed Captain A. P. Ketchum in charge of working out the details of the restoration. Ketchum, a believer in black land ownership had earlier worked with Saxton in distributing and recording reservation grants. He was serving on Howard's staff at the time of this appointment. Ketchum, according to the Commissioner "the most judicious officer . . . [available] for that duty," did his best to delay full restoration to white claimants, but in February 1866 Howard ordered him to return to Washington. The restoration process, however, continued under the assistant commissioners, who had little choice but to comply with the president's policy. Initially, Davis Tillson also delayed a speedy restoration in Georgia, temporarily returning to white claimants only land unencumbered by black settlers until Congress clarified a situation left so unclear by Sherman. (*See Document No. 11.*) During 1866, however, Tillson came to the conclusion that Sherman's order was of dubious value in part because of his clashes with black settlers and in part because of his fear that they would not turn their grants into productive farms.

On July 16, 1866, Congress renewed the Bureau and sealed the fate of the reservation freedpeople. Those once privileged ex-slaves with good "possessory titles" could remain on their grants to harvest their crops and then either sign contracts with white landowners, purchase land on the coast of South Carolina to which the government held clear title, or leave to work elsewhere. The Bureau began to carry out this final step in restoring reservation lands during the latter part of 1866, a process speeded by the imperfect claims the freedpeople produced for the Bureau. (*See Document No. 12.*) Incomplete certificates or the occupation of the wrong plots of land allowed the Bureau to blame the freedpeople, as South Carolina Assistant Commissioner Scott did in his report for 1866, for their ignorance in conforming to the conditions of Sherman's special field order. Tillson recognized that no freedpeople within his jurisdiction had valid "possessory titles" exactly conforming to all of the requirements set out by Sherman's order; nevertheless, he tried to work within the spirit of that order to help freedpeople who had at least met some of the requirements to claim South Carolina land.

It was unfair to blame all of the freedpeople for their incomplete or imperfect claims. Those faulty claims had resulted from Ketchum's inability while earlier working under Saxton to deal with all of those ex-slaves settling in the reservation, to make sure they complied with the conditions, to register their holdings, and to issue proper certificates. Time limitations and limited resources took their toll. In the reservation in Georgia, for example, the farther the distance the freedpeople were from Savannah, the less likely it was that they had had the opportunity to meet with Ketchum to have their claims recorded. Nevertheless, the consequences for the freedpeople remained the same: they would need to leave their holdings.

There were reservation freedpeople who took advantage of the offered South Carolina lands. In November 1867, Howard reported that 1,980 heads of families owned 19,040 acres of land in the Beaufort, South Carolina, Bureau subdistrict, having paid the government $31,000 for the property. Unfortunately not all reservation freedpeople could take or wished to take advantage of the government's offer. Some ex-slaves had already given up on their claims and had left to work elsewhere. Some violently and fruitlessly resisted the efforts of white landowners, the Bureau and the Army to oust them from the land they believed to be rightly their own. Some remained as squatters on marginal land or neglected property even after the government's policy turned against them. But for most of the reservation freedpeople, Sherman's promise went unfulfilled.

The Southern Homestead Act. Even as Bureau men restored property to white claimants, they sought out other means for helping freedpeople obtain property. In 1865, Davis Tillson attempted but failed to secure northern capital in order to purchase land that the investors could then divide and sell as family farms to Georgia's ex-slaves. He did, however, show a willingness to help freedpeople locate property that they could lease until they could afford to purchase land. O. O. Howard engaged in another plan to sell small plots of land to freedmen at Barry Farm in the District of Columbia. He continued to believe with unrealistic optimism that freedpeople elsewhere would benefit from the activities of capitalist investors who would sell them land on reasonable terms. In early 1866, the Commissioner also had his subordinates assess the possibility of settling freedpeople on public lands in the South, some of which proved to be unsuitable for farming. In the end, all such enterprises failed to satisfy the freedpeople's desire for some general redistribution of property and all required that the freedpeople who embarked on any plan to obtain land have some capital with which to start their enterprises. That latter difficulty as well as the Bureau's own limited resources figured in to the mixed outcome of Southern Homestead Act of June 21, 1866, the government's last significant effort to help the freedpeople obtain land.

The Southern Homestead Act set aside over 46 million acres of public lands in Alabama, Arkansas, Florida, Louisiana, and Mississippi. For two years from passage, the maximum claim would be 80 acres, with the claimant paying fees for entering the claim. The lands would be open only to loyal refugees and freedpeople until January 1, 1867. The government apparently delayed a general opening of the public lands not so much to give freedpeople a head start in staking their claims, but rather to give them an equal opportunity to compete for the land. Most freedpeople at the time of passage should have committed themselves to yearlong contracts or leases for 1866 that no federal official would have suggested they break to take advantage of the legislation. The homesteaders once they registered claims would need to hold onto their property for five years and pay the required fees to register and complete the claim.

The distribution of this land fell under the supervision of the federal government's General Land Office and the Bureau's role in implementing the law was technically a very limited one. However, as the guardian of the interests of the freedpeople, its officers and agents could not avoid participating to some degree in the freedpeople's efforts to find land under the law. On July 2, 1866, Commissioner Howard informed his subordinates that they should certainly urge the freedpeople take advantage of the Southern Homestead Act, essentially having his Bureau serve as an information gathering agency that would educate the freedpeople to the opportunities now available to them. Bureau officers did what they could to spread the word of the opportunities now available under the new law. In Alabama, Wager Swayne circulated information about the law, while in Arkansas Bureau agents urged freedpeople to homestead. In Georgia superintendent of education G. L. Eberhart assumed that burden as part of his duties, while Assistant Commissioner Tillson corresponded with his counterpart in Arkansas to learn of the status of the efforts of certain Georgia freedpeople to secure homestead lands.

As far as rendering financial assistance to the settlers, the Bureau limited itself to providing transportation and one month's rations. A few of these men understood that the physical assistance the government offered to the homesteaders was too limited to be of much help in providing a good start on a successful homestead. In 1866, Lieutenant J. S. Powers, the Bureau subassistant commissioner for the Beaufort, South Carolina, area, reported that "The freedmen are much exercised about the homestead act, and are holding meetings in each district to devise ways and means of emigration." However, Powers recognized that "without material aid form the government sufficient to carry them through the first year at their proposed new homes, much suffering will be the result of their move." Only failure could result, he concluded, "as the great majority of them will find themselves as destitute of means of the first of January, 1867, as they were at the commencement of 1866."

Powers, aware that the government would not assist these freedpeople beyond what it had already authorized the Bureau to do, warned his charges of the difficulties they would encounter and urged them to save as much as possible before attempting to migrate. Augustus Mitchell, a Maine native, an antebellum Georgia resident and the Bureau physician at St. Mary's, Georgia, on the other hand proposed that the government provide a year's worth of capital for the homesteaders. It was a suggestion that fell on deaf ears, even though so many homesteaders were hindered in their efforts by the need to work for someone while they fulfilled the requirements of the law.

Mitchell and the other Bureau men who thought as he did were out of step with the views of the majority of their colleagues who viewed homestead land as the reward for successfully participating in the free labor system, not as an unearned opportunity for the freedpeople to grab a head start in the new economy. Most Bureau men probably agreed with Louisiana Assistant Commissioner Absalom Baird's assessment that only freedpeople who had already accumulated a stake would succeed in the homesteading process. Davis Tillson willingly assisted those Georgia freedpeople who had what he believed were sufficient resources for making homesteads productive and withheld his support for those who had yet to earn such a stake.

Despite the apparent obstacles, freedpeople responded enthusiastically to the information Bureau men provided them about homesteading, but they found that the reality was not as satisfying as the promise. Michael Lanza, the historian of the Southern Homestead Act, concludes that it is difficult to determine from the records the number of freedpeople who took advantage of the law. Howard reported in late 1869 that about 4,000 families "have faced and overcome obstacles" to acquire homesteads; according to Lanza's estimates, almost 3,000 more achieved this goal by the end of the law's decade-long life when Congress repealed the law in 1876. Any number of freedpeople benefiting from the law was a good thing, but the low numbers underline the difficulties involved in the process. Homesteaders, black and white, registered a total of 67,600 claims. Of that total, about 28,000 claims led to actual land titles, a success rate of about 41 percent. Lanza concludes that blacks constituted from 20 to 25 percent of the total number of initial claims or about a maximum of 16,900. He believes that they enjoyed a rate of success equal to white homesteaders, which at an approximate 41 percent success rate would have been at best 6,929 claims. The majority of the South's freedpeople could not even try to take advantage of the Homestead Act of 1866 and the majority of those who did try failed to make permanent homes of their claims.

The practical limitations of a poor people seeking to use the law looms large in the story of the Southern Homestead Act. As Arkansas special agent Dr. W. W. Granger reported in April 1868, "the most extensive and most to be regretted cause" for the "slacking up of the homestead entries" of the freedpeople "is the poverty in which so many of them are involved." Reiterating Mitchell's observation, Granger concluded, "The result is in too many cases, entire inability to provide themselves with subsistence needed while putting a little patch in cultivation, and a shelter on it for their families—leaving seeds, tools and animals for cultivation out of the question."

There were, however, many other factors that complicated the freedpeople's efforts and hindered the fulfillment of the law's promise. Most of these problems were beyond the Bureau's power to control. Poor record-keeping practices, unopened land offices, poor land quality, lack of surveys and good maps, and confusion over land ownership all inhibited the implementation of the law, even when the Bureau tried to correct these problems. In Arkansas, the appointment of Dr. Granger as the Bureau's surveyor of public lands was an important advancement of the freedpeople's cause in connection with the homestead law and an good attempt to provide them with adequate information about prospective homesteads. In Louisiana, shortly after the passage of the law, Assistant Commissioner Absalom Baird tried to give working freedpeople —just the kind of individuals who should be rewarded in the free-labor system—a chance to take advantage of the law when he appointed an agent to locate land for freedpeople who were still tied to labor contracts. Later in 1867, the Bureau appointed land agents in Florida to locate public lands suitable for homesteaders to try to correct another serious problem. "Before the appointment of these agents," Commissioner Howard explained, "colored people would sometimes find that they had paid their money and made a costly pilgrimage to Tallahassee only to find that they were located in the middle of some Florida swamp."

Regardless, the problems were more than the Bureau could handle. Unenthusiastic or obstructionist land registrars, fraud, and the short time requirements for actually settling on registered claims also compounded these difficulties and figured into the law's failure or at best its very limited success. But Michael Lanza notes that the strong white opposition to black landholding and the postwar struggle between blacks and whites over the control of black labor played major roles in obstructing the freedpeople's use of the law. This was a struggle that also shaped the free-labor system to which most ex-slaves had to turn to keep together body and soul.

CHAPTER 6

NURTURING FREE LABOR

The Benefits of Free Labor. Bureau men worried that providing the freedpeople with a limitless dole or with free land would ruin the character of the ex-slaves, but they were just as certain that hard work and the resulting accumulation of even modest wealth would have the opposite effect. Hard work not only provided an avenue for permanently removing destitution from the South, it also had the added benefit of building character and thus preparing the freedpeople to earn their place as citizens. For Bureau men, labor not only had a practical economic consequence, but also an important, overarching moral quality that they assumed shored up or complemented all other virtues.

Such an understanding of work made even the hint of black laziness all the more pernicious and counterproductive, for idle freedpeople would undermine the fruits of victory. On the other hand, hard-working freedpeople would validate Yankee ideals and further strengthen the reunited nation. Bureau men assumed that the success of free labor would be an affirmation of their own wartime efforts as well as Lincoln's Emancipation Proclamation; its failure would reflect on Yankee beliefs, national policy, the martyred president, and, in particular, themselves. As Texas Assistant Commissioner Kiddo explained in October 1866, "The United States government remotely, but the Freedmen's Bureau immediately will be held responsible, by the political world at least, for this grandest experiment of the age."

The freedpeople's visible embrace of labor, Bureau men assumed, would also reinforce the ex-slaves' claim to their new status by proving beyond a doubt that they deserved their freedom, thus additionally confirming the wisdom of northern wartime policy. Through work the freedpeople would ultimately secure their freedom, for without labor there could be no real end to slavery. As Orlando Brown reminded the freedpeople of Virginia in July 1865, accept industry and frugality "and the glory of passing successfully from Slavery to Freedom, will, by the blessing of God, be yours."

Industrious freedpeople, however, would be able to claim more than being living examples of Yankee wisdom. Just as antebellum Northerners had benefited from their own efforts, so now ex-slaves would have the same opportunities, Mississippi Bureau chief Samuel Thomas explained in July 1865, to "enjoy the fair fruits of [their] labor." "A free man works for himself." Fisk explained, and "Every man is, under God, just what he makes himself." The opportunities in a free-labor economy were abundant, Bureau men reasoned; the freedpeople only had to take advantage of them.

Importantly, for these Bureau officials, work would bring to the freedpeople the ultimate material reward of property ownership, which was an important step in securing emancipation long after the Bureau had left the South. Bureau men assumed that once the freedpeople understood that land ownership was the great reward of hard work, they would accept the discipline of free labor, become as frugal as Yankees, and strive to achieve that cherished goal. But these same men were very clear about one thing: property ownership was sweet because it required effort. The Bureau men somewhat naively assumed that once the freedpeople understood the true nature of freedom and went to work initially as laborers on someone else's land, the free-labor system—in their minds fair, progressive, inevitably productive, and racially neutral—would deliver all the promised benefits of hard work.

Along with these political and economic dimensions of labor, the Bureau brought to the South an almost mystical conceptualization of work's place in the greater scheme of things. For Bureau men, turning away from hard work was near to turning away from the grace freely given by God. General Fisk, who claimed to love to spend his time in productive employment, pointed out in his 1866 advice pamphlet to the freedpeople that the angels in heaven were busy in God's name. Furthermore, God had commanded Adam and Eve to tend the Garden and then He came into the world to make His way as a working man. Work hard and provide for your families, he told freedmen, for such was "the most religious thing you can do." In January 1866, Davis Tillson also reminded a meeting of freedmen "that labor is not imposed by the white man, but by your Creator; that it is not a curse but a blessing." Plainly put, laziness was not only a sign that individuals were unworthy of all the considerations claimed by free men, but it was also sinful.

Of course, to make this transplanted labor system a success, white employers had to accept the end of slavery and treat freedpeople in a just and fair way. During the summer of 1865, there remained white Southerners who questioned the wisdom of emancipation, worried that only force would keep freedpeople at work, and resented any intrusion into their personal affairs by Yankees. And as early as the fall of 1866, there were white landowners who were quick to pronounce free labor a failure while doing their best to make it so. Bureau men were not blind to these attitudes. A number of officers and agents expressed their concern that slavery had corrupted the white population and had rendered ex-masters unreliable employers. Thus, whites, too, would need careful tutoring in the benefits of free labor.

Bureau men, however, could be optimistic, even if circumstances required them to be firm with their former enemies. J. B. Kiddo predicted that a successful free-labor system would be the "social, financial, and political redemption of the south," suggesting that blacks and whites would equally benefit. Other Bureau men stressed the mutual interests of blacks and whites. Orlando Brown, for example, told the people of Virginia that the interests of capital and labor had to be combined or "each is comparatively valueless," while Davis Tillson noted that the economic salvation of whites as well as blacks was at stake. Bureau men believed that once white Southerners grasped this relationship, they would accept the Yankee prescription for economic success. What Bureau men discovered, however, was that ex-slaves came to the new ways more willingly than did their ex-masters.

Initiating the Labor Contract System. In August 1865, O. O. Howard informed Maine's Freedmen's Relief Society that the Bureau's "first business was to regulate labor." To set his subordinates on to the right path for accomplishing such a task, the Commissioner issued a series of circulars during the spring and summer of 1865 that he hoped would set the tone for his agency's labor policies. On May 19, 1865, Howard made it clear that there was a sufficient need for labor to keep all refugees and freedpeople busily and productively employed. Therefore, he charged his subordinates with the task of introducing "practicable systems of compensated labor" in the erstwhile Confederacy to address the need to put freedpeople to work. Furthermore, they were to educate the black and white populations as they made their labor plans known to them.

Later in July, Howard reminded his subordinates that only the market would determine the wages of the freedpeople, while a lien on the crop or the employers' property would secure payment of those wages. Indeed, throughout the Bureau's existence, Bureau men accepted as an article of faith the idea that the freedpeople had first lien on the crop they

had raised. Howard also urged freedpeople to enter into written contracts to formalize their work arrangements, while reminding his subordinates that there could be no compulsion in the process. Neither ex-
masters nor Bureau agents could force the freedpeople either to sign
contracts or to work for employers not freely chosen. "Suffering may
result to some extent" from this laissez-faire approach to labor, Howard
explained, "but suffering is preferred to slavery, and is, to some degree,
the necessary consequence of events."

In August 1865, Howard addressed the charge that the Bureau-supervised contracts he recommended for the South smacked of the continu-
ation of slavery in another guise. He argued that they were in fact the
equivalent of contracts made in the North. Bureau men did not devise
a new system for freedpeople and the South. Rather, they used a device
that was known to them and one that they hoped would protect the
fledgling labor system in the South. "And the evils of the system,"
Howard argued, "are less than by any other known one."

Not all Bureau men believed that written contracts were the most ad-
vantageous way to arrange labor; some officers and agents feared that
they actually restricted the freedpeople's liberty, preventing them from
leaving unwholesome situations for better employment. A few remarked
on the way freedpeople worked on leased property and wondered about
contract labor. In July 1866, Thomas J. Wood, Mississippi's assistant
commissioner, reported that freedpeople working on abandoned lands
leased to them at Davis Bend were making crops "among the best in
the State." He asked Commissioner Howard, "May not this be an argument against the present labor system?"

Most Bureau men, nevertheless, at least initially believed that written
agreements would stabilize the labor situation to the benefit of both employers and employees and bring fine harvests back to the war-ravaged
South. Furthermore, contracts would provide the Bureau with tools and
opportunities by which the agency could educate freedpeople, as well as
ex-masters, in the workings of the free-labor system. Howard, later re-
flecting on the Bureau-supervised contract system during the fall of
1869, concluded, "To the freedmen, the Bureau office in this way became a school in which he learned the first practical business lessons
of life." At the same time, a Bureau-supervised contract system gave
agency personnel opportunities to perform their duty as guardians of
the ex-slaves, keeping documents on file in case disputes arose when it
came time to settle up.

During the summer and fall of 1865, Bureau men traveled throughout their jurisdictions explaining the new labor situation and continued to do so as required throughout the agency's lifetime. They urged freedpeople to refrain from wandering about the countryside and to work with their former masters or at least to settle into new positions as soon as possible, reminding them that the expectation of land redistribution was nothing but a distracting fantasy. They also lectured ex-masters about the requirements of free labor, warned them to put away the whips they had used during slavery, and reminded them that they as well as the freedpeople were responsible for the future economic and social stability of the land. (*See Document No. 13.*)

Some Bureau men believed that a laissez-faire approach worked best when it came to the terms of the contracts into which the freedpeople and their ex-masters entered, especially in areas where there was a noticeable demand for labor. There were other Bureau men, however, who assumed that novices about to engage in the free-labor system required some very specific guidance. Assistant Commissioner Fisk, for example, accepted that freedpeople should be at liberty to strike their own bargains with employers, but also instructed his men to establish guidelines for adequate compensation. Assistant Commissioner Wager Swayne issued labor regulations to reassure both white and black Alabamans, initiating a contract system that emphasized the "mutual securities and limitations" of both parties for a twelve-month period. Other officers and agents violated Howard's strictures against setting specific wages in their detailed printed regulations, as did Augusta Bureau agent John Emory Bryant. (*See Document No. 14.*) Bryant intended his regulations to safeguard the freedpeople, but in fact provoked at least one Northerner to protest what at first glance appeared to be the instigation of new forms of repressive labor control. (*See Document No. 15.*)

During the fall of 1865, some Bureau officials exceeded their authority and violated Howard's orders to refrain from forcing freedpeople to sign contracts. In general, however, the Bureau promoted an idea of contracting that emphasized the new status of the ex-slaves as free people. Freedpeople could choose their employers, bargain for their wages, and make the most of their situations. Even if the Bureau assumed that the freedpeople were junior partners in the new system, the very fact that it accepted the legitimacy of contracts as legally binding documents was significant. The nature of a contract as an agreement between two responsible and equal parties, one of those parties being black, was a radical departure from the past. With freedom, however, came responsibility. Once the freedpeople entered into agreements, the Bureau expected them to honor them. (*See Document No. 16.*)

Bureau men guaranteed the rights of black workers, but they understood that landowners and employers had rights, too. If freedpeople did not honor their contracts, sacred agreements according to Mississippi's assistant commissioner Samuel Thomas and most other Bureau men, the Bureau would make them do so or allow them to suffer the consequences of being discharged from employment. Indeed, for Orlando Brown, two of the "most essential conditions of a state of" freedom were "*a visible means of support, and fidelity to contracts.*"

The Response to the Bureau's Contract System. Many

if not most Bureau officials assumed that the freedpeople would command the greater part of attention if they expected the new free-labor system to function. Bureau men believed that first and foremost slavery had had a significant impact on the freedpeople, rendering them in need of greater guidance, while shaping their views of work in general and making them suspicious of the intentions of their ex-masters. Initially, freedpeople were wary of committing themselves to year-long contracts with their former masters. Some freedpeople objected to the contracting process not only because they expected land at the end of 1865, but also because they felt the documents limited their freedom. Others worried that the documents would bind them to their employers in some other way, perhaps longer than one agricultural year, or return them to slavery.

There always remained freedpeople who were suspicious of contracts. However, a significant number of them accepted the system promulgated by the Bureau to give agents and officers a degree of optimism. Furthermore, freedpeople came to understand that they could use the contract system to their advantage, holding out for better bargains and frustrating ex-masters along the way.

In some areas of the South, the freedpeople learned their lessons well. During the early years of Reconstruction there were Georgia planters who complained about the audacity of freedpeople who challenged the labor terms they offered them. In Maryland, historian Richard Paul Fuke explains, ex-slaves bargained for better agreements that would expand their independence, including the addition of garden plots for their families' use. Some ex-slaves became more sophisticated as their free-

dom matured. Historian John C. Rodrigue notes that by early 1868 in
Louisiana's sugar region, where there was a demand for black labor,
freedpeople encouraged by the Bureau accepted the free-labor system to
the point where they engaged in tough and smart bargaining with their
potential employers. They withheld their labor while they attended meetings where individuals urged them to demand as much as $25 a month
as well as their rations. These workers and other Louisiana freedpeople
came to accept the free-labor system as a useful part of their freedom
experience and came to consider the Bureau as their ally.

As freedpeople came to accept the new system, they also came to see
benefits in having written documents supervised by the Bureau. In practical terms, Bureau men could prevent employers from imposing inadequate compensation or unjust terms on the freedpeople, a benefit of
contracts that freedpeople recognized. The process of contracting, however, also forced ex-masters to acknowledge the ex-slaves' new status,
while the documents themselves often had clauses included by which
the agreement attested to the fact that the laborers were now free people.
Furthermore, freedpeople came to understand that such agreements
could confirm their own identities apart from the mass of workers that
slavery had made of them. By 1867 in Georgia, for example, freedpeople
and their employers began moving away from contracts that bound long
lists of workers to their terms to contracts that employers made with
single workers or families, a probable sign of a freedmen's desire to as-
sert their individuality. While some Arkansas planters continued to sign
contracts with large numbers of freedpeople, as historian Randy Finley
discovered, it became common for them to sign agreements with two
to four workers. In fact, throughout the South as Reconstruction progressed, the common work unit became the black family, a development
encouraged by the Freedmen's Bureau acknowledgement of the husband
and father as the individual who could command the labor of such
a unit.

As historian Mary J. Farmer has shown, the Bureau accepted the primary role of the husband in commanding a family's labor by willingly
voiding contracts forced upon women without their husbands' consent.
At times, Bureau men even accepted a marriage contract as having the
power to surpass a previously signed labor contract. Yet, even in these
cases, Bureau decisions reflected the diversity of interpretations concerning work, family and other matters that followed the agency across
the South. There were also occasions when officers and agents were re-

luctant to violate the sacred nature of a labor contract willingly signed by a woman in the absence of her husband even when confronted with the claims of patriarchy supported by marriage vows.

The freedpeople's search for the best return on their labor prompted many to leave their old homes with the encouragement of Bureau officials, forcing employers to bargain and compete amongst themselves for what they had long taken for granted. In Arkansas, freedpeople, encouraged by the Bureau, moved to where employers needed their labor. In some states, such as Virginia and Georgia, however, shifting labor within borders was insufficient for absorbing surplus workers. To deal with this problem, the Bureau provided transportation to freedpeople seeking better labor terms in western states, with some officials acting more aggressively than others and often in concert with private labor recruiters. As historian William Cohen has shown in his book *At Freedom's Edge: Black Mobility and the Southern White Quest for Racial Control, 1861–1915*, free labor ideally would have the market controlling the ebb and flow of workers. However, given the circumstances of the postwar South, Cohen notes, the Bureau could not ignore the need to intervene to help establish the new system by providing freedpeople with the best opportunities to secure favorable employment. This was especially true when white Southerners tampered with the market by attempting to prevent freedpeople from exercising their freedom of movement to keep an abundant supply of workers in their communities.

Some historians consider the Bureau's involvement in black migration as an attempt to curry favor with white employers or at least something that reduced the Bureau to little more than a labor agency. A more reasonable explanation of Bureau activity in this area is that the Bureau men simply wanted to make sure that the economy would recover from the war and that freedpeople would find productive employment. Commissioner Howard held to the belief that transportation of willing migrants was a better policy than allowing impoverished freedpeople to swell the relief lists.

White Southerners reacted in contradictory ways to the Bureau's contract system. Employers generally resented having outsiders insinuating themselves into their "family" affairs, telling them what to do with their workers; some of these individuals simply ignored the Bureau for as long as they could. There were white employers who were less passive and attempted to sabotage the system before it could take root. They tried to limit the impact of the system and circumvent competition by banding together to agree to set wage amounts they offered the freedpeople. During the fall of 1865, for example, Orlando Brown reported that in some parts of Virginia "the citizens had entered into covenant not to pay more than five dollars ($5) per month to able-bodied men, not to rent lands to freedmen, nor to give employment to any without a certificate from their former owners." In some areas of South Carolina and Georgia, planters also gathered together to agree upon imposing uniform terms on labor arrangements. Elsewhere, planters tried to keep their costs down by keeping their labor supply plentiful by forcefully preventing freedpeople from leaving their neighborhoods. Other planters made verbal arrangements of dubious value with agreeable but ignorant laborers beyond the eyes of Bureau men, while some employers compromised with the requirements of the new regime by signing legitimate contracts under the supervision of local magistrates instead of Bureau officers, still avoiding intrusive Yankee eyes. As late as the spring of 1868, the Kentucky Bureau reported that white employers continued to "use every means in their power to prevent them [the freedpeople] from entering into contracts" supervised by the agency.

Some planters who accepted Bureau contracts resigned themselves to the system for fear of some sort of federal disciplinary action, while others probably believed that they were signing contracts under duress, thus taking comfort in their mental reservations about the legality of the whole process. There were, however, planters who expected to make the system work to their advantage. They interpreted the Bureau's repeated proclamations to the freedpeople about self-discipline, responsibility and industry as indications that the agency would be an ally in controlling their ex-slaves. They assumed that they could use contracts to protect their own interests, even if the documents meant bargaining with their ex-slaves. These employers did their best to produce documents that made it clear that ex-slaves remained in an inferior position.

The Bureau's lack of real power combined with the agency's awareness of its own temporary nature to limit the lasting, beneficial role of contracts. The desire to facilitate the former Confederate states' resumption of control over the normal functions of government and the desire to see the freedpeople quickly rise to the responsibilities of their new status restricted the agency's involvement in the very system it expected to nurture. The agency's interaction with the events of Reconstruction in Mississippi illustrates the problem.

In November 1865, in the wake of Andrew Johnson's reorganization of the state, the Mississippi legislature passed a law defining the freed-people's legal privileges and civil rights. This infamous "black code," which provoked outrage in the North, also restricted the ex-slaves' freedom in a number of ways, including requiring that they have evidence by early January every year that they were settled into homes and had employment. Mississippi turned the contract into a restrictive document far beyond what the Bureau had anticipated it to be. Yet, the state's assistant commissioner of the Bureau, Colonel Samuel Thomas, accepted such documents as legitimate, although still worthy of Bureau supervision if not interference. On December 31, 1865, he informed his subordinates that they could advise freedpeople and act as their "next friend" but could not interfere with contracts made by local magistrates. It would be a learning experience for the freedpeople. "There can be no better time for the freedmen to familiarize themselves with business life and common forms of law, under civil government," he explained, "than at a time when officers of the general government are here whose duty it is to see that their rights are respected."

Thus, for different reasons, freedpeople and their ex-masters made contracts, many but not all of them under the supervision of Bureau agents. Standard printed forms supplied by the Bureau were common throughout the South and limited how far employers could go in circumscribing the independence of their workers, at least on paper. (*See Document No. 17.*) Through these documents as well as circulars from Howard and his assistant commissioners, the agency made it plain what it expected of labor arrangements. The Bureau generally required that the employer to provide wages, housing, medical care, fuel and food to their workers, while in return those workers were to be diligent in their labor, obedient in following legitimate orders, and respectful in their relations with their employers and their employers families. Furthermore, the Bureau prohibited using any kind of force, especially those practices that were common during slavery, to maintain labor discipline. But beyond these items, contracts played many variations on the free-labor theme, running the gamut of terms, especially when lengthy hand-written documents replaced the more concise Bureau form. (*See Document No. 18.*)

Some employers paid freedpeople wages in shares of the crops they raised, others promised cash, and Bureau men debated which approach was the fairer or the more efficient. Some Bureau men argued that a stake in the long-term health of the crop would keep the freedpeople constant while others argued that cash paid as frequently as on a monthly basis gave employees a sense of the rewards of free labor and the freedom to leave unsatisfactory situations. The amount of cash wages varied, being generally higher by a few dollars per month in the Mississippi River valley than in the eastern regions of older, worn land. In Georgia, for example, Assistant Commissioner Tillson believed that prime male hands should receive $12 to $13 per month while in Arkansas male field hands averaged about $17 per month. Throughout the South, shares as wages generally ran from one-quarter to one-third of the crop, depending on the mix of other benefits offered by the employer and the resources the freedpeople might have had at their disposal. A true sharecropping system, whereby freedpeople worked a plot of land technically independent of the landowner's daily supervision and then claimed a part of the harvest at the end of the season based on various conditions, eventually developed and began to appear in Bureau contracts in 1867. Historian Edward Royce in his study of the phenomenon argues that because of pressure from freedpeople who wished greater independence, the "radically new mode of labor organization" became more common in 1868. However, these economic developments, which eventually would lead to severe limitations on the ex-slaves' freedom, had more to do with the requirements and resources of the freedpeople and their employers than with any Bureau policy. The widespread and oppressive labor arrangements that eventually developed by the end of Reconstruction were far removed from what the Bureau had expected of the contract-based free-labor system.

Between 1865 and 1869, agents and officers watched over the terms of untold numbers of contracts, with assistant commissioners feeling sufficiently secure in their authority to nullify those contracts supervised by their subordinates that did not measure up to their expectations. But the best-intentioned officials could not guarantee that either party would do all that the documents required of them. Frequently, employers and employees failed to live up to their bargains and the Bureau men spent much of their time in the field attempting to resolve the conflicts that grew out of challenged and broken contracts.

Enforcing Contracts. Regardless of the type of payment noted in a contract, most contracts stipulated that the employer would settle his accounts with his workers only after the harvest. This requirement, reasonable in an agricultural economy that lacked cash until harvest time, gave planters the opportunity to break contracts during the slow summer period, thus depriving workers of their just wages. In October 1866, Orlando Brown noticed that "when the person who hired labor no longer needs it, it is not rare to find the laborer turned away and payment evaded on trivial pretexts." In November 1866, John Randolph Lewis shortly after becoming assistant commissioner of Tennessee also noticed that, "as the crops mature and are laid by, the employers take advantage of these special provisions to find all sorts of pretexts for turning away their hands without wages or share in the crops. Unfortunately for the freedmen, these bad men have ample facilities, by their knowledge of law and the prejudices of the courts, to make the worse appear the better part."

Some of the "pretexts" these officers observed were the results of poorly constructed contracts, either the result of white duplicity or Bureau inadequacy. Colonel J. Duwell Green, the Bureau officer in charge of the Columbia, South Carolina, district reported in 1866 that poor contracts made before his arrival forced freedpeople to go out and search for labor in order to feed themselves while they also tried to work the growing crop. The result of this necessity was that "evil-disposed employers" found "an opportunity to take advantage of the clause in their contracts which dismisses laborers for absence without leave, forfeiting all claim to their share in the crop which they had been laboring to perfect for the last six months." It became common, however, for Bureau men to try to prevent the inclusion in contracts of clauses that allowed the total forfeiture of wages or crop shares if workers were dismissed primarily because of the widespread use of violence to drive off workers during the slow period.

As Reconstruction progressed, Bureau reports more frequently than not pointed to white employers as the culprits in broken contracts. Brevet Major L. Walker, Bureau officer in charge of the Anderson, South Carolina, district, believed that freedpeople violated their contracts out of ignorance while pure malice motivated delinquent whites. In late 1866, he complained about the high percentage of contracts broken in the Edgefield area. Of 646 contracts approved in that subdistrict, his subordinate reported, "at least thirty per cent of the employers have violated them" in their efforts to undermine the free-labor system and the prospects of the ex-slaves as well as "to revenge themselves on the blacks for what loss they may have suffered from the authorities of the United States." The problem persisted. In 1867 some Edgefield Dis-

trict, South Carolina planters "gathered and disposed of crops and retained the entire proceed, not allowing the negroes for their year's work
any compensation whatever."

Bureau men reported common practices across the South. In Kentucky after the 1867 harvest, employers simply ignored verbal contracts
that lacked written documentation and the signature of witnesses. From
Georgia to Arkansas and Texas, planters used violence to drive their
workers away from their lands after they had harvested crops, especially
if that harvest was not an especially good one. Bureau men discovered
planters shipping crops beyond the reach of their workers, even though
the Bureau insisted that the workers had the first claim to payment from
the harvest.

During the early days of Reconstruction, Bureau men exercised their
authority more directly upon the offending planters than at any other
time. During late 1865, freedpeople in South Carolina, Georgia and
Florida kept Bureau men busy by demanding their presence at year-end
settlements, where the supervised the distribution of the profits of the
year's labor. Also in December 1865, Alabama Assistant Commissioner
Wager Swayne, advised his men to enforce contract settlements by directly intervening in the division of crops if necessary and if possible.
Even so, Bureau investigations could drag on for months as planters
either obstructed the process with various tactics. Frequently, Bureau
men who lacked a resident army guard required the wronged freedpeople
to act as their bailiffs to carry back orders to the very employers who
were causing the difficulties to appear before the Bureau to answer the
complaints. The ex-slaves often returned to the Bureau men beaten and
discouraged, carrying insulting messages to the officials from employers
who urged them to mind their own business. In the end, there never
were sufficient troops, even after the inauguration of Military Reconstruction in March 1867, to give agency's efforts real power to break
this increasing white awareness of the Bureau's impotence.

Dishonest employers used a number of tactics to avoid settling with
their workers. Some employers intimidated the complainants, who withdrew their charges or left the area in fear for their lives. Some employers
appeared before the Bureau with false financial records that showed
their workers to be in their debt. There were employers who promised
to appear before a Bureau official and then failed to keep the appointments. Others actually settled with their freedpeople under Bureau supervision, but gave promissory notes to cover their debt to employees,

which they then failed to pay, thus causing the process to start all over again. Even when Bureau men accomplished something and were able to put money into the hands of the freedpeople, the settlement amount frequently was a compromised figure, one that failed to cover all that the employer owed his workers. Better to put some money into the pockets of the workers, Bureau men might have reasoned, than to let them starve another several months while the case remained unsettled. (*See Document No. 19.*)

As the federal government came to expect civil courts to function equitably for black and whites, Bureau men became involved in a tangled legal process that further frustrated the free-labor system they had hoped to establish. Agents and officers were encouraged to observe the civil courts and become actively involved after civil authorities had failed to act justly in entertaining the freedpeople's complaints. If civil authorities failed to take cognizance of a case or if civil authorities failed to do justice for the freedpeople, the Bureau could intervene and could seize crops until the involved parties achieved a fair settlement. (*See Document No. 20.*)

Too often, however, such an approach meant that the federal government came to the aid of the freedpeople too late to be of great help, especially if a dishonest employer had the foresight to ship his crops beyond the reach of the Bureau man. It was a practice that the Bureau tried to prevent in Louisiana, Georgia and elsewhere—Georgia and Alabama Bureau officials, for example, cooperated to try to seize crops moved across state lines—but it remained one that some planters found effective. Also, courts learned how to follow the letter of the law and still delay the freedpeople's ability to claim their wages; indeed, there were cases in Georgia that dragged on for over a year as courts followed common legal procedures.

There were times and places where the promise of Bureau intervention was sufficient to make employers behave; a threat to seize crops and withhold them from the market, for example, was a good way at least to bring employers to the table. When word spread that the agency would soon withdraw from a jurisdiction, conditions worsened for the freedpeople. In February 1868, Lieutenant George W. Kingsbury, the Bureau subassistant commissioner stationed at Burkesville, Kentucky, reported that "complaints came in rapidly of the mistreatment of the blacks by whites and they being unable to collect pay for their work of the whites" when planters learned of the discontinuance of the Bureau. However, when it became apparent that the Bureau would remain for a while longer, circumstances improved for the freedpeople. Nevertheless, it was clear to Kingsbury that when the Bureau ceased its operations, "the freedmen would be unable to collect one half of their rightful dues." Elsewhere, even before the termination of the Bureau, planters anticipated the event. In Georgia during 1868, planters, aware that a greatly reduced Bureau would confine its activities to black education and bounty matters during 1869 chose to ignore the agency. Bureau men continued to advise freedpeople and act as their next friends in court matters, but their ability to do much more no longer remained.

By1868, white and black Southerners were aware that the Bureau would not continue to supervise labor after the end of the year and went about conducting their business as they saw best. During that year, Freedmen's Bureau officers and agents could not help but comment on the small number of contracts that came to their attention for their approval. Work arrangements were in the hands of black and white Southerners and if economic conditions improved for the ex-slaves it was because whites needed black labor. However, the Bureau's message as embodied in the contract system of free labor had a lingering importance for the ex-slaves. Their experience with the agency confirmed their status as free people who had economic and civil rights that at least some white men had respected.

CHAPTER 7

FACILITATING EDUCATION

Educational Philosophy. From the earliest days of the Bureau's work, Commissioner Howard expected his agents and officers to give assistance to the northern charitable organizations and the freedpeople in establishing schools. Most Bureau men were amenable to this charge because they understood that education, in the broadest sense of the word, was a task informing all aspects of their work. Supervising labor contracts, lecturing on the rights and obligations of freedom, cleaning up the homes of freedpeople, registering marriages, promulgating temperance, publicizing savings banks, and just about every other task taken on by the agency had the underlying didactic purpose of informing black and white Southerners about how to behave as good Yankees. Even so, formal schooling had an important and special place for many Bureau men. Few of them had to be convinced of the agency's renewed commitment to the task when in February 1867 Howard strengthened the Bureau's relationship to black education by instructing all of his subordinates to give their close attention to educational matters as they performed their other duties.

Bureau men never abandoned their commitment to the agency's other goals as they pursued the call to educate the black South; officers and agents understood that they were all intimately connected. Indeed, Bureau men, despite their faith in the power of education, could never completely separate education's success from the success of their labor program because they always expected the freedpeople to assume a large portion of the financial burden of education. In December 1865, for example, Joseph Warren, the Mississippi Bureau's school superintendent, cautioned that it would do the freedpeople "no good, to indulge them in the practical mendicancy, to which they are inclined" by giving them too much help with their schooling. The Bureau would extend what assistance it could to help the ex-slaves obtain buildings or materials for constructing them, but when it lacked needed resources, "the people must put their own shoulders to the wheel. The vehicle will otherwise stop."

Watching the agency's power ebb, however, convinced many officials that the Bureau's best hope for guaranteeing the future of the freedpeople, especially after the agency's termination, was by directing its greatest efforts to education. During 1866, Wager Swayne came to consider education the most important of his duties as circumstances diminished the power of his Alabama agency. John Randolph Lewis agreed. During 1866, while serving as the Tennessee assistant commissioner, Lewis accepted that economic and civil rights remained primary, but he came to see the limitations under which the agency increasingly functioned in enforcing those rights and accepted education as the "controlling element" in the freedpeople's efforts to claim them.

Certainly, from the start, Bureau men recognize the pragmatic day-to-day significance of education in dealing with "the practical business of life," as John Alvord, Howard's education chief, referred to it in January 1866. In October 1865, Joseph Warren noted that education provided the means by which freedpeople could "protect themselves from imposition and fraud." And Clinton B. Fisk explained to freedpeople that education "makes the mind strong, gives greater vigor and endurance to the body, and adds to the years of a man's life," while opening "numerous roads to competence and to wealth." Education, in other words, had important economic benefits for the freedpeople, as it would cultivate the intellectual discipline that a free-labor system required of its participants. When trying to convince white Southerners to support or at least tolerate black education, the Bureau often used this line of reasoning while pointing to the salutary consequences an educated work force would have for entire communities. As North Carolina Assistant Commissioner Eliphalet Whittlesey explained in July 1865, "No one thing will so much contribute to present content and good order among the freedmen, and to the future well-being of all classes, as a good, general system of education."

Southerners might not have been entirely open to such an argument in part because the system allegedly conferring such good was consciously rooted in northern educational practices. Bureau men and teachers expected to transplant the content, the style, and the consequences of learning with which they were already familiar. Thus, when Bureau men advocated education as an engine of enduring change, they also assumed that the curriculum of the schools they helped to support would do more than teach practical things necessary for navigating daily agricultural life. For these Bureau men, education could help to erase the bad habits and the moral laxity they attributed to slavery and remake the freedpeople into disciplined, sober, thrifty Yankees. Education would not only prevent freedpeople from falling into a new kind of bondage, but also provide them with the means to reach new levels of personal achievement. Even practical industrial education, which the Bureau willingly assisted, could have important consequences beyond training freedpeople in skills given the Bureau's understanding of the uplifting consequences of hard work.

In the process of helping to develop a Yankee-style system of education, Bureau officers also put into place one more tool for maintaining the reunited nation many of them had fought to preserve. Carl F. Kaestle in his study *Pillars of the Republic: Common Schools and American Society, 1780–1860* notes that antebellum Yankee reformers shaped a school curriculum "dedicated to moral education and good citizenship." They designed such a curriculum to instill virtue in the pupils and nurture a common culture, thereby preserving the nation's republican form of government.

After the war, Bureau men and the educators they assisted expected the same results from their new field of endeavor. In October 1866, F. A. Fiske, the North Carolina Bureau's superintendent of education, argued that by building character, black students would become "good and useful citizens and members of society." About the same time, Fiske's counterpart in Alabama, R. D. Harper, also made the connection between helping the freedpeople and a felicitous future for the reunited nation. "To liberate them without giving them the benefits of education, is only to increase their power to do evil, and to put in jeopardy the best interests of our country," he wrote in an appeal to a northern philanthropic organization in September 1866. "Their own welfare mental, moral and physical, and the safety of the Government alike, urgently demand that vigorous efforts be made for the education and consequent elevation of the freed people of the South."

If such an education would help freedpeople come to understand who their true friends were and lead them into the Republican party, some Bureau men reasoned, so much the better. To be sure, Bureau headquarters made it clear that partisan politics had no place in the classroom, while state-level officials cautioned politically enthusiastic teachers to avoid obviously partisan activities at school. However, E. A. Ware, a Georgia Bureau education superintendent, understood that the connections between the good effects of Bureau-sponsored education and the Republican party would become apparent to freedpeople without overt indoctrination from Yankee teachers.

An Advocate and Coordinator of Private Educational Efforts. In May 1865, Howard instructed his subordinates to "systematize and facilitate" the work of northern benevolent associations in their efforts to help to educate these freedpeople. Neither Congress nor Howard expected the Freedmen's Bureau to establish and maintain a south-wide school system for the freedpeople. It therefore became critical for the agency to harness the enthusiasm already shown by philanthropists and freedpeople who had begun their work during the war, reinvigorate any of their flagging endeavors, and bring order to their old and new efforts. By the end of the war, according to historian Ronald E. Butchart, there were already over four dozen northern organizations involved with black education that had raised over a million dollars for supplies and teachers. The Bureau's supervisory role served in varying degrees of success as a moderating influence on the rivalry, jealousy, and redundancy spawned by these competing educational missionary associations. Furthermore, its role as coordinator of Reconstruction's educational efforts helped to head off blind false starts in unpromising fields of endeavor, preventing the squandering of limited resources.

Howard expected the Bureau to deal with the educational challenges of Reconstruction under the direction the Reverend John W. Alvord, pastor, abolitionist and educator. Alvord, who joined the agency in September 1865, served the Bureau and the freedpeople until October 1870, supervising educational work during the agency's active years. As Alvord learned soon after his appointment if he had not realized it earlier, being an advocate and coordinator of black education required stamina as well as dedication. The superintendent engaged in inspection tours and lecturing while reporting on educational matters to his superiors and maintaining extensive correspondence with the societies and his subordinates. Such activities served the purpose of collecting, digesting and disseminating to the right people extensive information about the needs of the freedpeople and matching those needs with the resources offered by the societies. Alvord, for example, began his first inspection tour shortly after his appointment in October 1865, covering thousands of miles as he traveled through the South from Baltimore to New Orleans and back to Washington. During his association with the Bureau, his detailed semi-annual reports, based on the extensive information submitted to him by his subordinates as well as his own experiences, provided Howard and the North with much information about the state of education among the emancipated slaves.

State education superintendents pursued a similar line of activity within their jurisdictions; they traveled, lectured and collected information, while assessing the needs of their states and attempting to coordinate the activities of the associations and the freedpeople. Superintendent Fiske corresponded with a hundred teachers and numbers of freedpeople and whites, all "without the aid of any clerical help," to assess the progress of North Carolina's educational advancement. (*See Document No. 21.*) Some of Alvord's state superintendents conveyed the information they had gathered directly to the northern people by embarking on lecture tours, but the convenience of the pen attracted all those concerned with spreading news of the needs and triumphs of black education. Superintendent Fiske and his counterparts in Bureau offices across the South directed northwards a steady stream of letters soliciting aid from the societies, reassuring them that they would do all in their power to assist the teachers. They never appeared to see these needs sated and renewed calls went northward prior to the commencement of each school year.

Bureau field officers and agents also contributed to an understanding of their jurisdictions' educational requirements, even before Howard instructed them to pay particular attention to furthering education. While pursuing their usual Bureau business, they also observed the progress of freedmen's schools, noted promising fields of endeavor, and received the complaints and appeals of teachers and freedpeople. Their general assessments concerning what could be done to improve educational opportunities for freedpeople provided crucial information that assisted the Bureau in formulating its appeals to the northern societies. Some wrote directly to the associations, as did Lieutenant Douglas Risley, who during 1867 through 1869 conducted an extensive correspondence with the American Missionary Association from his Brunswick, Georgia, headquarters. Most men reported directly to their Bureau superiors, providing useful information for the agency's decision making. In January 1867, Joseph C. Rodriguez, for example, informed the Bureau's regional officer about the availability of buildings for potential use as schoolhouses in the Bowling Green, Kentucky, region. He also noted the potential for black support, the education associations formed by freedpeople in Bowling Green and Franklin, and the opposition to black education in some areas as well as the need to solicit teachers "from abroad."

The Bureau also engaged the freedpeople in an educational dialogue

that lasted as long as the agency's active years in the South. By war's
end, the freedpeople had already shown their desire for education, flock-
ing to schools in Louisiana, Maryland, South Carolina and elsewhere.
In some black communities, black teachers and churches provided ral-
lying points for schools even before they had any contact with white
educators or the Bureau. When the Bureau came, its men talked with
black leaders and groups of freedpeople, while encouraging associations
in the freedmen's community that would work to support schools and
teachers. During 1866, Superintendent Fiske engaged "in awakening"
an interest among the freedpeople in education "by public address, private efforts and correspondence." In July 1867, William Kirkman arrived
at his Texas subdistrict and immediately began to discuss establishing
schools with the local freedpeople. Some assistant commissioners appointed special agents to deal exclusively with such tasks. In Georgia,
two such agents, John A. Rockwell and William J. White, one of the few
black men to work for the Bureau, traveled the state urging freedpeople
to organize educational committees, raise money, acquire property for
schools, and construct buildings. (*See Document No. 22.*) John H. Butler,
another "efficient colored agent," according to his assistant commissioner, "has, also, been kept constantly at work traveling from neighborhood to neighborhood throughout lower Maryland."

The Response to the Bureau's Call. In July 1865, *The American Missionary*, the official journal of the philanthropic American Missionary Association, reminded its readers that "The Bureau should have
the countenance and support of all Christians and Philanthropists." For
the most part, it did. The various northern aid societies that had rallied
to the freedpeople's cause before the end of the war continued to do
impressive work once the Bureau began to try to coordinate their work,
especially in their efforts to recruit and help pay teachers during the
early years of Reconstruction. In South Carolina, for example, the New
England Freedmen's Commission worked with B. F. Whitemore, a former army chaplain appointed an assistant superintendent of education
by Rufus Saxton, to establish 13 schools in eastern South Carolina by
the spring of 1866.

Repeated across the South, such efforts helped to give rise to the
blossoming of a system of freedmen's education to which the northern
associations and the Bureau funneled assistance. By December 1865,
Alvord noted, benevolent societies were involved with 740 schools, serv-

ing 90,589 students and staffed by 1,314 teachers; the numbers continued to increase, he assured Howard, even as he was writing his present
report. Later in October 1870, Howard reported that 2,039 schools
regularly reported to the Bureau, a requirement for schools desiring Bureau aid. The existence of these schools continued to owe much to the
help sent South by northern philanthropists. During the last half of the
1860s, according to historian Ronald E. Butchard, philanthropic organizations raised about a half a million dollars a year for educational purposes and supported upwards to 2,000 teachers each year.

The freedpeople's ability to meet the Bureau's expectations for contributing to their own education varied with the harvests and the honesty of their employers and there were instances of schools closing down
because of black poverty. Nevertheless, despite their financial difficulties, the ex-slaves generally greeted the agency's educational efforts with
great enthusiasm because it was one of the black community's top priorities. Even without Bureau officials reminding them of it, they almost
intuitively understood the connection between education and freedom.
"This great multitude," Superintendent Alvord reported to Howard in
January 1866, "rise up simultaneously, and ask for education." It was a
desire, he noted, that the freedpeople matched with "A willingness, even
an ambition, to bear expenses." In his June 1867 report, Alvord noted
that the freedpeople paid the expenses for 555 schools, partially contributed to the expenses of another 501 out of a total of 1,839 day and evening schools, and actually owned 391 school buildings. Later in October
1870, Howard reported that the freedpeople were partially or entirely
supporting 1,324 schools of a regularly reporting total of 2,039 and held
title to 592 school buildings.

Freedpeople gratefully gave their hard-earned money to the support
Yankee school teachers, but in taking an active role in their own education they frequently expressed a desire to see their funds support black
teachers. Freedpeople were willing to pay these teachers and in some
states there were considerable numbers of black instructors. However,
support from outside of the freedmen's communities was harder to
come by. There was a fear on the part of the Bureau that at least at the
outset of this great endeavor the black teachers available were second
rate and capable of doing as much harm as good. The preference of
Freedmen's Bureau and the northern aid societies was for white teachers
with good references and their help tended to flow in that direction. In
his June 1867 report, Alvord noted that of the 2,087 teachers who re-

ported to the Bureau, a procedure suggesting that they received some outside assistance, 699 were black. The number of black teachers either supported by the freedpeople themselves varied from state to state, but Bureau statistics, according to historian James D. Anderson, underestimate the number of African Americans teaching during Reconstruction by discounting the impact of Sabbath schools. Students in these schools, Anderson notes, studied the fundamentals as well as the lessons of the Bible. If one learned how to read the Bible, one still learned how to read.

Regardless, the Bureau men realized that sooner or later necessity would require black teachers to assume a larger role in educating the ex-slaves in the regular schools because the associations never furnished enough teachers. School superintendents recruited or hired some white Southerners who wished to teach, but even this resource did not fill all the vacancies. Bureau men, therefore, could not ignore the fact that they had better help prepare freedpeople for the day when they would be the ones who stood in front of the classrooms.

One ready solution was C. W. Buckley's approach to the problem. In March 1868, Buckley reported that in Alabama "It is in our policy to convert colored pupils into teachers as fast as possible. It is cheaper if not so beneficial, and it has good effects in many ways." As Reconstruction progressed, Buckley's "colored pupils" moved through their grades and they eventually provided many country schools with teachers. On a more formal level, in 1867 Commissioner Howard urged the associations and philanthropic organizations in the North to establish normal schools for the freedpeople and the Bureau contributed over $400,000 to such institutions over the next several years. In his October 1870 report Howard noted that were 74 schools functioning among the freedpeople and refugees sufficiently sophisticated to train teachers. His figures suggested that the system was having some impact on school staffing even as the associations' efforts were on the wane. Of the teachers reporting to the Bureau in the fall of 1870, 1,312 were black and 1,251 were white.

Helping to Maintain the Educational Network. After the associations and the freedpeople responded to the Bureau's call, they continued to cooperate with and rely upon the agency for all sorts of things. The Bureau's efforts prompted the American Missionary Association in October 1867 to praise Howard's organization for having "shielded and assisted the laborers sent forth by Northern benevolent societies." Once teachers made up their minds to embark on their missions, they counted on Howard's Bureau to provide them with transportation to their southern destinations and the Bureau expended thousands of dollars to move them to their schools. Over the first six months of 1867, for example, the Bureau paid transportation costs for 975 teachers. School superintendents, field officers, and agents directed these teachers to their assignments, securing housing for them in increasingly hostile environments, while providing them with rations at reduced rates.

Bureau men also helped teachers with various and sundry problems, including finding textbooks and adequate furniture for their schools. When funds from the associations or the freedpeople failed to appear on time, teachers turned to Bureau men who reminded the freedpeople of their obligations or wrote appeals to the northern offices of the concerned associations. Joseph Warren once even asked the American Missionary Association to add a little extra when it sent salary money to Mississippi to improve the diet of its teachers there.

The Bureau had no authority to step in to make up for delinquent teachers' salaries from its budget when the associations' home offices or the freedpeople failed to meet their obligations. Nevertheless, assistant commissioners tried to deal with the problem. In 1866 and 1867, Wager Swayne went beyond his proper authority when he actually paid teachers from Alabama Bureau funds, but others tried methods within the boundaries set by regulations. In February 1866, for example, Absolam Baird initiated a tuition system with mixed results and for some teachers an actual reduction in their pay. His attempt to collect money through the freedpeople's labor contracts did not fare any better. After he assumed his position in the spring of 1866, Assistant Commissioner Joseph Kiddo tried to pay for his Texas Bureau's education work and promote free tuition for the freedpeople by collecting a fee on contracts, but the practice lapsed after he left the agency in January 1867. However, the Texas Bureau continued to maintain a fund from the sale of confiscated and abandoned property from which it drew money for educational purposes.

Headquarters negotiated the limits Congress had placed on the Bureau's relationship to education with more success when Commissioner Howard worked out a scheme whereby he could keep the teachers in funds. By paying their sponsoring associations rental fees for school buildings, he provided a pool of money from which teachers could then draw part of their salaries. In November 1868, Howard facilitated this plan by turning over Bureau-controlled buildings to the various associations, which would allow them to claim more rent and thus meet the needs of more teachers. The fact that Howard had school buildings to turn over to these associations was one of his agency's measurable contributions to the furthering of black education.

The Bureau's School Buildings. One of the more pressing concerns of the benevolent associations was whether there would be a place for teachers to teach if they sent personnel to promising fields identified by the Bureau. The freedpeople, too, were concerned about the physical symbol of education and frequently pressed the Bureau for assistance in securing a place in which to educate their community. Initially, the Bureau had no financing to build or buy structures suitable for school use, but it could command other resources to help black communities meet their needs.

At the outset of Reconstruction Bureau officials set aside abandoned and confiscated property, including barns, for use as schoolhouses, not an altogether enduring solution to the educational needs of the freedpeople after President Andrew Johnson began to return such property to its white owners. Assistant commissioners also found lumber for freedmen's schools by allowing officers and agents to have old barracks moved or torn down and reconstructed as school houses where needed. But Bureau educational officers struggled with the notion that they would have to rely on inadequate buildings to meet the needs of the freedpeople. In December 1865, John Ogden, the Tennessee Bureau school superintendent, argued that old buildings and barns were simply not good enough for schools, "the exponents of a higher civilization, the stepping-stones of *right thinking and right living*." Later in October 1866, Superintendent Fiske complained about North Carolina's overcrowded and inadequate school buildings. "Many of those buildings have not only been distasteful and unsightly," he reported, "but so uncomfortable in cold and stormy weather as to endanger the health of both teachers and pupils." Such buildings would "seriously retard" the progress of students. Thus, when Bureau men did assist freedpeople with schoolhouses, they could be fairly specific about the type of building that they expected the freedpeople to construct, at times giving detailed plans for the building, including diagrams and dimensions.

Congress gave the Bureau a better opportunity to help the freedpeople acquire schoolhouses when it included in the Army Appropriation
Act of July 1866 an allocation $500,000 for "repairs and rent of school-
houses and asylums." The Bureau law of the same month gave the agency
the power to "seize, hold, use, lease, or sell" property that had belonged
to the erstwhile Confederacy for the benefit of black education and required the agency to lease buildings for school purposes when benevolent societies provided teachers to staff them. Howard and his Bureau
made good use of these measures. Indeed, the commissioner contrived
to stretch the letter of the law by being very generous with his definition
of "repairs." If freedpeople acquired sufficient resources to secure land,
to begin a structure, and to agree to use the building from then on for
educational purposes—sure signs of ambition and good faith—the Bureau would step in and complete the construction as a "repair."

The results of this reinvigorated effort were noticeable. On Juy 1,
1867, Superintendent Alvord reported that the Bureau by various means
had provided the freedpeople with 428 schoolhouses over the past six
months and spent a total of almost $221,000 for educational purposes,
including the construction and rental of school buildings. In July 1870,
Alvord reported that for the preceding year, the Bureau had continued
its good efforts to place roofs over the heads of black scholars by constructing or partially constructing 334 buildings, including one for Lincoln University in Pennsylvania and another for Storer College in West
Virginia, and repairing another 198. The agency, according to Commissioner Howard's October 1870 annual report, also rented 598 school
buildings during this period. Howard did his best to make sure that his
work in this area would outlast the agency, requiring that trustees who
wished the Bureau's assistance with their construction projects acquire
the deed to the lot on which they intended to build and that they "bind
themselves and their successors to hold and use the same" and the completed schoolhouse "for educational purposes forever." Furthermore, he
required that they pledge never to exclude pupils from the benefits of
the school or any proceeds that might come from the future rental or
sale of the building "on account of race or previous condition of servitude." It was right that he should be so concerned about the future. By
the time the Commissioner made this report he admitted that the Bureau's resources were exhausted and that the freedpeople were now on
their own. "All I can do is counsel the freedmen to make every effort
and sacrifice necessary to keep their schools open," he explained, "and

agitate the subject of free schools until they secure their establishment."
(*See Document No. 23.*)

The End of Bureau Educational Work. At the American
Missionary Association's annual meeting in 1869, its membership expressed thanks to Bureau for all that it had done to further the education
of the freedpeople. The agency "has stood as a rampart of defense between the Freedmen and their foes; and by the wise disposal of funds
to this Association, and to others, for the erection of school buildings, it
has given a firm basis to some of the most promising efforts that have yet
been made to promote education at the South." The Reverend Alvord's
final report dated July 1, 1870 suggested that the Bureau deserved the
praise. He noted 2,039 schools were regularly reporting to the Bureau
with another 638 irregularly reporting. In these schools, 3,300 teachers
educated 149,581 pupils.

Despite such successes, both Alvord and Howard remained cautious
about the future. "This Bureau has only inaugurated a system of instruction, helping its first stages," Alvord warned, "which is to be continued and perfected." Indeed, he recognized that "The masses of freedmen are still ignorant." Bureau schools had touched the lives of only a
minority of freedpeople, with historian George Bentley estimating that
agency-assisted schools reached only 10 percent of school-aged freedpeople. Also, by 1870 the benevolent associations were retrenching at
the same time that the Bureau was closing the last of its state offices.
Howard had hoped that eventually the "States should severally adopt a
good wholesome school system whereby all the children of every color
and description should have the same facilities as those of Massachusetts or Ohio." But by 1870, there already was sufficient evidence of
white hostility or at best indifference to black education.

Some white Southerners had accepted the fact that education might
allow them greater control over their workforce, especially if they could
convince freedpeople to avoid Yankee teachers, and some used their support for schools to attract laborers to their plantations. But being unop-
posed to black schools was not exactly the same thing as being suppor-
tive of them. As one Texas Bureau man wrote in November 1868, "The
whites profess to be in favor of education, but their actions contradict
their professions." By way of illustrating the kind of environment whites
created for black education, he reported "A white teacher cannot find a
boarding house." Furthermore, "If the teacher is a woman, she is per-

secuted and abused, her character blackened and the foulest reports circulated."

There were white opponents to black education who used less subtle approaches to retard educational progress. Throughout the Bureau's existence, whites disturbed school sessions, harassed teachers and students, burned down schoolhouses, and chased away Yankee teachers. Whites Southerners on occasion subjected the teachers who tried to stand by their commitments to violence. Bureau assistant commissioners provided military protection when they could, but some of them considered it unadvisable and contrary to the ultimate restoration of civil government. As with so many other aspects of the Bureau's work, the agency expected civil authorities to deal with these problems. Only after the authorities proved to be unresponsive would they take up the case, and by then it might already be too late to do much good.

In the end, the federal government expected the states to take on the burden of education both blacks and whites in a public system, but by the time the Bureau closed its offices, the signs were not encouraging. New Orleans and Louisiana made headway in developing a system to educate blacks at the public expense, but elsewhere governments were not very successful in developing alternatives to private or Bureau sponsored education. In Florida during 1866, black men had to pay a school tax, but the state did little for their children. Also during 1866, Texas taxed blacks and whites for educational purposes, but provided funds only for whites. During the late 1860s in Charleston, South Carolina, freedpeople paid their taxes while the city government denied their children access to free schools. "The excuse was," Howard later explained, "that the general Government had freed the negroes and might now educate them." In 1870, E. L. Dean, the Bureau's superintendent of education in South Carolina complained about "the ignorance and stupidity of the county school officials, and the comparative indifference of our legislature to this cause" of black education, while Benjamin Runkle, his Kentucky counterpart, reported that "the State refuses to do anything whatever" about the matter.

Bureau officials recognized that there was no historic commitment to public education in the southern states and urged continued and greater federal involvement in black education. Captain James McCleery, the Bureau's superintendent of education for northwestern Louisiana and northern Texas, judged the public system in Louisiana to be good and noted the beginnings of one in Texas, "but the people generally regard it with apathy." "The whites own the property," he explained, "and are opposed to being taxed to support schools for blacks." His experiences led him to argue for federal involvement. "The State has a right to make soldiers for its defense, has its military schools for that purpose," he argued. "It has an equal right to see that every child is properly prepared for citizenship." Nevertheless, by the early summer of 1870, the Bureau had divested itself of what remaining school properties it held and turned over its efforts to newly the developing state-supported systems established by Republican legislatures.

CHAPTER 8

DEFINING AND PROTECTING THE RIGHTS OF FREED SLAVES

The Rights of Freedpeople. Practical considerations contributed significantly, but not exclusively, to the Freedmen's Bureau's considerable concern for the economic rights of the ex-slaves. Those same pragmatic concerns infused the agency's efforts to secure a range of rights for the ex-slaves. Without the same constitutional rights enjoyed by white men, the ex-slaves would not be able to stand on their own feet, thus remaining in some sort of limbo between slavery and freedom requiring the Bureau's and the nation's continued guardianship. However, this pragmatism generally worked in tandem with a sincere belief that ex-slaves deserved to claim the same array of rights held by their former masters. Helping the ex-slaves achieve that goal was a critical aspect of the agency's efforts to secure the fruits of victory and leave a lasting impression on the post-war South. The Bureau and the nation were limited in their imagination as to how to go about achieving that goal, but their failure was as much a consequence of the southern white opposition as their own ideological limitations.

Bureau men accepted that freedpeople could rightly expect to enjoy their human rights—life, liberty and property—and use the rights embodied in the federal constitution to protect them. Furthermore, they were consistent advocates for equal consideration before the laws of the state and the nation. (*See Document No. 24.*) In circulars and letters, Bureau officials made it clear that the freedpeople had the right to freedom of movement, the right to assemble peaceably and the right to security in their persons and in their families. Bureau men, for example, condemned the common practice of illegally apprenticing the children of ex-slaves often without the knowledge or the informed consent of their parents and worked to have such children returned. (*See Document No. 25.*) While the Bureau could not force states to accept black testimony in their courts, it refused to abandon its judicial roles until they did. During the early years of Reconstruction, Bureau men acknowledged that the vote was a privilege granted by states and, therefore, could accept state-imposed restrictions on black political participation. However, when in March 1867 Congress conferred that privilege upon the

91

freedmen, the agency attempted to protect the freedmen's exercise of it in the face of escalating violence.

The Bureau's defense of the ex-slaves' Second Amendment right to bear arms, a right that had no apparent practical benefit to free-labor discipline and one that white Southerners openly opposed, provides a good example of the agency's commitment to helping freedpeople enjoy all of their rights. In December 1865, Davis Tillson acknowledged that the freedpeople must obey all laws concerning the use of weapons, but he explained to white Georgians that "All men, without distinction of color, have the right to keep arms to defend their homes, families or themselves." And Clinton B. Fisk argued in March 1866, "To prevent a freedman from purchasing or owning a shotgun, a squirrel rifle, or the musket he carried honorably through the war, would be an outrage calling for prompt interference on the part of the United States." In taking this stand, Bureau men challenged white racial sensibilities. They probably further aggravated white resentment when they actually turned to armed ex-slaves to assist them in performing their duties, as did the Athens, Georgia, Bureau officer in 1867 when he recruited twelve armed freedmen to act as a posse to pursue a white criminal.

White Southerners had long equated the possession of firearms as a privilege of white men and before the war slaves had handled them only at the forbearance of their masters. After the war, across the South whites employed different tactics to deprive the freedpeople of their Second Amendment rights, prompting the Bureau's concern. During 1866, various grand juries and courts unsuccessfully requested that the Georgia Bureau disarm freedpeople. Earlier in December 1865, Wager Swayne arrested two members of the Alabama militia for disarming freedmen and held them for trial by military commission. "There must be 'no distinction of color' in the right to carry arms, any more than in any other right," he explained. As long as the freedmen violated no laws, Swayne proclaimed, they "are not to be deprived of guns."

Ideological Limitations. The Bureau did not assume that any rights claimed by free men were absolute. Consequently, the agency had to balance the freedpeople's rights with their obligations and with competing rights as well as the enduring belief in the federal system of government. For example, officials often accepted the idea that the obligations of contracts freely entered could trump competing rights, such as a husband's claim to his wife's company or labor. Also, Bureau men could not grasp the freedpeople's conception of family connections and the rights freedpeople believed grew from them. There were Bureau officials, for example, who failed to acknowledge the custody claims of relatives other than parents over apprenticed children; in such situations orphans legally apprenticed were likely to remain so even if grandparents or uncles and aunts tried to claim them.

Freedmen's Bureau officials also could make distinctions that would appear unfair or limiting to modern Americans. In 1866, for example, Davis Tillson, admonished freedmen to wait patiently for access to the ballot box and the jury box, while promising them protection in their right to life, liberty and property. He also made it quite clear that social equality or a sense that there could be no distinctions based on accomplishments, wealth, or education did not exist among whites. Freedpeople, therefore, should not expect different treatment. Furthermore, "All persons white and black, have the right to select their associates, and to live on terms of intimacy and social equality with those only whom they may chose, and who may have like convictions, feelings, and tastes with themselves."

The acceptance of the Bureau's temporary nature also limited the agency's understanding of what its personnel could do for the freedpeople. Bureau officials realized that in their efforts to protect the freedpeople in their rights as free individuals they were encroaching on concerns that the national government had previously left to the states. They, along with most Republicans, had not abandoned their belief in federalism. The Bureau realized that it must soon turn over the protection of the freedpeople's rights to civilian justice. This assumption held arguably the greatest ideological limitation on the Bureau's and the nation's aggressive protection of freedpeople's rights: the widespread belief that equality before the law would be sufficient for securing the ex-slaves' freedom and happiness. Bureau men expected that local and state officials in the South would quickly accept the requirement that they give freedpeople equal protection before their laws, thus removing any necessity for the national government's intervention into these affairs, because they assumed that the benefits of doing so would be obvious. If freedpeople secured equal protection before the law, they would need nothing more than their own ambition to succeed. What Bureau men did not initially grasp, however, was that even state laws that purportedly guaranteed no distinction based on race or previous condition did not guarantee protection from the prejudices of those men who were to enforce such laws.

From Bureau Courts to White Justice. In May 1865, Commissioner Howard authorized his subordinates to handle cases involving freedpeople where "there is an interruption of civil law, or in which local courts, by reason of old codes, in violation of the freedom guaranteed by the proclamation of the President and laws of Congress, disregard the negro's right to justice before the law, in not allowing him to give testimony." Thus, during the early months of Reconstruction, Bureau assistant commissioners looked after the freedpeople's rights by allowing their agents and officers to adjudicate minor cases while instructing them to turn over major cases to military tribunals where local and state courts refused to accept black testimony. Commissioner Howard preferred three-man panels made up of a representative of the involved freedpeople with a second individual representing white parties, the third being the local Bureau official. Because Howard was always reluctant to impose rigid uniformity on his subordinates, variations developed throughout the southern states. Some assistant commissioners accepted the three-member panel, while others authorized agents and officers to act alone. In North Carolina, the assistant commissioner only suggested that his subordinates form judicial panels with the help of local citizens. In Georgia, Alabama, and Florida, assistant commissioners initially used local magistrates as agents and allowed them to deal with minor cases involving freedpeople, assuming that their white neighbors would transfer any respect that they had for their local judicial offices to the Bureau. All the while, the Bureau had to improvise to meet unexpected circumstances resulting from local conditions. For example, sometimes the Bureau could not establish three-man panels because whites refused to cooperate, especially when the freedpeople selected a black man to represent them.

The Bureau began to withdraw from direct involvement in exercising judicial functions as states began to pass laws that had the appearance of giving freedpeople equal access to the civilian justice system. In Mississippi, Bureau officials became observers during the fall of 1865 when civilian officials promised that they would be impartial in giving justice to the freedpeople and in December 1865, the Georgia Bureau deferred to civilian courts, a decision confirmed in April of the following year.

Throughout 1866, other Bureau assistant commissioners restricted their agencies' judicial functions, although, as Texas Assistant Commissioner J. B. Kiddoo cautioned in October 1866, "it has not yet transpired to what extent these courts will do justice to such cases."

Bureau men, however, remained closely involved in the freedpeople's quest for justice. Frequently, they did their best to compromise disputes over apprenticeship agreements, labor contracts, and other areas of conflict between blacks and whites, well-aware of the difficulties freedpeople would face in the courtroom. The freedpeople themselves continued to approach Bureau agents to help settle or compromise disputes among themselves and between themselves and their employers down to the last days of their duty in the South.

When freedpeople did end up before the bar, Bureau men were there, hoping their presence would encourage white Southerners to deal fairly with the ex-slaves. In March 1866, for example, Virginia Assistant Commissioner Orlando Brown restricted his subordinates to observing civilian courts and to acting as the "next friends" of the freedpeople. At the same time, he required that "no person of color will be examined or brought to trial on a criminal charge until he shall have had sufficient time and opportunity to notify" the local Bureau officer. Virginia Bureau agents, therefore, appeared in defense of freedpeople in courts when possible, although they preferred to arbitrate matters before they had gone that far, an activity that for some men "engrossed almost their entire attention." Officials in other states found themselves in similar circumstances. In Tennessee and Georgia, Bureau officials were to be judicial watchdogs and advisers to the freedpeople, a task that consumed significant amounts of time for conscientious Bureau men. And North Carolina officers regularly attended the "sessions of the county court in their respective districts to protect the interests of the freedmen" during 1867.

The Bureau's retreat from formal judicial activity assumed that white officials would impartially enforce the laws that their state legislatures had enacted, thus providing the freedpeople with ample opportunity to protect their rights through the states' courts. It was an assumption that widespread and vigorous white resistance to Reconstruction proved wrong. White Southerners began to resist giving freedpeople equal consideration before the law almost as soon as the Bureau withdrew from acting as judge and jury in cases involving the ex-slaves. Throughout the South, Bureau men provided their superiors with evidence that suggested justice was an elusive thing for freedpeople. As historian Barry Crouch has shown, Texas laws did not make distinctions based on color or race. Nevertheless, the Texas legislature saw its handiwork as a way to control blacks and hurry the Bureau from the state, while the judiciary only enforced those laws with vigor on the black population.

Even when whites throughout the South followed the form of law, they used numerous tactics to deprive it of its substance. Racially neutral laws did not stop threats and violence from interfering with the freedpeople as they attempted to file complaints against whites. Freedpeople risked losing their jobs if they spent too much time waiting for cases to come to trial because judges frequently postponed them. Exslaves who brought their complaints before a magistrate lacked funds for lawyers and for court costs; if they found themselves jailed they were too poor to post bail. Black plaintiffs and defendants were at the mercy of white judges and juries who, in Tennessee Assistant Commissioner John R. Lewis's opinion, failed to take their testimony seriously, if it was admitted at all; Lewis learned that it was common practice for courts to exclude black testimony by claiming that it was "*not offered.*" Even if a jury convicted a white perpetrator of violence, Lewis complained, he could "expect the lightest punishment." On the other hand, Tennessee juries "often convicted [freedpeople] on the slightest testimony" and judges meted out "the heaviest penalty." Lewis, a firm believer in the importance of education, also believed that ignorance left freedpeople the victims of "the grossest kind of lawyers' trickery." He concluded that the only way for freedpeople to obtain justice in the state of Tennessee was to have the Bureau station an agent who was "a firstclass lawyer" in every judicial district.

When white officials did intervene, there were no guarantees that they would do nothing more than satisfy the form and not the substance of justice. Consequently, the Bureau reserved the right to reestablish its courts where there were blatant violations of the freedpeople's legal rights. The agency was ever cautious, but it did act in extreme circumstances, especially when the July 1866 Bureau law gave them the authority to do so. In Virginia during July 1866, for example, Orlando Brown reestablished three-member Bureau panels in three counties where "the magistrates . . . refused to administer justice, and those districts being left wholly without law or order." In Kentucky in October 1866, Bureau officer Charles F. Johnson, instructed one of his agents to avoid establishing a permanent court, but authorized him to act alone in hearing cases "where civil authorities refuse negro evidence" when it is essential to the case.

Bureau men accepted security of person as a basic right of free people. Consequently, few things revealed their frustration with white justice more than their reports of violence directed against the freedpeople and the lack of action on the part of civilian authorities in dealing with its perpetrators. (*See Document No. 26.*) In Georgia, for example, the Bureau reported 41 cases of murder committed during 1865 and 1866; only four of those cases had come to trial by the fall of 1866 and the defendants were acquitted. In November 1866, Kentucky's assistant commissioner reported that between June 1, 1866 and October 31, 1866 of the 237 "outrages" against the freedpeople, meaning crimes involving violence of some sort, the civil authorities had made only 42 arrests. In Tennessee, the assistant commissioner's "Register of Outrages" dated February 1867 was peppered with comments about the civil authorities' inability or unwillingness to bring whites to justice. Accused white Tennesseans had gone free on bail and never tried or had fled with no effort made by the authorities to arrest them.

Legal and material limitations required Bureau officials to pursue justice on a case-by-case basis and only after particular violations came to their attention. In October 1866, Assistant Commissioner Charles H. Howard reported significant abuses in executing the Maryland apprenticeship law. He believed there was a total of some 1200 cases in Ann Arundel and Calvert Counties in which parents did not give their consent for the apprenticing of their children, with other counties producing comparable figures. "The agents of this bureau have given attention to this subject and some apprentices have been released by *habeas corpus*," he reported. "But each case of unlawful apprenticeship must be brought separately before the court, no decision having yet been made, or State law enacted which operates generally for the release of parties unjustly and illegally apprenticed."

Officers and agents in various jurisdictions tried to pressure civilian authorities to take up freedmen's cases by threatening them with military intervention and even arresting and holding white perpetrators until they had their day in court. The Bureau's imperfect access to policing resources, however, further complicated its duties in responding to the inadequacies of the civilian legal system. It was a common practice, for example, for Bureau agents to use the complaining freedpeople to carry summonses to those whites who had wronged them. In April 1866, Virginia Bureau officer J. Arnold Yeckley had to rely on the mother of an illegally apprenticed child to act as his bailiff to carry the order to the white guardian to give up the child. "He threatened to kill her and she came back," Yeckley explained. A visit to Yeckley, prompted by a policeman, convinced the guardian to return the child to the mother, or so he told the Bureau officer. "They knocked her down several times, put a rope around her neck, dragged her to the fence and choked her," Yeckley learned when the mother returned empty handed a second time. "These men then took whips and whipped her on her bare back. *This is chivalry*," Yeckley complained. "I will try & have them punished, but do not think it can be done in the civil courts."

After May 1866, Bureau assistant commissioners could more readily make good on their threats to arrest and hold perpetrators or to use military force when they assumed regular positions as state-level commanders within the military chain of command and could ostensibly order local Army post commanders to assist Bureau agents. Ulysses S. Grant's General Order No. 44, issued July 6, 1866 also provided authority for such aggressive action by calling for the arrest of anyone who attacked a federal official or a citizen where civilian officials failed to act and the authority to hold the perpetrators until the local courts prosecuted them. Days after the War Department promulgated the order, North Carolina's assistant commissioner ordered his men to arrest individuals who violated anyone's rights if civilian courts refused to act and to "detain such persons in Military confinement, until such time as a proper judicial tribunal may be ready and willing to try them." During 1866, both Georgia's and Tennessee's assistant commissioners also ordered their men to arrest individuals and hold them until the civil authorities took action.

Despite these changes, the Bureau's policing ability remained at the mercy of military men, some who were cooperative, others who were not. In August 1866, Subassistant Commissioner Thomas Leddy investigated a case in northern Florida in which a known murderer shot a young freedman. He left the execution of justice up to the civil authorities, observing how the case progressed. When the civil authorities failed to take action, he traveled to Gainesville, Florida, to secure military assistance to arrest the perpetrator. Unfortunately, by the time he returned to Stark, the scene of the crime, the perpetrator had fled to Liberty County, on the southeastern Georgia coast. Determined to see justice done, he traveled to the military post at Fernandina and requested the commander to dispatch some men to arrest the gunman at a ferry on the St. Mary's River that separated the two states. The commanding officer refused to act, "as he deemed it unwise to do so."

Importantly, Bureau men who reported these conditions expressed their dismay in ways that revealed their understanding of their role of the freedpeople's guardians. During the fall of 1866, for example, officers throughout South Carolina complained about the exercise of civilian justice. Benjamin P. Runkle, Anderson District's Bureau officer, bemoaned the fact that the restoration of civil law led to a worsening of conditions because white South Carolinians assumed that the Bureau no longer had any power to interfere with their actions. Civilian officials were all the more popular among their white constituents, he claimed, for their inactivity. "I beg leave to renew my recommendation that these districts be taken in hand," Runkle recommended, "and that the evildoer and their aiders and abettors taught that the United States is prompt to enforce law." His counterpart on the coast in the Edisto District complained that there were no courts where freedpeople could receive justice and argued that "some other power must intervene." He concluded, "It is a stupendous wrong to emancipate and then desert" the freedpeople. Throughout the South, Bureau men begged for the power to do something, but the solutions that the government presented to them failed to have the desired effect.

On September 19, Commissioner Howard, aware of these complaints, used the authority granted by the July 1866 Bureau law to move his subordinates towards reestablishing three-member tribunals. However, such an action would have required presidential support to sustain it, an unlikely occurrence given the chief executive's conservative constitutional inclinations. By this time, President Johnson had already declared the rebellion to be over and the Supreme Court in the Milligan case restricted military tribunals to places where a state of war actually existed. In January 1867, Howard sought to test this decision and the July 1866 Bureau law by finding a suitable case into which the Bureau might insert itself, but failed to accomplish his end. The reintroduction of the Bureau and the military as arbiters of freedmen's rights in the erstwhile Confederacy would need to await further congressional action, which did come to pass in March 1867.

The Civil Rights Act of 1866. The Civil Rights Act of April 9, 1866, which Congress passed over the president's veto, provided Bureau men with another weapon in its attempts to protect the freedpeople's rights by using the courts. The law recognized freedpeople as having citizens' rights and provided federal courts and civil rights commissioners with the authority to intervene in cases in which local authorities failed to protect those rights. The law also gave Bureau officials the power to arrest violators and the reasonable expectation to receive assistance from military commanders to carry out this duty. Bureau men could then present cases of injustice to the commissioners who were required to investigate the charges before turning them over to the federal judiciary.

Unfortunately, as historian Donald Nieman has convincingly argued, the law had numerous flaws, not the least of them being the inability to deal with local and state courts that appeared to follow the letter of non-discriminatory laws and yet failed to do justice to the freedpeople.

Even if Bureau men derived some benefit from the law as Congress had narrowly conceived it, they encountered all sorts of problems in its execution. President Johnson did not care to pay much attention to the law's enforcement and consequently neither did his Justice Department. Federal attorneys in the South received little guidance from Washington in how to proceed; in come cases they stymied the Bureau when they failed to prosecute cases because they believed the law failed to give them adequate authority where there was no clear legislative discrimination. Investigations too often became bogged down in the slow movement of paper up and down the chain of command and officers and agents frequently found that they lacked ready access to the military force that was necessary for making the law work.

There was also confusion sown by local jurists. In October 1866, Charles H. Howard, the assistant commissioner of the District of Columbia, complained that "In Maryland, while one judge sustains the civil rights act by his decision, another decides it unconstitutional." Across the Potomac in Virginia, he found the same situation "and until this point be finally settled, that act will be of little practical avail to the freedmen." In Mississippi, Commissioner O. O. Howard reported at the end of the year, some district judges declared the law unconstitutional. He concluded that the law was not "in full operation in some portions of the south, for many criminals that ought to be brought to trial under that bill are at large."

In Kentucky, according to historian Donald Nieman, the Bureau was able to make use of the federal law because state law prohibited blacks from testifying against whites, a clear act of legislative discrimination. Furthermore, Commissioner Howard noted that the state in general "was slow to modify objectionable laws" that recent federal constitutional amendments and laws challenged; he also noted that the state court of appeals "retarded progress" by declaring the civil rights law unconstitutional. Nevertheless, the federal district court there "strongly sustained" the Civil Rights Act.

There were other problems, however, that slowed the Bureau's pursuit of justice in Kentucky and reinforced the conclusion that what happened in the federal courts was not sufficient to give freedpeople equal treatment before the law. In March 1868, Bureau officer Benjamin Runkle reported that there were freedpeople, victims of violence, who could not appear before United States Commissioners because they could not afford the cost of transportation. In April 1868, he reported that when freedpeople came forward and the commissioner issued warrants "it has been found impossible to make arrests." Runkle bemoaned the fact that a continued and general resistance to the federal government among white Kentuckians interfered with enforcing the law. The Bureau needed the assistance of cavalry troopers to make arrests of fleet-footed criminals, but it lacked cooperation of the military commander who said "No action could be taken by the commanding general with a view to procuring cavalry, until the United States civil authorities should represent their inability to execute the law without mounted men." In Lebanon, Kentucky, the federal marshal said no person in town could be found to act as bailiff and execute warrants, while at the same time the military commander believed that it was not right to use troops to protect the local law enforcement officials or to act as bailiffs. "It will be impossible for the bureau officers, under these circumstances, to do any more towards securing the arrest of any of these parties," Runkle complained. In the end the Bureau could not enforce the civil rights law "without the sword." "All this is humiliating, but it is true," Runkle concluded, "and I repeat again that the bureau officers are not responsible for this condition of affairs, and they cannot prevent it."

Military Reconstruction and Justice. By late 1866, it was apparent that without additional assistance, Bureau men would be unable to protect themselves let alone freedpeople and southern Unionists. Congress, aware of the agency's difficulties and concerned about the security of the freedpeople and Unionists in the South, passed Military

Reconstruction Act of March 2, 1867. It was followed by additional laws passed on March 23 and July 19 that collectively gave the appearance of a reinvigorated push to change the South and make it safe for allies of the federal government.

The March 2 act of Congress divided the erstwhile Confederacy, excluding an already restored Tennessee, into five military districts under military commanders who had the option of bringing criminals before military tribunals. It also provided that the states were to form new governments with new constitutions that embodied the principle of universal manhood suffrage. The states also had to approve the Fourteenth Amendment, which would recognize black citizenship, but in return Congress would consider restoring their full and proper relationship to the union. The second Reconstruction law provided more specifics for executing the first, while the July law, in addition to other things, gave the commanders of the military districts the power to remove civilian officials. These laws were important steps towards reasserting Bureau authority in the South. They continued to reflect the assumption that equality before state laws was the key to protecting the freedpeople's rights, but providing the freedmen with a political role in Reconstruction was a new departure, one based on the assumption that the vote was also important for their security. The first assumption recommitted the Bureau's officers and agents to a job that they had been performing with mixed results since they had come South; the second assumption gave them more duties to strain their already full schedules.

Military Reconstruction brought the Bureau's assistant commissioners under the direct control of the district commanders, an indication of Commissioner Howard's loss of complete control over his own agency. The situation created some confusion as the Bureau officers served two masters, but the trouble might be rewarded with greater success in dealing with recalcitrant white Southerners that came from an increase in military power. Subassistant commissioners and agents now assumed that they would be able to have more forceful tools in their arsenal than merely their persuasive abilities. One Georgia officer even concluded that the Reconstruction laws of March made the agency's power "absolute" when applied to securing the freedpeople's rights in the state's courthouses.

Reality, however, did not match these assumptions. If Bureau men expected a reinvigorated Reconstruction effort to come from these laws, they were only partially gratified in their hopes. Military commanders did interfere with civilian authorities in their efforts to secure the freed-people's rights and provided the Bureau with authority to seize property in contract disputes to secure the freedpeople's unpaid wages. The military tried to force civil authorities to expand the jury selection lists in an effort to seat freedmen on juries, but only with limited success. Also, Bureau men brought their complaints about civil officials to the military when they could document blatant discrimination against freedpeople and found some commanders willing to remove the offending individuals. Commanders on occasion instituted military commissions upon the detailed recommendation of Bureau men to provide freedpeople with justice. In all cases Bureau men were obliged to produce a substantial amount of paperwork to convince the commanders that the military should interfere with the normal course of civilian justice.

The Military Reconstruction Acts did not change the routines and disappointments of the Bureau men. In executing the promises made by the laws, Bureau men soon ran up against district commanders who were conservative in their use of their authority. In Georgia, George G. Meade, commander of the Third Military District, frequently stymied aggressive Bureau action. He cautioned agents and officers not to inter-fere in judicial cases without first allowing them wend their way through the usual civilian channels, something that continued to frustrate the freedpeople's quest for justice, and without first receiving his permis-sion. Bureau officials, therefore, continued to assist the freedpeople as best they could much in the same way as they had done before March 1867, serving as next friends, attorneys, arbitrators, and information gatherers.

Military Reconstruction and Politics. Early on in Recon-struction, Bureau men had shown interest in advising and educating the freedpeople about politics. While Howard instructed his men to remain politically neutral, he nevertheless promoted the cause of the Republi-can party and did not object to discrete political activity on the part of his subordinates. For example, in October 1865, he had his subordinates distribute pamphlets for the Union League, founded in 1862 in support of the war effort that developed into an arm of the more radical faction of the Republican party. Subordinates such as John Emory Bryant, the Augusta, Georgia, agent and Thomas Osborn, the assistant commis-sioner for Florida, helped to nurture black political awareness before the beginning of Military Reconstruction.

The very presence of sympathetic Bureau men in the South encouraged ex-slaves to look to the party of Lincoln, but after 1867 the besieged agency became more obviously tied to the Republican party. Not insignificant was the reorganization of the Bureau in early 1867 that allowed the agency to pay salaries for agents. Such a change allowed assistant commissioners to hire union men and veterans, while military policy allowed the agency to tap into the manpower of the Veteran Reserve Corps. One might expect these men to hold political sympathies that would encourage them to protect the fruits of victory. Always aware of the temporary nature of the Bureau, they came to understand that black political activity that favored the Republican party was an important part of preserving any advances the agency had made in areas such as education and labor.

There certainly remained Bureau men who were Democrats or unsympathetic to black political ambitions just as there were officers who tried to control their more politically enthusiastic subordinates. As Michael Fitzgerald has shown in his study of the Union League in Alabama and Mississippi, much depended on the inclinations of individual Bureau officials. In Mississippi, Assistant Commissioner Alvan C. Gillem, who assumed his position in late January 1867, was a Democrat and a friend of Andrew Johnson; there were Mississippi agents who were inclined to work with Republican politicians, but Gillem reigned in the political activity of his subordinates. Wager Swayne, the long-time Alabama assistant commissioner, on the other hand, was an enthusiastic Republican whose activities, according to Richard Abbott, the historian of the Republican party in the nineteenth-century South, contributed mightily to that state's restoration to the Union.

During Military Reconstruction, district commanders required their subordinates, who also happened to be Howard's assistant commissioners, to perform a number of tasks relative to the political requirements of Military Reconstruction. They were to supervise the voter registration process in their states, to recommend individuals to act as voter registrars, to disseminate information to voters, to keep peace at and observe elections, and to investigate and report fraud. These officers turned to their Bureau subordinates to assist them with these matters.

Bureau agents and officers became an important source of recommendations for registrars and some of them served in that capacity. They gave speeches at political meetings of the freedpeople to apprise them of their political rights and duties, a task that provided them with the opportunity to remind freedpeople that Lincoln's party was the party of emancipation and that they should use their vote to preserve the Union victory. They protected the freedpeople's right to hold such meetings in most cases, as long as they did not interfere with their work. During elections, Bureau men made sure that polls were open to the freedpeople. They also investigated cases of freedpeople dismissed from employment because they had registered to vote, attended a Republican political meeting, or voted for a Republican candidate.

Bureau men under normal circumstances investigated violence against freedpeople, but during periods of heightened political activity learned that politics bred its own brand of violence. With politics now a part of the freedmen's lives, the Bureau had to deal with planned violence that came from white terrorist organizations such as the Ku Klux Klan. Indeed, Bureau men were on the receiving end of comparable violence because of their connection with black politics. In Georgia, for example, one Bureau agent believed that the political activities of Military Reconstruction put him at greater personal risk, while in 1868 John J. Knox's violent confrontation with an ex-Confederate was a direct consequence of his activities during the November election.

Howard's warning to refrain from becoming embroiled in political activity at a personal level did not discourage some of his subordinates from using the Bureau as a spring board to their own political careers. Robert K. Scott, South Carolina's assistant commissioner, was only the most prominent example when he won election as governor of that state in 1868. A number of Bureau men turned up at state conventions and as historian Richard Abbott discovered, a noticeable number of officials became involved in politics after the reorganization of their states. At the same time, Abbott is correct to note that despite complaints from white Southerners, conservative northern Democrats and the president, the Bureau simply did not have sufficient personnel to dominate state organizations in the South.

In the end, Military Reconstruction failed to help the Freedmen's Bureau secure justice or the larger rights of the freedpeople. Reports from officers and agents throughout the South described some progress, but on the whole drew a pessimistic portrait of race relations and the freedpeople's ability to secure their rights without federal intervention. In late 1867, Commissioner Howard reported that while higher state courts appeared to be functioning fairly, the lower courts were not. Magistrates and juries continued to favor whites, while local authorities continued to ignore violence directed against the freedpeople. In October 1868 Assistant Commissioner J. J. Reynolds reported his frustration with the situation in Texas. "[T]he sentiment of the entire people is so demoralized and they are so specially averse to recognizing the equality of the Negro before the law," he wrote to Commissioner Howard, "that I cannot report any very great amount of progress in that direction."

In June 1868, Congress accepted that Arkansas, Alabama, Georgia, Florida, North Carolina, and South Carolina had sufficiently conformed to its Reconstruction requirements to be readmitted to their proper relationship with the rest of the union, further limiting the Bureau's role. In North Carolina, the governor appointed the remaining Bureau men as magistrates, which gave them some real power to deal with the complaints of freedpeople. But for the most part, the Bureau's agents and officers continued to deal with the complaints of the freedpeople from their position as advisors and mediators as the agency prepared to restrict its operations to educational activities and assisting freedmen secure their military bounty claims at the end of the year. Georgia, relapsing into an unreconstructed state after expelling black legislators from its government, along with Texas, Mississippi and Virginia found their way back into the union in 1869, but by that time, as far as white Southerners were concerned, the Bureau did not matter.

Bounties. At the same time that the Freedmen's Bureau began to assume the additional duties commensurate with Military Reconstruction, its officials became the source of all bounty and other claims of black veterans and their heirs. On March 29, 1867, Congress declared it the duty of Commissioner Howard and "the Officers and Agents of the Freedmen's Bureau, to facilitate as far as possible, the discovery, identity and payment of the claimants." Commissioner Howard later recalled, at this point he became responsible for the payment of all claims, thereby assuming ultimate responsibility for protecting the freedpeople's financial rights before the federal government.

From the Bureau's inception, it had been involved in helping black veterans and their heirs secure their financial claims against the government. In July 1865, Howard had ordered his subordinates to help freedpeople process monetary claims against the federal government and in March 1866 he established a Claims Divisions to oversee the Bureau's activities with regard to securing the pensions, bounties and back pay of black veterans. The duty was plagued by the same bureaucratic red tape that often delayed the Bureau's actions in other matters. In October 1866, Lt. A. Coats complained from New Bern, North Carolina, that the Bureau had appointed him to handle claims without providing him with full instructions. Consequently, the claims he filed for freedpeople bounced between his office and Washington, sometimes several times, in order that he comply "with some new rule" about which he had known nothing. After five months in his position, he had yet to collect a claim. Later in January 1870, John H. Wager, the Huntsville, Alabama, agent, complained about the various rules with which he had to contend to submit a bounty claim. Furthermore, requirements weighed heavily on the widows of black soldiers who had neither the resources to travel to his office to provide him with the necessary information for filing their claims nor the funds to pay notary fees. Nevertheless, the Bureau men dispensed information and advice and helped freedpeople with the necessary paperwork.

Bureau officials naturally urged freedpeople to be thrifty with the funds they received and advised them to deposit their money in the "Freedmen's Bank." (*See Document No. 27.*) Not a part of the Bureau, the Freedmen's Savings and Trust Company began operation after receiving its charter from Congress in March 1865. Howard endorsed the bank and urged his subordinates to promote it. The commissioner also helped it secure office space for bank branches and appointed some of its cashiers to act as Bureau bounty agents, no doubt helping to create the impression among some freedpeople that there was more than a casual connection between the two organizations. Fortunately, the Bureau officials could do no more than encourage freedpeople to deposit their funds in the bank. The institution failed in 1874.

The Freedmen's Bureau also assisted the freedpeople by investigating cases of fraud perpetrated by private claims agents. Freedpeople either because they wished to avoid delays in securing what the government owed them or because they knew no better often used private claims agents and lawyers, who compiled the necessary paperwork, and, if dishonest, claimed exorbitant fees for processing their claims. Congress's action in March 1867, therefore, was an attempt to keep money due the freedpeople out of the hands of private claims agents and lawyers who had been profiting from the promises of quick payment to the freedpeople. In the end, Howard believed that even though he dispersed reasonable fees to private claims agents, he saved the freedpeople over $62,000 while securing them much-needed funds. From March 29,

1867 to the end of September 1870, the Bureau Commissioner reported that he had paid out $7,683,618.61; in October 1871 at the end of the next reporting period, he noted the Bureau had settled claims totaling another $56,581.79. He later claimed that his agency had settled over 40,000 cases before the agency discharged the last of the claims agents in March 1872 and turned over its files to the Secretary of War on July 1 of that year.

PART II

DOCUMENTS

DOCUMENT NO. 1

SENATOR CHARLES SUMNER'S SPEECH IN DEFENSE OF ESTABLISHING A FREEDMEN'S BUREAU, JUNE 13, 1864*

Massachusetts Senator Charles Sumner, a longtime advocate for blacks since his election to the Senate in 1851, offered the following remarks in defense of the Freedmen's Bureau bill on June 13, 1864, during the Senate's debate of the measure. These remarks, along with Sumner's additional comments made on June 15, supported active intervention by the federal government on behalf of the South's slaves. They were published in pamphlet form, whereby they gained some wider circulation for the senator's thoughts on the issues surrounding the legislation. Sumner continued to serve in the Senate until his death in 1874.

γ   γ   γ

Mr. President, the Senate only a short time ago was engaged for a week in considering how to open an iron way from the Atlantic to the Pacific. It is now to consider how to open a way from slavery to freedom.

I regret much that only thus tardily we have been able to take up the bill for a Bureau of Freedmen. But I trust that nothing will interfere with its consideration now. In what I have to say, I shall confine myself to a simple statement. If I differ from others I beg to be understood that it is in no spirit of controversy, and with no pride of opinion. Nothing of this kind can enter justly into any such discussion.

I shall not detain the Senate to expose the importance of this measure. All must confess it at a glance. It is at once a charity and a duty.

By virtue of existing acts of Congress, and also under the proclamation of the President, large numbers of slaves have suddenly become free. These may now be counted by the hundred thousand. In the progress of history they will be counted by the million.

As they derive their freedom from the United States, under legislative or executive acts, the national Government cannot be excused from

* Charles Sumner, *Bridge from Slavery to Freedom: Speech of Hon. Charles Sumner, on the Bill to Establish a Bureau of Freedmen, in the Senate of the U.S., June 13 and 15, 1864* (Washington, D.C.: H. Polkinhorn & Son, Printers, 1864), on deposit at The Ohio Historical Society, Columbus, Ohio.

making such provisions as may be required for their immediate protection and welfare during the present *transition period*. The freedom that has been conferred must be rendered useful, or at least saved from being a burden. Reports, official and unofficial, show the necessity of action. In some places it is a question of life and death. . . .

It is evident, then, that the freedmen are not idlers. They desire work. But in their helpless condition they have not the ability to obtain it without assistance. They are alone, friendless, and uninformed. The curse of slavery is still upon them. Somebody must take them by the hand; not to support them but simply to help them to that work which will support them. Thus far private societies in different parts of the country, at the East and the West—especially at all the principal centers—have done much toward this charity. But private societies are inadequate to the duties required. The intervention of the national Government is necessary. Without such intervention, many of those poor people, freed by our acts in the exercise of a military necessity, will be left to perish.

The service required is too vast and complex for unorganized individuals. It must proceed from the national Government. This alone can supply the adequate machinery, and extend the proper network of assistance, with the unity of operation which is required. The national Government must interfere in the case precisely as in building the Pacific railroad. Private charity in our country is active and generous, but it is powerless to cope with the evils arising from a wicked institution; nor can it provide a remedy where society itself has been overthrown.

There are few who will not admit that something must be done by the Government. Cold must be the heart which could turn away from this call. But whatever is done must be through some designated agency, and this brings me to another aspect of the question.

The President in his proclamation of emancipation has used the following language: "I recommend to them"—that is, to the freedmen—"that in all cases, when allowed, they labor faithfully for reasonable wages." Such is the recommendation from that supreme authority which decreed emancipation. They are to labor, and for reasonable wages. But the President does not undertake to say how this opportunity shall be obtained; how the laborer shall be brought in connection with the land; how his rights shall be protected; and how his new-found liberty shall be made a blessing. It was enough, perhaps, on the occasion of the proclamation that the suggestion should be made. Faithful labor and reasonable wages! Let these be secured, and everything else will follow.

Different subjects as they become important are committed to the care of special bureaus. I need only refer to patents, agriculture, public lands, pensions, and Indian affairs, each under the charge of a separate Commissioner. Clearly the time has come for a Bureau of Freedmen. In speaking of a Bureau of Freedmen, I mean a bureau which will be confined in its operations to the affairs of freedmen, and not travel beyond this increasing class to embrace others, it may be of African descent. Our present necessity is to help those who have been made free by the present war; and the term freedmen describes sufficiently those who have once been slaves; and it is this class which we propose to help during the *transition period* from slavery to freedom. Call it charity or duty, it is sacred as humanity. . . .

I do not know how extensive the desire may be to set slavery again on its feet under another name. But when we take into consideration the selfish tendencies of the world, the disposition of the strong to appropriate the labor of the weak, and the reluctance of slave-masters to renounce their habitual power, I have felt that Congress would not do its duty on this occasion if it did not by special provision guard against any such outrage. There must be no slavery under an *alias*. This terrible wrong must not be allowed to skulk in serfdom or compulsory labor. "Once free, always free:" such is the maxim of justice and jurisprudence. But any system by which the freedmen may be annexed to the soil . . . will be in direct conflict with their newly acquired rights. They can be properly bound only by contract; and considering how easily they may be induced to enter into engagements ignorantly or heedlessly, and this become legal victims of designing men, it is evident that nor precautions in their behalf can be too great.

It is well known that in some of the British West Indies an attempt was made, at the period of emancipation, to establish a system of apprenticeship which should be an intermediate condition between slavery and freedom. But the experiment failed. . . .

But surely there is no need of eloquence or persuasion to induce you to set your faces like flint against any such half-way system. Freedom that has been declared must be secured completely, so that it may not fail through any pretension of fraud of wicked men. . . .

For the sake of plainness, I ask your attention to th[e] main features of the bill, under the following heads:

1. It provides exclusively for freedmen, meaning thereby "such persons as were once slaves," without undertaking to embrace persons generally of African descent.

2. It seeks to secure to such freedmen, the opportunity to labor or

apprenticeship, by requiring contracts between the freedmen and their employers to be carefully attested before local officials.

3. It provides positively against any system of enforced labor or apprenticeship by requiring contracts between the freedmen and their employers to be carefully attested before local officers.

4. It establishes a careful machinery for the purposes of the bill, both as regards the freedmen and as regards the lands.

But the bill may be seen not only in what it does, but also in what it avoids doing.

It does not undertake too much. It does not assume to provide ways and means for the support of the freedmen; but it does look to securing them the opportunities of labor according to well-guarded contracts and under the friendly advice of agents of the Government, who shall take care that they are protected against abuse of all kinds.

It is the declared duty of these agents "to protect these persons in the enjoyment of their rights, to promote their welfare, and to secure to them and their posterity the blessings of liberty." Under these comprehensive words all that is proper and constitutional will be authorized for their welcome and security, while Labor will be made to go hand in hand. But the case at last will be reversed. It will be Liberty that will conduct the freedman to the fields, protect him in his toil, and secure to him all its fruits. . . .

DOCUMENT NO. 2

CONGRESS ESTABLISHES THE FREEDMEN'S BUREAU, MARCH 3, 1865*

The legislation establishing the Freedmen's Bureau was much more than what some people had expected and much less than what many people had hoped for. The law gave the new agency control over more than just the ex-slaves, including within its jurisdiction the care of white refugees and the control of abandoned lands in the erstwhile Confederacy. But it established an organization that was limited in power, strapped for funds, and temporary in nature.

* *Statutes-at-Large of the United States of America, 1789–1873*, 17 vols. (Washington, D.C.: Government Printing Office, 1850–1873), 13: 507.

ϒ   ϒ   ϒ

An Act to establish a Bureau for the Relief of Freedmen and Refugees

Be it enacted by the Senate and House of Representatives of the United States of America in Congress assembled, That there is hereby established in the War Department, to continue during the present war of rebellion, and for one year thereafter, a bureau of refugees, freedmen, and abandoned lands, to which shall be committed, as hereinafter provided, the supervision and management of all abandoned lands, and the control of all subjects relating to refugees and freedmen from rebel states, or from any district of country within the territory embraced on the operations of the army, under such rules and regulations as may be prescribed by the head of the bureau and approved by the President. The said bureau shall be under the management and control of a commissioner to be appointed by the President, by and with the advice and consent of the Senate, whose compensation shall be three thousand dollars per annum, and such number of clerks as may be assigned to him by the Secretary of War, not exceeding one chief clerk, two of the fourth class, two of the third class, and five of the first class. And the commissioner and all persons appointed under this act, shall, before entering upon their duties, take the oath of office prescribed in an act entitled "An act to prescribe an oath of office, and for other purposes," approved July second, eighteen hundred and sixty-two, and the commissioner and the chief clerk shall, before entering upon their duties, give bonds to the treasurer of the United States, the former in the sum of fifty thousand dollars, and the latter in the sum of ten thousand dollars, conditioned for the faithful discharge of their duties respectively, with securities to be approved as sufficient by the Attorney-General, which bonds shall be filed in the office of the first comptroller of the treasury, to be by him put in suit for the benefit of any injured party upon any breach of the conditions thereof.

SEC. 2. *And be it further enacted*, That the Secretary of War may direct such issues of provisions, clothing, and fuel, as he may deem needful for the immediate and temporary shelter and supply of destitute and suffering refugees and freedmen and their wives and children, under such rules and regulations as he may direct.

SEC. 3. *And be it further enacted*, That the President may, by and with the advice and consent of the Senate, appoint an assistant commissioner for each of the states declared to be in insurrection, not exceeding ten in number, who shall under the direction of the commissioner, aid in the execution of the provisions of this act; and he shall give bond to the Treasurer of the United States, in the sum of twenty thousand dollars in the form and manner prescribed in the first section of this act. Each of the said commissioners shall receive an annual salary of two thousand five hundred dollars in full compensation for all his services. And any military officer may be detailed and assigned to duty under this act without increase of pay or allowances. The commissioner shall, before the commencement of each regular session of congress, make a full report of his proceedings with exhibits of the state of his accounts to the President, who shall communicate the same to congress, and shall also make special reports whenever required to do so by the President or either house of congress; and the assistant commissioners shall make quarterly reports of their proceedings to the commissioner, and also such other special reports as from time to time may be required.

SEC. 4. *And be it further enacted*, That the commissioner, under the direction of the President, shall have authority to set apart, for the use of loyal refugees and freedmen, such tracts of land within the insurrectionary states as shall have been abandoned, or to which the United States shall have acquired title by confiscation or sale, or otherwise, and to every male citizen, whether refugee or freedmen, as aforesaid, there shall be assigned not more than forty acres of such land, and the person to whom it was so assigned shall be protected in the use and enjoyment of the land for the term of three years at an annual rent not exceeding six per centum upon the value of the such land, as it was appraised by the state authorities in the year eighteen hundred and sixty, for the purpose of taxation, and in case no such appraisal can be found, then the rental shall be based upon the estimated value of the land in said year, to be ascertained in such manner as the commissioner may by regulation prescribe. At the end of said term, or at any time during said term, the occupants of any parcels so assigned may purchase the land and receive such title thereto as the United States can convey, upon paying therefor the value of the land, ascertained and fixed for the purpose of determining the annual rent aforesaid.

SEC. 5, *And be it further enacted*, That all acts and parts of acts inconsistent with the provisions of this act, are hereby repealed.

APPROVED, March 3, 1865.

DOCUMENT NO. 3

A MEETING OF PLANTERS HELD IN SAVANNAH, GEORGIA, JUNE 6, 1865*

At outset of Reconstruction, planters throughout the South considered the Freedmen's Bureau a means for stabilizing their labor force. A group of planters meeting in Savannah, Georgia, appealed to the Bureau to bring discipline back to the cotton fields and rice fields of the state. To assume that the Bureau would be an ally in such work was not just wishful thinking on the part of the planters; their views were not all that contrary to the Bureau's own policies concerning the enforcement of labor discipline. However, planters in Georgia and elsewhere would soon learn that the agency's agenda was more complicated than simply making sure ex-slaves once again assumed the role of docile workers.

γ   γ   γ

At a large and intelligent meeting of Planters held in the City of Savannah on the 6th day of June 1865, the novel position in which the Planters of our state, have been placed by the results of the war which has just been closed, occupied their serious attention exciting fearful forebodings [*sic*] of the distress awaiting the future for themselves. For their State, and for that unfortunate race of people who have for generations composed a part of their families, and whose interest and happiness, have been so mutually dependent, and interwoven with each other.

The results of this sad war, if not having already effected[,] is threatening to sever that long existing relationship between Masters and Slaves; and placing the slave in the new condition of freemen, dependent upon his own judgement[,] industry, energy[,] and economy, to advance his happiness and success in life; and on the wisdom of his determination depends the success of the Planter, and the prosperity of the State, and as the wellbeing of the colored Race. The consequence of such reflections, was a conviction—

* Robert Habersham [and other planters] to [O. O. Howard], June 6, 1865, reel 74, Registers and Letters Received, Records of the Commissioner, Bureau of Refugees, Freedmen, and Abandoned Lands, 1865–1872, National Archives Microfilm Publication M752.

1st The necessity of a wise system for the management of labor, being devised as a permanent measure for the future, and 2nd The necessity of the adoption of speedy and effective means to secure the cultivation, and harvesting of the growing crops this last, requiring immediate attention.

Should the effects of the Presidential Emancipation Proclamation be the same throughout the State, as they have been in our immediate vicinity, an almost total loss of the crops must ensue. The desire for freedom being so natural to all men, and the conception of its value being so fanciful in the slave, generally considering, its essential quality, is the exemption from all labor—that so soon as he is aware, that he is made a freeman by the power of the government, and from the experience of others, learns that the same power provides him with the needed rations for the support of himself and family, all control of the Planter is lost, and labor terminates.

At this season of the year, when the growing crops of the State call for the most devoted care, and the whole suc[c]ess of the year, culminating, in the attentions of the present; a few weeks loss of labor—the fruits of the Past and the hopes for the future of the crops, pass beyond reach of the planter, rendering abortive, all of his preceeding [*sic*] labor and expenditure. [A] few weeks abandonment of labor and all is gone—leaving our State for the ensuing year, without a crop of its own for a support, and without the means of procuring it from abroad[.] Such must be the condition of the white and colored race unless speedy and effective means, be devised and applied to avert the evil, by retaining the services of laborers until the crops shall have been secured. What is the remedy? And how shall it be applied? Compensation, liberal compensation, will not the present year, secure generally the services of the so recent slave. Like the child with its new play thing [*sic*], it must enjoy it, to its full. To congregate in the cities and towns mingle in social gatherings, enjoy free rations from the government, is a boon to him to great to be resisted. [N]or do the wants of the future disturb his present perfect bliss. For the present year at least, to protect our State from the loss of its promising growing crops, and from famine, as the planter has bee, and is soon to be deprived of his physical and moral control of his laborers, reliance and hope alone can be placed on the power of government, in its military or civil capacity and each day's delay in its exercise, depressing the hope of the planter, and demoralizing the character of the laborer.

So serious and appalling are our apprehensions for the future of our State, that this meeting feels constrained by the conviction of duty to its states and for the cause of humanity to appeal to Maj. Gen[era]l Howard, Chief of the Freedmen's Bureau, that he would for the good of the Black man, as well as the white, speedily adopt such measures, as may secure the fruit of the growing crops at the South and receive for his consideration, from the planters such suggestions, as may result from their long experience and which may conduce to the speedy formation of a system and its application, as shall secure for the people of our State a support, and a deliverance from impending famine. In connection with this important subject we would respectfully call attention to the notorious fact, that since the issuance of the President[']s Emancipation Proclamation, many hundreds of colored laborers, have deserted their former owners, and are now roaming at large, throughout the State, and have become more or less dependent upon the public charity, and the plunder of private property for a livelihood, and it [is] seriously apprehended that unless this evil is speedily arrested by the prompt attention of the government, it will become still more alarming and disastrious [*sic*], in its consequences.

In conclusion, this meeting of Planters, would respectfully submit for the consideration of General Howard as the most practicable means, which occurs to them to save the growing crops in the Southern states the following:

1st—The distribution and application, of an effective Military or other physical force, to enforce discipline & labor.

2nd—A published order from the Freedmen's Bureau, requireing [*sic*] all laborers on Plantations, and Farms, to remain faithfully discharging their duties, in cultivating and harvesting the growing crops.

3rd—A published notice, that no government rations, will be allowed to any laborers, who may desert, or abandon, the plantation, on which he or she may have been employed since the planting of the present crops.

All of which is respectfully submitted.

Rob[er]t Habersham
Chairman

William H. Miller
Secretary

DOCUMENT NO. 4

O. O. HOWARD'S RULES AND REGULATIONS FOR ASSISTANT COMMISSIONERS, MAY 30, 1865*

Major General Oliver Otis Howard formally assumed command of the Freedmen's Bureau on May 19, 1865 and immediately began the Herculean task of giving substance to the legislation authorizing the agency. His Circular No. 5 gave his assistant commissioners, his immediate subordinates, a set of guidelines to follow in their own organizational efforts and revealed his own views about the nature of his new agency.

γ   γ   γ

[Circular No. 5.]
WAR DEPARTMENT,
BUREAU OF REFUGEES, FREEDMEN, AND ABANDONED LANDS

Washington, May 30, 1865.

Rules and regulations for assistant commissioners

I. The headquarters of the assistant commissioners will, for the present, be established as follows, viz.: for Virginia, at Richmond; North Carolina, at Raleigh, N.C.; South Carolina and Georgia, at Beaufort, S.C.; Alabama, at Mongomery, Ala.; Kentucky and Tennessee, at Nashville, Tenn.; Missouri and Arkansas, at St. Louis, Mo[.]; Mississippi, at Vicksburg, Miss.; Louisiana, at New Orleans, La.; Florida, at Jacksonville, Fla.

II. Assistant commissioners not already at their posts will make haste to establish their headquarters, acquaint themselves with their fields, and do all in their power to quicken and direct the industry of refugees and freedmen, that they and their communities may do all that can be done for the season, already so far advanced, to prevent starvation and suffering, and promote good order and prosperity. Their attention is in-

---

* *House Executive Documents*, No. 70, 39th Congress, 1st session (serial 1256), pp. 180–81.

vited to circular No. 2, from this bureau, indicative of the objects to be attained.

III. Relief establishments will be discontinued as speedily as the cessation of hostilities and the return of industrial pursuits will permit. Great discrimination will be observed in administering relief, so as to include none that are not absolutely necessitous and destitute.

IV. Every effort will be made to render the people self-supporting. Government supplies will only be temporarily issued to enable destitute persons speedily to support themselves, and exact accounts must be kept with each individual or community, and held as a lien upon their crops. The ration for the destitute will be that already provided in General Orders No. 30, War Department, series 1864. The commissioners are especially to remember that their duties are to enforce, with reference to these classes, the laws of the United States.

V. Loyal refugees, who have been driven from their homes, will, on their return, be protected from abuse, and the calamities of their situation relieved as far as possible. If destitute, they will be aided wit transportation, and food when deemed expedient, while in transitu, returning to their former homes.

VI. Simple good faith, for which we hope on all hands from those concerned in the passing away of slavery, will especially relieve the assistant commissioners in the discharge of their duties towards the freedmen, as well as promote the general welfare. The assistant commissioners will, everywhere, declare and protect their freedom, as set forth in the Proclamations of the President and the laws of Congress.

VII. In all places where there is an interruption of civil law, or in which local courts, by reason of old codes, in violation of the freedom guaranteed by the proclamation of the President and the laws of Congress, disregard he negro's right to justice before the laws, in not allowing him to give testimony, the control of all subjects relating to refugees and freedmen being committed to this bureau, the assistant commissioners will adjudicate, either themselves or through officers of their appointment, all difficulties arising between negroes themselves, or between negroes and whites or Indians, except those in military service, so far as recognizable by military authority, and not taken cognizance of by the other tribunals, civil or military, of the United States.

VIII. Negroes must be free to chose their own employers, and be paid for their labor. Agreements should be free, *bona fide* acts, approved by proper officers and their inviolability enforced on both parties. The old system of overseers tending to compulsory unpaid labor and acts of cruelty and oppression is prohibited. The unity of families, and all the rights of the family relation, will be carefully guarded. In places where the local statutes make no provisions for the marriage of persons of color, the assistant commissioners are authorized to designate officers who shall keep a record of marriages, which may be solemnized by any ordained minister of the Gospel, who shall make a return of the same, with such items as may be required for registration at places designated by the assistant commissioner. Registrations already made by United States officers will be carefully preserved.

IX. Assistant commissioners will instruct their receiving and disbursing officers to make requisitions upon all officers, civil or military, in charge of funds, abandoned lands, &c., within their respective territories, to turn over the same in accordance with the orders of the President. They will direct their medical officers to ascertain the fact and necessities connected with the medical treatment and sanitary condition of refugees and freedmen. They will instruct their teachers to collect the facts in reference to the progress of the work of education, and aid it with as few changes as possible to the close of the present season. During school vacations of the hot months special attention will be given to the provision for the next year.

X. Assistant commissioners will aid refugees and freedmen in securing titles to land according to law. This may be done for them as individuals or by encouraging joint companies.

XI. This bureau being in the War Department, all rules and regulations governing officers under accountability for property apply as set forth in the revised regulations of the army. All other persons in the service of the bureau are also subject to military jurisdiction.

XII. Assistant commissioners will require regular and complete reports from their subordinates, and will themselves report quarterly, as directed by law, and correspond frequently with this bureau, directing to the commissioner in person.

O. O. Howard

Major General, Comm'r Bureau Refugees, Freedmen &c.
Approved June 2, 1865.

ANDREW JOHNSON,
President of the United States

DOCUMENT NO. 5

ELIPHALET WHITTLESEY ASSUMES COMMAND OF THE NORTH CAROLINA BUREAU, JULY 1, 1865*

Colonel Eliphalet Whittlesey had been a minister and a professor at Bowdoin College in Maine before the war. He had served during the war as Oliver Otis Howard's judge advocate and had received a brevet or honorary rank of Brigadier General. He remained assistant commissioner of the North Carolina Bureau until May 15, 1866, when he was arrested for misconduct. Despite the accusations, he was acquitted of wrongdoing and went on to serve with Howard's staff until 1872. As with many Bureau officers, even the more radical ones such as he, Whittlesey at first approached his task with optimism, assuming that white Southerners would eventually cooperate with the new regime at least because it was in their own interest to do so.

γ   γ   γ

Bureau of Refugees, Freedmen &c
Hd. Qrs. Asst. Commissioner, State of N. C.
Raleigh, N. C. July 1ˢᵗ, 1865

Circular
No. 1

Having been appointed by the President of the United States Assistant Commissioner in the Bureau of Refugees, Freedmen and Abandoned Lands, and having been assigned by Maj. General Howard to the State of North Carolina, I hereby assume control of all subjects relating to Refugees and Freedmen in the State, and request all officers and others now in charge of Freedmen, to report to me the condition of their work.

In entering upon the duties of this office, I invite the hearty co-operation of all who desire the welfare of the State.

A great social revolution is going on. The united wisdom of all classes will be required to guide it to a successful issue. The negro has become

---

* Circular No. 1, July 1, 1865, reel 20, Records of the Assistant Commissioner for the State of North Carolina, Bureau of Refugees, Freedmen and Abandoned Lands, 1865–1870, National Archives Microfilm Publication M843.

free, but he has not become an object of indifference. His interests and those of the white man are the same. He cannot with safety be treated with neglect, or scorn, or cruelty. He is human, and is entitled to all the rights of a man. Withhold from the Freedmen fair wages for their labor, deny them a right to a fair hearing before courts of justice, discourage their efforts to accumulate property, and to acquire learning, and you will drive from the State its real wealth— its productive labor. On the other hand, give to the Freedman that which is just and equal, give them all the facilities possible for improvement and education, and you will secure in the States its best supporters and its truest friends. The School House, the Spelling Book, and the Bible will be found better preservers of peace and good order, than the revolver and bowie knife.

I invite the co-operation of Freedmen also. Without your help this Bureau can do but little for you. Our freedom imposes upon you new duties. Some of you have families: it is your duty to support them. Some of you have aged parents and relatives, to whom liberty has come too late: it is your duty to minister to their comfort. Some of you will meet with helpless orphans: it is your duty to supply to them, as far as you can, the places of their lost parents. It is your duty, in common with all men, to obey the laws of the land, to live honestly, uprightly; and in fear of God.

Your freedom will expose you to some new trouble. Bad men will take advantage of your ignorance and impose upon you. Some will try to defraud you of your wages, and a few may be wicked and cowardly enough to revenge their losses upon you by violence. But let none of these things provoke you to evil deeds. It is better to suffer wrong than to do wrong. By manly patience and modest fortitude, you will live down hate and gain the respect of all good men.

Your freedom gives you new privileges. You can now live in families. The marriage tie is as sacred among you as among your neighbors. As soon as you acquire the means, you can have your own homes, and continue to improve them in comfort and beauty. You can learn to read and write, and you can support schools for your children. You can select your own religious teachers, and in due time will be able to sustain your own churches. Your conduct hitherto has been worthy of much praise. Your quiet demeanor, and industrious habits are winning for you a good name. You have many friends. Not only the officers of this Bureau, but good men every where will encourage and aid you. And God, the author of all good, will be your friend. Be true to Him and He will not fail to protect and bless you.

E. Whittlesey
Col. and Asst. Commissioner

Official:

    Asst. Adjutant General

DOCUMENT NO. 6

FREEDPEOPLE OF YORK COUNTY, VIRGINIA, PETITION FOR A BLACK REPRESENTATIVE ON A FREEDMEN'S BUREAU TRIBUNAL, JULY 14, 1866*

The following petition was but one part of an effort of the freedpeople in York County on the Virginia peninsula to have Dr. Daniel M. Norton, a black man, initially selected by them in late 1865 and rejected by the state assistant commissioner, appointed as their representative on the freedmen's court for their county. The Virginia Bureau at this time used three-man panels to settle disputes between whites and blacks, with one sitting member representing whites, another blacks, and a third the Bureau. The significance attached to the appointment of Norton suggests the importance the freedpeople attached to the Bureau. Commissioner Howard forwarded this petition to Assistant Commissioner Orlando Brown on July 17. Brown returned it to Howard on July 19. Explaining why he objected to acting on the petition, Brown argued somewhat disingenuously that the representative should be nonpartisan; therefore, an advocate for the freedpeople would be inappropriate. More to the point, he informed Howard that no white man would serve with Norton and that he expected to discontinue the courts in the near future. Further protest on the part of York County freedpeople failed to change the Bureau's mind about Dr. Norton, a runaway slave who had studied medi-

---

* Rev. J. Cary [and 29 other petitioners] to Maj. Gen. O. O. Howard, July 14, 1866, reel 31, Registers and Letters Received, Records of the Commissioner, Bureau of Refugees, Freedmen, and Abandoned Lands, 1865–1872, National Archives Microfilm Publication M752.

cine in Troy, New York, and returned to become a l eader in the black com-
munity in Hampton. In the end, however, the freedpeople had their way.
Norton, among his other political accomplishments, held office as justice of
the peace in York County for 40 years.

γ   γ   γ

York County[,] Virginia[,] July 14th, 1866

To Gen. O. O. Howard

Commissioner of Freedmen[']s Bureau

We the Colored people of the County whose names are appended, Respectfully petition the Commissioner, that he allow Dr. Daniel M. Norton to Represent us in the Freedmen[']s Court of York County Va. He
was Elected Agent for the Colored people according to orders last fall
and did Act as Such until the arrival of Lt. Massey with orders from
Col. O. Brown, Commissioner for the State of Virginia. Stating that he
Could not Act as Agent, and as we learn it was on account of his being
Colored, and whereas we your petitioners believe that those Restrictions
have been Removed, we Respectfully petition the Commissioner to Re-
consider this case and allow Dr. Daniel M. Norton to Act and Represent
us in the Freedmen[']s Court. We your petitioners Look about ourselves, and see the Whites people in our midst having all the Rights of
choice, through the Ballot Box of those who Shall Rule over them or be
Executioners of the Laws under which they live. This they have irrespective of what has been their Cause for the last four years, we have no
such Right, and as the Right of petition is the only one Granted to us
whereby we may indicate a choice we hope the excuse of it may not
prove offensive.

The Freedmen[']s Bureau being the only protection we have against
the unjust demands, the exorbitant exactions [*sic*] and lawless violence
of the Whites amongst ourselves it is not unnatural that we Should be
[frustrated?] about his Removal, and as we cannot appreciate the fact
that we could better our cause by giving up our choice Dr. D. M. Norton who is highly Respected by all good union men of the County and
Elect A White man in his place as we have been ordered to do by
Lt. Massey, saying that no other counties had Colored men, as Agent.
Dr. Daniel M. Norton is in good standing with the Missionary Soci-

ety[']s and a true upright Christian much Respected by all, and a man
of good judgement[.]

Names
Rev J. Cary
[and 29 others]

DOCUMENT NO. 7

A BUREAU SUPERINTENDENT REPORTS ON THE ORGANIZATION OF THE AGENCY IN NORTH CAROLINA, AUGUST 7, 1865*

Officers and agents of the Freedmen's Bureau encountered any number of difficulties as they attempted to give some shape to the fledgling agency during the unsettled summer of 1865. Assistant commissioners required monthly reports from their officers. Reports such as this one from North Carolina Bureau officer Lieutenant Colonel Dexter E. Clapp, formerly an officer in a black regiment, were common in form and content throughout the South at this time. This report indicates the several problems that were still awaiting solutions at the hands of the new Bureau. Until the Bureau's end, agents and officers filed similar monthly reports to their superiors.

γ   γ   γ

Office of the Bureau of Refugees &c
Hd. Qrs. Central Dist of N.C. Raleigh Aug. 7th 1865

Lieut Fred. H. Bucher
    Act. Asst. Adjt. Genrl.

Lieut[:]

In obedience to orders, I have the honor to make the following report
for the month of July 1865, for the Central Dist of N.C.

There have been issued to Destitute Freedmen in Hospitals, Desti-

* Lt. Col. Dexter E. Clapp to Lt. Fred. H. Bucher, August 7, 1865, reel 22, Records of
the Assistant Commissioner for the State of North Carolina, Bureau of Refugees,
Freedmen, and Abandoned Lands, National Archives Microfilm Publication M843.

tute Camp, City and Surrounding Country, Since the 11ᵗʰ day of July, at which time I took charge of this Office, 12223 Rations, also to Destitute Refugees (White) in Camp 140 Rations. Aside from this there have been issued to Destitute Freedmen in the Surrounding country 4687 Rations of Hd. Brd. which was turned over to me by the Officer whom I relieved. At Goldsboro N.C. there have been issued to Destitute Freedmen 28789 Rations.

Total issues of Meat & H[ar]d Br[ea]d 41352 Rations. Total issues of Hd. Brd. alone 4687 Rations.

I have almost entirely Stopped the issue of Rations to Destitute Freedmen who are not in Camp and Hospital. I am thoroughly convinced that the general issue of rations to Freedmen of the City and vicinity has been productive of much more harm than good by fostering idleness &c. Since this issue has been stopped, I have heard of no cases of actual suffering.

From the distant Counties of the District where there are no Officers of this Bureau on duty, I have received a large number of complaints of gross abuse of Freedmen, for the want of Officers I have been able to investigate only a few of these complaints, Some of these cases which have been investigated have been found to have no foundation; other cases indicate an intention to oppress and abuse the Freedmen. From observation, I am thoroughly convinced that the presence of an Officer in each of the Sub Districts of two or three Counties each, would effectually prevent all such abuses.

There appears in some Districts among the Freedmen a disinclination to work. I think this arises in a great measure from a lack of proper information, as to their true condition as Freedmen, and from the practice of employers in those Districts paying the men wages insufficient for the support of themselves and families, this is the case in Warren County. Licentious ideas of freedom prevail to some extent in the Districts above referred to, arising in part from statements made to the Freedmen by the Straglers [sic] of the Union Army.

In Nash County, I am informed there are among the white people some fears of an insurrection, the Local Police of that County have dealt with the persons suspected of this in a manner both cruel and calculated to produce the very evil dreaded; gentlemen from Warren County mention the same danger as somewhat feared there; hints of the same danger also come from Johnston County, all of these evils will be, I am confident, avoided or remedied by the sending of judicious officers to these sections. While I believe the fears of insurrection are imaginary, I also feel that I cannot too strongly represent the importance of stationing officers of this Bureau in each of these Sub Districts which are practically beyound [*sic*] my supervision.

The case of Sarah Hogan, former slave of Alexander Hogan of Orange County, who was cruelly whipped by Wm. Robinson has already been brought to your notice; William Robinson is a member of the Local Police and whipped this girl without any authority for so doing, and in my opinion without any sufficient reason for punishment.

Guion Earp[,] Sergeant of the Local Police of Johnston County, brutally maltreated Stephen Stanstell Freedman, searching his house for pork alleged to have been stolen, without any proper authority for so doing, yet he, Earp, seems to have been persuaded by his superiors and neighbors, that he had a right to administer these punishments as he did, he is also represented as having been a Union man, he is now under arrest, and charges have been sent to the District Commander, with the request that he may be brought to trial before a Military Commission. Very many other similar complaints have been made to us which we could not investigate, and I repeat that I believe that the assignment of Officers to the Sub Districts would almost entirely obviate these evils.

Very many misunderstandings of late have arisen between Freedmen who have been cultivating crops for citizens with the expectation of receiving a portion of the crop from the fact that when the cultivation of the crop was completed, they claim that they were to perform no other work on the farms. Such complaints have come by hundreds from all parts of the District. I have succeeded on satisfactorily arranging all these cases when I could obtain the attendance of both parties, but in places that cannot be reached by one of our Officers, misunderstanding, idleness and their concomitant troubles must arise.

There is another very serious evil connected with the employment of Freedmen by Officers of the U.S. Government to which I wish to call your attention. A large number of Freedmen have entered complaints at this office, that they had been at work for different Quartermasters and Commissares [*sic*] of this place and that they had been discharged with little or no pay[;] they invariably stated that when they commenced work, they [had] been promised $15.00 per Month and their rations. In the cases which I have communicated with the Officers for whom they had [worked,] I received reply that these men were never promised any wages, but were informed that they would receive no pay, except rations.

The men in close examination without an exception reiterated that they had been promised the above mentioned wages. It is not necessary for me to enumerate the evils resulting from such treatment of Freedmen by Officers of the U.S. Government but it appears to me that not least among these evils, is the destruction of the implicit faith which they have had in the Government and its Officers, and the increase, among them, of the disinclination to work. The disinclination to work resulting from their former condition of unpaid laborers, and from too frequent practice, by Officers and men of our Army requiring them to labor without pay, I believe to be the greatest difficulty which will have to be overcome in making them honest and industrious citizens.

Very Respectfully

Your Obdt. Srvt.

Dexter E. Clapp

Lt. Col. 38th Regt. U.S.C.I. and Supt. Freedmen

U[nited] S[tates] C[olored] I[nfantry]

DOCUMENT NO. 8

A BUREAU AGENT'S EXPERIENCES AS AN OUTSIDER IN CARNESVILLE, GEORGIA, AUGUST 29, 1868*

Freedmen's Bureau agents and officers rarely found their posts to be welcoming places in which to live but conditions worsened for Bureau men after it became clear that Congress had set the agency's termination date. J. W. Barney, a former captain in the 1ˢᵗ Delaware Volunteer Infantry, had relocated to Georgia after the war long before "carpetbaggers" could take political advantage of the South, probably to nurse his health and his financial prospects, as did so many other veterans. He started working with the Bureau in November 1865. Frustrated with the Bureau's diminished authority and fearing for his safety, he tendered his resignation from the agency in August 1868 to be effective on September 1. One may translate the Latin phrase in

* J. W. Barney to Bvt. Brig. Gen. C. C. Sibley, August 29, 1868, reel 58, Registers and Letters Received by the Commissioner of the Bureau of Refugees, Freedmen, and Abandoned Lands, 1865–1872, National Archives Microfilm Publication M752.

the threat reproduced by Barney in this letter as "a word to a wandering
viper" or, in plainer terms, "a warning to a snake in the grass."

γ   γ   γ

Atlanta Geo.

Aug. 29th 1868

Bvt Brig. Gen. C. C. Sibley

Asst Com'r State of Geo.

General

I have the honor to submit the
following report at the request of his Excellency Gov. R. B. Bullock for
your consideration and for his sattisfaction [*sic*] &c. showing why it was
compulsory on my part to resign my post as Agent of the Freedmen[']s
Bureau at Carnesville in northeast Georgia. I entered upon my official
duties as Agent of the Freedmen[']s Bureau at Carnesville on the 1st Day
of Sept. 1867. The moment I entered upon my duties as such I became
obnoxious to the citizens of Carnesville and the surrounding country
Even beyond the limits of my offices jurisdiction I soon discovered this
fact and governed myself accordingly. I had no society whatever, organized no political clubs, nor delivered no public addresses, except to the
colored people upon the subject of education and such matters as per-
tained to their general welfare with reference to contracts &c. I had not
been long in Carnesville when an education convention was called by
the Supt. of Education for this State to be held at the city of Macon. I
was directed to send delegates to that convention. I put out the report
to the freedpeople requesting them to assemble at their church on a certain evening. They came, as many as could make it conveniant [*sic*] to
attend. I stated to them the object of our meeting, and in the mean time
seven or eight white men, some of whom I recognized as citizens of the
village, came in and I was asked the question if we had not met there
for the purpose of organizing a "Union League". I answered in the
negative, whereupon I was then told by one man that he had been so informed, and that he wished me to distinctly understand that no "God-
Damd [*sic*]" Union League should be organized in that town, or county
This report soon spread thro [*sic*] the country and had a strong tendency
to inflame the passions of a prejudiced people against me without provo-
cation. Shortly after this event I notified a white man (officially) to appear at my office, he disregarded my notice and denied my authority. I
notified him the second time, only to be again disregarded. I then di-

rected his arrest by the Sheriff not however until after he had threatened
my life. Another man who while in my office transacting business in
which he was concerned took the liberty of calling me a "damd liar
[sic]" and him I knocked down, which the people did not like nor did I
like to be called that. On the following day a crowd of fiendish white
men aroused by the effects of corn whiskey (for I think it is the only
kind they have there and make it themselves without regard to law) ar-
rayed themselves in a hostile manner against me, giving me no reason
for it. They followed me to my Boarding house[.] I went in and kept to
my room until they left the town that day. A colored woman was told
soon after that a reward of one thousand dollars would be given to any
one who would get me out of town for the purpose of murdering me.
Soon after this thirty five came in town, armed with shot guns and pis-
tols, broke down the stables and took there from a yoke of oxen which
the Revenue Officer had seized upon legally, for some violation of law.
The citizens winked at this riotous proceedings of this mob, which gave
rise to the sending of United States troops to that place. The troops
were there about two months and order prevailed on the part of the citizens for the time being. As soon as the military left the Revenue Officers
left with a firm belief that they could no longer remain there with any
degree of safety. This left me alone at the mercy only of a single union
white man who was as much despised by the rebels as I was myself. The
people were then free to act and talk as they pleased, and they did both
beyond the bounds of all human Justice. They then soon began to hold
their political caucuses and public meetings. Inflamatory [sic] appeals,
revolutionary in their character, were made repeatedly and publicly to
the passions of an illiterate class of people, such as control public opinion in the north-eastern part of this State. Many letters were sent to me
bearing threats against my life, some of which I have in my possession
at present. These letters were all signed K.K.K. but in different hand-
writing and bearing different dates. These letters I paid but little attention to, it shows however the little regard the people had for Gen. Meade's
orders with reference to such secret organization, for I rec'vd them all
after Gen. Meade[']s order had been issued. I took my wife one Sunday
to Franklin Springs nine miles from Carnesville a place of resort. There
were many persons from Elbert County there and a few from Franklin
County. I went in the morning intending to return the same day, but it
rained and I was compelled to remain at the Springs all night; on the
following day I was notified to leave the premises by parties unknown

to me from Elbert County. They told me that my presence was objectionable to southern gentleman. The following is a copy of a letter sealed and addressed to me while I was at the Springs. I found it at my door when I came out of my room on the following morning.

                    "Verbum Sepi [Eūti]"

                              Franklin Springs, Ga.

                              Sunday 26" day of the Bloody Moon

Carpet Bagger Barney

We are somewhat surprised to see you offer to ensconse [sic] yourself among or offer to stop at a resort of southern gentlemen. You have concluded we suppose that this would be beneficial to your health. On the contrary we think it would be very sickly, especially for cattle of your stripe and we advise your to postpone your visit for a few weeks. For further particulars enquire of

                              Elberton

After I had left the Springs, two men came to Carnesville from the Springs and reported that they wanted to get hold of me. One of the citizens of Carnesville came to me and state that these was some plot being conspired against me he thought, and advised me to not go where those men were, to have anything to say to them. A few says after this, one G. W. Lecroy, a citizen of Carnesville, called me out in the street under the pretence of seeing me on some business. I went, he offered his hand. I shook hands with him and he began by saying, well Capt. the military has turned everything over to the civil authorities and I want to inform you that our people have been imposed upon long enough, and God-Dam [sic] you if you are not out of this town in twenty four hours, I will take your life you damd [sic] Yankee Radical scoundrel. You think our people are whip[p]ed, but we will show you before you are thro with your radical rule.

I left Lecroy when he first began to raise a difficulty, he went to his house enquiring for his gun—swore he would shoot me at that moment. When I heard his threat, I went in my Boarding-house, took the proprietors gun and approached the door, notified my wife to get back in another room. A few of the better class of citizens had been attracted to the place and saw what was likely to occur when they went to Lecroy and told him he must be quiet and they succeded [sic] in quieting him for that day.

The people thro[ugh] the country have laid-by their crops and have nothing to do but assemble at those little towns, here some person like

Ben Hill deliver an incendiary speech and get drunk &c. I was assaulted
the night before I left the place by several drunken white wretches and
not a friend near me except my wife, and it was more on her account I
got my own consent to resign. Had I been alone or single, I certainly
should have killed some one and left the place. My wife was constantly
in dread, if I went from the house to the Office, knowing the intense
hatred that existed against me, and the many threats that had already
been made against my life. I was asked to attend their rebel meetings,
and hear their rebel speeches, I refuse, and some where [*sic*] heard to
say we ought to make the Damd [*sic*] Yankee go and listen to a Democratic speech. I refused to attend any of them, it was not my way of
thinking and I did not feel disposed to mix with them. Such are the
state of affairs that exist in north-east Geo. Today and the few instances
of heathenism and lawlessness herein mentioned are but a unit compared to the great host of their treacherous deeds perpetrated almost
hourly thro the mountains of Georgia. The people seem to be born mi-
nus the moral attributes of every thing is manly or good. The great mys-
tery to the many is that a man of my stamp could live in that section of
country one year.

> Very Respectfully
> Your Obt. Servt
> Jno. W. Barney

DOCUMENT NO. 9

A PETITION FOR ASSISTANCE FROM NORTH CAROLINA FREEDPEOPLE AND A BUREAU OFFICER'S RESPONSE, JULY 10, 1867*

*Freedpeople understood the Bureau to be the federal agency to which they
should turn when they needed assistance and they often did not hesitate to
go straight to the top with their concerns. The following petition with its
endorsement by the local Bureau subassistant commissioner provides an ex-*

* S. B. Hunter and others to Maj. Gen. O. O. Howard, July 10, 1867, reel 11, Records of
the Assistant Commissioner for the State of North Carolina, Bureau of Refugees,
Freedmen, and Abandoned Lands, 1865–1870, National Archives Microfilm Publication
M843.

ample of black expectations as well as the Bureau's handling of relief and land questions and its belief in freedpeople's need to earn their own way. The freedpeople of the Trent River Settlement near New Berne, on the North Carolina coast, reportedly numbered 5,000 in September 1865. In December 1865, Assistant Commissioner Eliphalet Whittlesey attempted to secure property for freedpeople in the settlement, an initiative that failed. The petition suggests that the settlement had fallen on hard times. Howard sent the letter down the chain of command for final action. A number of endorsements are not reproduced here.

γ   γ   γ

Kimble Hill
New Berne July 10th 1867

Major General O. O. Howard, sir

We call for your Assistence [*sic*] in the time of need[.] We are over on A Hill Branched of[f] from New Berne call[ed] Kimble Hill Where Many of our People are [going] to New Berne Begging for something to Eate and We are living in little shantys and When it Rains We are intirely [*sic*] in it[.] We are Where the Government Put us When We Was Brought from our Hom[e]s[.] The[y] Say that the land is turned over and they [are] after Rent Which We are not Able to Pay it[.] We are now Living Where We Was Put for Pertection [*sic*] of the Wo[r]se Whites[.] We are Hardly Able [to] Buy Bread[.] They are Calling on us for Ground Rent[.] We Want to Know Wheather [*sic*] it is Just or un-just[.] We are Willing to Do the Best We can[.] The Whole Majority of the Hill are in Distress and are Begging for your Assistance Hoping that you Will Do the Best you can for us, Which We think you Will certainly do toward We Poor Peoples and if We should be taxed to see that We should be Reasible [*sic*] taxed so that We should meet that De-mand.

Please Write soon

Respectfully yours [*sic*] Honor
(Colored)   (Committee)

S. B. Hunter [and eleven others]

If you be so Please to Write us Please Direct your Letter to
Southey B. Hunter
[J. Didon ?] Box 214
New Berne
No[rth Ca[rolina]

[endorsement]
Bureau of Refugees Freedmen & AL
Office of Sub Asst Comr Sub Dist No. 3
New Berne[,] N. C. Aug 10th 1867

Respectfully returned to Lt. Col. *J. F. Chur, A. A. A. Gen.* With the information that the tract of land, variously known as *James City, Trent River Settlements and Kimbals Hill*, has been turned over to the owners, who have allowed me to fix rents for the houses and lots occupied by the Colored People, which I have done, at sums ranging from *50cts* to *$1.00* per month. The Destitute I have supplied with Rations and Clothing. They are now in a condition with nothing to complain of. They have had the idea that they never would have to pay rents, from which I have endeavoured to disabuse their minds.

> Stephen Moore
> Lieut Col. V. R. C.
> Sub Asst Comr

DOCUMENT 10

THE BUREAU ACTS AS A PUBLIC HEALTH AGENCY IN HELENA, ARKANSAS, MAY 11, 1867*

The Bureau's medical division staffed and supervised hospitals and clinics throughout the South, treating thousands of blacks and whites during the late 1860s. These facilities often provided the freedpeople with their only access to medical care. Crises larger than individual ailments also required Bureau medical men to serve as public health officials, as was the case in Helena, a town in eastern Arkansas on the Mississippi River where sixty freedpersons died during the cholera outbreak of 1867. Diseases that could be devastating to freedpeople living in crowded quarters prompted Bureau officers and agents to discourage ex-slaves from congregating in towns and cities.

γ   γ   γ

* E. V. Duvell to Bvt. Col. L. A. Edwards, May 11, 1867, reel 14, Records of the Assistant Commissioner for the State of Arkansas, Bureau of Refugees, Freedmen, and Abandoned Lands, 1865–1869, National Archives Microfilm Publication M979.

Bureau of Refugees Freedmen and Abandoned Lands,
For Arkansas and Indian Territory
Office of Surgeon in Chief
Little Rock Ark May 11th 1867

Sir

In accordance with the provisions of Special Orders No. 12 issued from these Headquarters upon receipt of your letter of instruction with reference to epidemic cholera reported at Helena dated April 22nd 1867, I have the honor to submit the following—

The disease reported to be *cholera*, first appeared about April 3^{d} in a deserted tenant house, known as the "Glass house", one and a half miles distant from the city, and situated at the base of a line of bluffs in the rear of same; here were crowded in great confusion hundred[s] of indigent and laboring classes, both blacks and whites—refugees from the recent inundation of the city—thus closely packed, shut in for warmth, the weather being stormy and cold, with no attention to the common laws of health, rebreathing the noxious gasses from their exhalations, subsisting upon fish, without vegetables, and drinking the turbid water of the flood—a disease, as certain of its victim as cholera, appeared and was followed by as rapid mortality.

As soon as the condition of these people was made known to the Bureau Medical Officer and the people dispersed, the disease disappeared as quickly as it came but few cases occuring [*sic*] subsequently. Several cases of violent disease also occured [*sic*] in the city, but only where the same conditions were present.

In my opinion the mortality reported was principally due to the poisonous influence resulting from the crowding of great numbers into small badly ventilated quarters, with improper diet regimen, and not due to cholera influence. Had the water receded, exposing the surface to the action of the sun, later in the season, cholera influence might have been present—but the disease appeared and mortality greatest, when the flood was at its height. The hospital building being submerged but few of these cases were treated in hospital, which may account for their now-appearance on weekly reports as previously mentioned.

About April 30th the last case appeared—and now the usual degree of health appears restored—though with the receding of the water the town is left in a most wretched condition.

Maj. Sweeny, Ag't, with the Medical officers at that point are energetic, and actively cooperating with the civil authorities to improve the sanitary condition of the city.

An ample supply of lime & disinfectant have already been purchased and an order issued directing all citizens to drain, police & whitewash the premises. To the indigent freed & white people, lime is furnished without charge by the Q[uater] M[aster] Dep't of the Bureau. The blacks especially I have found whitewashing and renovating their quarters—with many of the white citizens however peremptory measures should be adopted—the time for action being *now*.

The hospital at this point has not received due attention heretofore, the building is found in a most dilapidated condition, and the hospital property in quantity little, and in quality almost worthless. Have recommended that the building be repaired at once (being unable to procure a better one) and a new issue of property will be promptly made.

As a result of the recent inundation of this almost entire District, the approaching sickly season is expected by the faculty generally to be greatly aggravated. By reason of this, it is thought proper to visit each station as early as practicable, with a view to a more perfect establishment of the hospitals, also to confer with the Medical Officers, in detail upon the most improved plan of treatment together with diet and general regimen in the management of epidemic and other pernicious disease due to this climate.

> Very Respectfully
> Your obt svt
>
> (Sign'd)   E. V. Duvell
>   A. Asst. Surg. USA.
>   Actg in Chief for Ark.

Bv't Col. L. A. Edwards
Surg. USA., Chief Medical Officer

DOCUMENT NO. 11

THE RESTORATION OF THE SHERMAN RESERVATION LANDS ON THE GEORGIA COAST, FEBRUARY 14, 1866*

The political maneuvering in Washington over the future of the Bureau and the land it supervised on the southeastern coast led Georgia Assistant Commissioner Davis Tillson to attempt to reconcile the coastal planters' desire for the restoration of their land with the claims freedpeople had on the same under General William T. Sherman's Special Field Order No. 15. Tillson expected that the Freedmen's Bureau legislation sponsored by Senator Lyman Trumbull, which gave these freedpeople three-year "possessory" titles, would become law, allowing the Bureau time to convince planters to give or sell land to the freedpeople. The presidential veto of that piece of legislation derailed Tillson's plan, although the assistant commissioner believed that his approach to restoration could still work.

γ   γ   γ

Bureau RF&AL
Office Asst Com'r State of Ga
In the field Savannah Feby 14th 1866

Special Field Orders}
No[.] 3   }

I.   Mr. *W. F. Eaton* is hereby appointed supervising Agent of this Bureau for St[.] Simons Island and of the Sea Islands South thereof on the coast of and belonging to the State of Georgia[.]

II.   The former owners of land upon St[.] Simons and the Sea Islands South, thereof on the coast and belonging to the State of Georgia will be permitted to return and occupy their lands or a portion thereof subject to the terms and conditions hereinafter specified[.]

* Special Field Orders, No. 3, February 14, 1866, reel 34, Records of the Assistant Commissioner for the State of Georgia, Bureau of Refugees, Freedmen and Abandoned Lands, 1865–1869, National Archives Microfilm Publication M798.

First[.] No owner will be allowed to make use of any threats against the freed people or the authorities of the United States or to use any violence or to say or do anything to disturb the peace on said Islands but all disputes will be referred to Mr. *W. F. Eaton* the Agent of this Bureau for said Islands for adjudication[.]

Second[.] Grants of land made the freed people in compliance with Genl Sherman's Special field order No. 15 dated Jany 16 1865 will be regarded as good and valid but Mr. Eaton the Agent of this Bureau may set apart and consolidate them contiguous to each other on one portion of the plantation upon which such grants have been given in such manner as to give the freed people a part possessing average fertility and other advantages and at the same time place no unnecessary obstacle in the way of the owner occupying and cultivating the remaining portion of the plantation[.]

Third[.] The former owners of land on said Islands will be allowed to occupy and cultivate the same when not assigned to freed people as described in proceeding section or other portions of their estates that may be made vacant by the consolidation hereinbefore mentioned. Such owners will be permitted to hire freed people on terms satisfactory to both parties, and approved by the Bureau[.]

Fourth[.] The freed people now on the Island not having grants of land will not be forced to leave their present domicile until the owners of the land upon which they may be located or their representatives shall have offered them opportunity of labor upon such terms and conditions as shall be satisfactory to the Bureau. Should such freed people refuse to accept this offer thus made them, then they shall remove from such plantations and allow the owner thereof the opportunity to hire others to cultivate the same[.]

> [Davis Tillson]
> Brig Genl Vols
> & Asst Comr

DOCUMENT NO. 12

THE RESTORATION OF PROPERTY IN THE SHERMAN RESERVATION ON THE SOUTH CAROLINA COAST, MAY 30, 1866*

Assistant Commissioners issued special orders to restore property to owners who had complied with the government's requirements, but agents and officers in the field investigated these cases and attempted to enforce such orders. The following report from Lieutenant Erastus Everson, a Massachusetts native who served with the Bureau through 1868, illustrates the problems these men encountered while performing their duty as well as the imperfect nature of many of the possessory titles held by the freedpeople under Special Field Order No. 15. Several related enclosures and endorsements are not reproduced here.

γ   γ   γ

Edisto May 30th 1866

Lt Col H W Smith A A Genl
  thro[ugh] Office Major J. E Cornelius ASA Comr
  Col,

      I have the honor to report in the application of John Townsend, for an examination of the possessory claims on his "Sea Cloud" plantation this island as follows—*Jacob Holms* holds certificate dated Aug 29 '65, which is not upon the original records of Mr. Alden the former agent of Bu[reau]. Jacob states he was on the adjoining plantation (same owner) now restored, last year; that he located his land here in January of this year (1866) that he didn't locate at all last year, but they all planted together. He also states that in De. '65 or Jan'y 1866, he with the two succeeding names, were called up to Mr Wittemore's office and had their paper signed—(they are dated in *Aug-1865*) The above is the case with *Abram Brown* planted with *Jacob Holmes Billy Williams* holds certificate same date, which is on the record he states however that he did not locate any ground on this plantation until January of this year,

---

* 1st Lt. Erastus Everson to Lt. Col. H. W. Smith, May 303, 1866, reel 9, Records of the Assistant Commissioner for the State of South Carolina, Bureau of Refugees, Freedmen and Abandoned Lands, 1865–1870, National Archives Microfilm Publication M869.

141

but last year planted the other side of the creek on Townsend's ["]Bleak Hall" place. The record shows he did not locate until January 1866 but has been on the plantation since January 1865, that he planted with the crowd last year. I asked this man to show me his land paper, explaining to him my object and duty, and telling him who I was. I waited for him ¾ of an hour and then searched for him; he had locked himself in the room, and refused to show me the paper, and regarding his paper I am unable to learn more.

The other people who were given land certificates have not located on this plantation, nor could I learn their whereabouts: the people said they were never there, and that they never heard their names before. In my opinion there is no strictly valid possessory claim, in accordance with present instructions on this plantation.

I have the honor to report also that I was beset by the women on this place in a very serious manner, and was obliged to use decisive measures for the preservation of the property as well as for my own head—After I had made known my errand, and told them who I was, and what I came form, and being also in uniform, they absolutely refused to give me any information, and what I got was by cross questions, and by much trouble: I wish to except from this Jacob Holmes, Billy Williams, & Abram Brown, who live in another settlement. The remainder of the people live in the dwelling house on the place: I told them that they must give me the information I desired, as I was an officer &c, sent for that purpose, both to benefit them, as well as the owner of the land and to put matters to rights between them: they then said I wouldn't have durst come there has not part of the men gone to the city: and made sundry surly demonstrations and remarks, more *enlightening* to look upon, than pleasing, and not easy to describe.

I then told them they were living in Mr. Townsend's house: on his land: and that I might as well tell them the truth at once, that if they had no valid claims, they would have to make some arrangement, or vacate the house, for that has been restored to him. They said they would not make any arrangement whatever for me or anybody else: that they cared for no United States officer: the Govt brought them to the island & they would burn down the house before they would "move away" or "from it themselves until put out." I then told them what were the consequences: when they derided me so much that I arrested the two who threatened to burn the house, vz [*sic*] Leah Jenkins & her daughter Jane.

The people followed me about a halfmile [*sic*] with hoes and sticks, and I got sick of this business and told them to go back, and said to them "this is the last time I tell you this"[;] they refused to obey, and I drew my revolver faced my horse about and charged them back to camp. I then carried the two I had a little way: talked to them severely and they promised to see the rest and mend matters. I think however Jane Jenkins, Leah Jenkins, Mary Ann-(the oracle) and Francis Weather should be brought to trial. I do not think I can unaided arrest them, but if you order it, I will try, begging to be excused from any consequences arising from the attempt.

I enclose copy of former}   Very respectfully
report on this place   }   Erastus W. Everson
                                  1st Lt. VRC ASA Comr

[endorsement]
Edisto May 30th 1866
Respectfully forwarded
to Major James E[.] Cornelius
VRC ASA Comr
with report enclosed
    Erastus W. Everson A.S.A.
    1st LtVRC A.S.A.Comr Edisto Island

[enclosure]
Copy of the Report of D. H. Whittemore in relation to Bleak Hall & Sea Cloud
Jany. 30th 1866.

                            Head Quarters Agent
                            Bureau Freedmen &c
                            Edisto Island Jany 30th 1866

Capt. A. P. Ketchum
        Dear Sir
                    I respectfully forward the following particulars in relation to the two plantations of Mr[.] Jno Townsend both of which I visited this day in company with Mr[.] Townsend. On his plantation known as "Sea Cloud" which we first visited and which is occupied entirely by *strangers*, the people received us much to my surprise with feelings of angry excitement, owing to the presence of Mr. Townsend. I

remonstrated with them, but for some time with no effect. They refused at first to give me the desired information, being very suspicious and fearing lest they should commit themselves, but after reassuring them to the contrary I effected a hearing & found there were (18) eighteen able bodied Freed people on the Plantation (2) two old & infirm & about (15) fifteen children. All these people came to the Plantation during February 1865 & planted [—] last year. Some of them hold or say they do Certificates for land on this Plantation, but for some unaccountable reason none would provide them, and those representing to have the certificates did not give their names as registered in the book, where those to whom Grants were given are recorded. I could therefore to day obtain nothing definite in relation to the Grants of land given on this Plantation. This Plantation consists of about 700 acres and fifty acres were cultivated by the people last year. All these people are strangers to this place, coming from the mainland.

On Mr. Townsend['s] Plantation known as "Bleak Hall" which we also visited to day I found thereon (61) sixty one able bodied Freed people (40) Forty children and (14) fourteen old infirm & helpless. All these people belong to this Plantation and came thereon during January 1866[.] None planted crops here last year and three hold certificates for land on this Plantation. This Plantation consists of 600 acres and 190 were cultivated by people during last year who were strangers to the place, and have since left the place & Island. The dwelling house on the Sea Cloud Plantation is occupied by the people & is in a very dilapidated condition, a few poor out houses are still standing. The dwelling on "Bleak Hall" was burned, but a great many out buildings are standing, a portion being occupied by the hands

I am Sir with respect
Yours Truly
D. W. Whittemore
Agt Bureau

I certify that this is a correct copy of the report made to Capt. A. P. Ketchum in relation to the Plantations of Mr. John Townsend, by D. W. Whittemore agent of the Bureau Edisto Island Jany 30 1866

S. H. Jenkins
J. Jenkins Mikell
Richard Roper

DOCUMENT NO. 13

ASSISTANT COMMISSIONER EDGAR M. GREGORY LECTURES WHITE TEXANS ON FREE LABOR, JANUARY 20, 1866*

Bureau officials lectured freedpeople on the benefits of free labor, believing that slavery had made them less reasonable in their willingness to adjust to the realities of the new system than their former masters. However, when they encountered intransigent whites, most Bureau officers such as Texas Assistant Commissioner Edgar M. Gregory did not hesitate to turn their attention to the foot-dragging planters. Gregory, the Texas Bureau's first assistant commissioner, took command of his agency in September 1865 and remained in that position until replaced by Joseph B. Kiddo, who assumed command in May 1866. In his last report, written in June 1866 after a tour of western Texas, a pessimistic Gregory bemoaned the continued and increasing disloyalty of white Texans while speaking well of the freedpeople. Panola County is in east Texas on the Louisiana border.

γ   γ   γ

Headquarters
Bureau R. F. and A. L.
State of Texas
Galveston January 20th 1866.

Benj. G. Harris, Esq. and
Foreman, Grand Jury of
Panola County, Texas
Gents,

I have received your communication dated Carthage, Texas, Decr 9th 1865 addressed to *Col. Hall* Sub Asst. Comr and by him referred to these headquarters.

In your complaint the freedmen of that County are charged with vio-

* Brig. Gen. E. M. Gregory to Benjamin G. Harris and the foreman of the Grand Jury, Panola County, Texas, January 20, 1866, reel 1, Records of the Assistant Commissioner for the State of Texas, Bureau of Refugees, Freedmen, and Abandoned Lands, 1865–1869, National Archives Microfilm Publication M821.

lation of contract[,] with vagrancy, Insolence, robbery, drunkenness, and General vicious conduct. [T]he appointment of a Provost Marshal is requested in order to restrain and govern said Freedmen, and one of your fellow citizens is recommended for that position.

While from by far the larger part of the state we learn by the most ample testimony that the blacks are the most docile, industrious[,] orderly free from serious crime, and with all the substratum that goes to make the good citizen, it is but natural that those who live remote from the offices of our agents, not knowing whom to trust or what to believe, comprehending their relations but imperfectly as to their former masters but imperfect masters, will gain the knowledge of their rights and duties more slowly than those who live nearer the points of information and relief.

But the disorders arising from this cause are local and transient. They are fast remeding [sic] themselves. The freedmen at the most distant points are learning the duties of the hour.

The same incitements that quicken the industry of other men in free societies are felt by them.

Just treatment furnishes all the incentives they need, though they are not over anxious to work for nominal wages with the prospect of being defrauded even of these, as has happened to thousands during the year just past.

In those counties where the people are well inclined the Negro where they comprehend a narrow and unjust policy towards them does not pay, he is rendering faithful Services for wages and doing better work than the lash could whip out of him, the business goes bravely on. Complaints are few. Idleness and theft are unknown and the prospects of an abundant crop are so flattering that the planters, having engaged all the available labor of the neighborhood, are sending long distances for freedmen of other localities, and hiring them fair prices.

In general the Freedmen of Texas present a record which, for Service and order, is most commendable. Turned headlong into freedom, without preparation, without premonition, by men at war with their masters, and told that they have been wronged and have a heritage of vengence [sic], they exhibited in their industry, docility and patience an example beyond the expectation of man. No people have ever been so tried. - None ever so stood trial. . . .

The wonder is not that disorders, misconceptions, wrongs should have sometimes occurred, but that they are so few and slight.

The Bureau of Freedmen is here to superintend and organize their labor[,] to defend their rights and inculcate thier [*sic*] duties, and to give them the control of themselves subject only to the common law.

While this Bureau has jurisdiction over all matters that concern the freedmen, its uniform policy is to avoid class legislation.

It cordially invites the civil authorities to take cognizance of all offences committed by or against the negro, and it interferes only when the state refuses to act, or when manifest injustice is done. In a word the Bureau leaves the Freedmen as other men are left—to the protection of equal law, insisting only that no distinctions against one race be made in favor of the other, shall be allowed.

If, then, disorder prevails in your county the remedy lies ready to your hand.

Apply the Vagrant and criminal laws of the state to Black and White alike, and meet out to each offender the stern discipline of Justice.

You have courts, Juries, Judges and all needful officers of law. [U]se then this machinery against all disturbers of your peace, irrespective of color or caste. Special Legislation is uncalled for and unwise when every occurance [*sic*] of disturbance, Violence and crime amongst the Colored people can be met by the Civil Authorities.

If in your locality, the laborer refuses to work it may be because though slavery be dead its collatoral [*sic*] influence still exist and Survive, and new inducements have taken the place of the lash and the chain. It may be that the planter as well as the negro has not yet learned what free labor means.

The former still hugs the idea that he has the power to fix the wages, restrain the personal liberty, and exercise authority over the latter. Past hatreds are still fed and false ideas nurtured.

The governing class are today what the past has made them, and the cannot cut loose at a single blow from their past traditions, beliefs, hatreds and hopes. [A]fter all the rough Schooling of the war they have still a lesson and a hard one, it is to be just to the Black man.

I sometimes think that long after the oppressed race shall rise into rights, duties and capacities so haughtily denied[,] the dominant class will not have overcome their contempt for the negro. Its roots will even then exist and trouble the land.

For years to come the crops of Texas must be raised by the black man. He has done this from the beginning. He is here on the spot and will if well treated remain. The desire to better his condition is deep in him.

Appeal to this inborn desire, this deep incentive in man gives rise to civilization[.] Out of it springs production, agriculture an wealth. . . .

Texas can become prosperous only through the concord of its labor with its capital. Its products, Cotton, Sugar[,] Corn[,] must be grown[.] The labor is free, and is picularly [*sic*] adapted by nature and training, as a tropical race, to cultivate these products.

But to make their labor available an entire change in the old system of of [*sic*] industry is needed. The spirit that has made the great states of the Northwest must be at work in Texas—and villages and small farms, the Steamengine [*sic*] and Water Wheel, the school House and church shape its society. A generation that has never been in the school House is even now knocking at your door.

When the farmers of the West and North are in want of hands, they offer every inducement to their workmen. Besides enhanced wages, care is taken that they have pleasant homes. Schools are built for their children[.] Churches are built, and studious provision made for their comfort.

This course will bring the Same Success to the banks of the Brazos, the Colorado, or the Trinity as on the Ohio.

Treat your laborers with liberality and on a basis of Justice. Give them a chance to secure themselves from fraud and inequality before the law. Tramell [*sic*] them not with any attempts at serfdom under a new form, and permitt [*sic*] them to run without a load the race of life.

Then your locality will settle down into it[s] abnormal state of Peace. The gulf between the two races will be bridged over by a vital sympathy, and your labor unite with your capital and become productive force.

> I am Gents
> Very Respectfully
> Your Obedt Servt
> E M Gregory
> Brig Genl and Asst Comr

DOCUMENT NO. 14

JOHN EMORY BRYANT'S LABOR
REGULATIONS, JUNE 12, 1865*

Bureau agents also saw a need to enforce some degree of order on the new free-labor system of the South. John Emory Bryant, a man who would make a reputation for himself as a radical when it came to Reconstruction matters, issued a set of regulations that became widely known in Georgia, thanks to repeated printings in the various newspapers of the state. Because Bryant was but one of only a few Bureau agents stationed in Georgia at the time he issued these regulations, his guidelines became a standard used by planters even beyond his jurisdiction until a new Bureau administration arrived in late September and expanded the state organization.

γ   γ   γ

Office Gen'l Sup't Freedmen
Augusta, Ga., June 12, 1865

The following rules are prescribed for the hiring and government of colored laborers at Augusta and vicinity, and for the treatment of freedmen:

Laborers will be allowed and encouraged to make voluntary contracts, either with their former masters, or any other person wishing to employ them. These contracts, when submitted to the general superintendent of freedmen, will be examined by him, and if found to be fair and equitable, will be by him approved[.] But, owing to the extent of country over which his jurisdiction now extends, and the great importance to the people of making a good crop the present season, it will not, at present, be considered necessary, by the general superintendent, that contracts to be binding, shall be submitted to him; but if equitable, and based upon the schedule of prices hereafter mentioned, will be considered binding.

If the freedmen desire to remain on the plantation of their former master, and he also desires that they should remain, and the workers consent to support the non[-]workers, the employer shall give to all, wholesome food, comfortable clothing, quarters, fuel and medical atten-

* Macon, Georgia, *Daily Telegraph*, June 16, 1865.

dance, and divide among the workers, *pro rata* what may be due them, if any thing, after deducting the expense of supporting the freedmen on the plantation. The government is not, at present, prepared to support the infirm or helpless; therefore, until further orders, no person will be allowed to turn away the infirm or helpless, to become a burden upon the public; they must be clothed, fed, and properly cared for when sick deducting the actual expenses from the wages of the able bodied hands. Should it be proven, that any have been turned away, an assessment will be made upon the persons, on whose premises they were living, when this order was issued, for their support, and he will be held guilty of a misdemeanor.

In cases, when it is absolutely necessary to make exceptions to this rule, permission must first be obtained from this office. The following rates are fixed as the compensation to be given laborers:

FIELD HANDS

Male hands $7	per month
Half hands . . . . $3[.]50	" "
Female hands $6	" "
Half hands $3	" "

HOUSE SERVANTS

Male servants	1st class	$10 per month
Male servants	2d class	8 " "
Male servants	3d class	6 " "
Female servants	1st class	8 " "
Female servants	2d class	6 " "
Female servants	3d class	5 " "

These classes will be determined by merit, and on agreement between the employer and employee. Mechanics and persons having trades, will be allowed and encouraged to make their own contracts.

The money wages for field hands will be paid on the 1st day of October, and 24th day of December; for house servants, at the end of each month; for mechanics, persons following trades and laborers who work by the day, as often as agreed upon between the parties. All contracts for field hands, will be for the balance of the year. For field hands, house servants, and laborers excepting mechanics and persons following trades, there must be secured to the laborer, in addition to the pay, just treatment, wholesome food, quarters, fuel, and medical attendance. The freedmen are reminded, that their freedom imposes upon them burdens and duties. They must labor and support themselves, their wives and children; and if they desire to become the owners of lands, they must buy them, as other freedmen are required to do. They must fulfill all equitable contracts; and if any contract is broken by them, without just cause, they will lose all that may be due them. They are free in all parts of the State of Georgia and South Carolina, and their rights as freedmen will be protected, by the whole military force of the United States government, if necessary. Every act of injustice or cruelty done him, will sooner or later be investigated, and the wrong-doer severely punished. Idleness and vagrancy will not be tolerated; and the government will support none, able and yet unwilling to work.

Wages for time lost on account of sickness, unless protracted, will not be deducted from the field hands or house servants; nor any time lost from any faults of the employer, or on account of inclement weather. But both wages and rations will be deducted when the sickness is feigned for the purpose of idleness or refusal to work, when able to do so, the offender may be discharged by the employer.—Whenever any freedman is discharged by the employer or his agent, and thinks himself wronged, or whenever they are maltreated, or deprived of any right due freedmen, they should report the case at this office, and the complaint will be promptly attended to.

But if the freedman, so discharged, refuse[s] to leave, or prowls about the premises to the injury of any person; or, in case any freedman commits an offence for which he should be punished, or is considered a dangerous person, he may be arrested by competent authority and brought to trial before the Provost Marshal. Whenever a military force cannot be obtained[,] a request may be made at this office, where it will receive prompt attention.

House servants are informed that they will be expected to remain one half each Sabbath with their employers, and field hands, that they are expected to work each day in the week except the Sabbath.

Complaints have been made at this office, that certain parties refuse to allow wives to leave their premises with their husbands, or parents to take charge of their children. Such persons are notified that freedmen in this regard, have the same right that white citizens have, and if they interfere with these rights, they are guilty of a grave offence, which will subject them to severe punishment.

These regulations are subject to the approval of Brevet Maj. Gen. R. Saxton, commissioner of the freedmen for South Carolina and Georgia.

J. E. Bryant
Gen'l Superintendent

DOCUMENT NO. 15

NORTHERN REACTION TO BUREAU LABOR GUIDELINES, JULY 1, 1865*

White Southerners generally reacted in a negative way when confronted with regulations that limited their ability to do as they wished with their laborers. John Emory Bryant's labor regulations also prompted some negative reaction among radical circles in the North, where at least this editorialist found them to be as restrictive to the rights of freedpeople as the Union army's wartime regulations in Louisiana had been.

γ   γ   γ

THE FREEDMEN'S BUREAU

Has the Bureau a system? If it has, is the circular of Mr. J. E. Bryant, Superintendent of Freedmen for Georgia, to be taken as a sample of what is to be enforced upon other States of which the Bureau has charge? Of Mr. Bryant we know nothing except from his published circular, and, judging from that, we should like to know as little as possible of him in the future. He seems to consider his duty to establish a schedule of wages for the freedmen under his charge—a reminiscense [*sic*] of the infamous Louisiana system which Gen. Banks created. . . .

We should be glad if somebody would explain to us the proper duty of the Freedmen's Bureau and its superintendents. Where does it get a right to regulate the price of labor for a State? Where does it get a right to fix it at this scandulus [*sic*] rate? Was the Bureau meant for the protection of the planter? The schedule above quoted is very little better

* *National Anti-Slavery Standard*, July 1, 1865.

than that which the planters of a dozen Virginia counties lately conspired together to impose on the negroes, and for ought that yet appears
under Gen. Howard's administration, the negroes would do better to
trust to their own protection than to his. As against the planter, they
have at least the right to refuse to work on extortionate terms, but how
will they hold out when the Government becomes a party to the fraud,
and under pretence of befriending the blacks, fixes a rate of wages that
is little short of stealing.

Nor is the inadequacy of the amount the worst feature in this scheme.
The Superintendents of Gen. Howard have no business to be fixing *any*
rate of wages. Are not blacks free? Can they not make their own contracts? The planters need and must have their labor, and eventually must
pay a decent price for it, if the blacks are left to deal with them on equal
terms. But Mr. Bryant intervenes with his schedule, and if military authority is backing him, will prove competent, as he is willing, to deprive
the freedmen of their chance for just wages. Even Banks did not venture
to put his price below eight dollars a month. The Freedmen's Bureau
seems to be going behind the intelligence of the Louisiana régime of
two years ago. Be it lack of capacity or lack of intention—we know not
which; but this we know, that under its present administration the Bureau is proving itself no friend to the Emancipated negro, and unless it
is speedily and radically reformed will prove a disgrace to the country.

DOCUMENT NO. 16

A BUREAU OFFICER ENFORCES A CONTRACT ON FREEDPEOPLE IN LOUISIANA, APRIL 20, 1867*

*Freedmen's Bureau officers and agents believed that for the new labor sys-
tem to be successful, both employers and employees had to abide by their
agreements. Few Bureau men tolerated or supported freedpeople who asserted
labor rights beyond those to which their contracts outlined. Lieutenant Ira*

* Lt. Ira D. M. McClary to Capt. William H. Sterling, April 20, 1867, reel 8, Assistant
Subassistant Commissioner for St. Bernard and Plaquemine Parishes, Field Office Records Relating to New Orleans, Louisiana, Bureau of Refugees, Freedmen, and Abandoned Lands, National Archives Microcopy M1483.

*McClary served as the assistant subassistant commissioner for St. Bernard
and Plaquemine Parishes from April into December 1867.*

γ   γ   γ

Office Agent Bureau of R F & A L
Parishes of St. Bernard & Plaquemines (SB) La
                        April 20, 1867

Capt. Wm. H. Sterling
1st U.S. Infantry & A. A. A. Genl.
        Captain
                In making Tri-Monthly report for this date: I have the honer
[*sic*] to state that within the past ten days I have Inspected five Plantations. Approved Contracts for one plantation. Friday April 19th I was
called upon to visit Scarsdale Plantation worked by H[.] P. Kernschan,
Esq. to settle a little trouble. I learned that the Freedmen went into the
field to work at the usual hours, after working about one hour one of the
hands stopped working & said that it was Good Friday, that he would
not work for any body, upon which the whole gang quit work and went
to their houses. The Overseer not knowing certain whether the day was
set apart by the Bureau regulations as a day of rest did not say anything
to them but went to Mr. Sawyer General Manager of the Plantation and
reported what had taken place. Mr. Sawyer ordered the Overseer to visit
other Plantations and learn if the Laborers were at work. The overseer
finding the hands all at work on other Plantations returned home and
reported the same. At the usual hours for the hands to go to their work
after Breakfast Mr. Sawyer sounded the Bell, but they all refused to go
out, saying that it was Good Friday and they would not work on that
day. Mr. Sawyer them sent for me. I arrived on the plantation about 10
½ O'clock A.M. I immediately called the Freedman together and informed them that this day was not set apart by the Bureau regulations
as a day of rest and also informed them of the consequences of refusing
to work when called upon. They were very saucy and made use of very
impudent language to me. I at once ordered that the Plantation Bell
should be sounded for them to go to their work at 1 O'clock P.M. and
that every man and woman that did not go to his or her work should
move from the Plantation and forfeit all back pay due them. At 1 O'clock
the Bell sounded fifteen out of forty went into the field, the remainder
moved their furniture out of their houses and went in search of employment, but finding that nobody would employ them they came back in

the evening and begged that they be allowed to go to work in the morning. I informed them that they could go to work but that they would forfeit all their back pay. Twenty five of the forty went to their work this morning before I left Mr. Sawyer informed me that if there was no more trouble with those men they would pay them the same as though nothing had taken place.

> I am Captain
> Very Respectfully
> Your Obedient Servant
> Ira D. M. McClary
> 2" Lt V.R.C. & Agent Bureau of RF&A.L.

DOCUMENT NO. 17

A BUREAU LABOR CONTRACT FORM FROM MUSCOGEE COUNTY, GEORGIA, FEBRUARY 24, 1866*

Bureau-sponsored contracts varied depending on the inclination of the agent and the dispositions and needs of the involved parties. Many officers and agents resorted to printed forms, which imposed a degree of uniformity on the style if not the content of contracts. Printed form contracts became more common as the agency matured. The italicized information in the following document indicates information written in the blanks of the printed form.

γ   γ   γ

Georgia Muscogee **County**

THIS CONTRACT, made this the *24* day of *February* 1866, between *Thos. P. Bartie* of the one part, and *Isaac & Wife* of the other part, WITNESSETH, that the said *Isaac & Wife* promise and agree to work for the said *Thos P Bartie* or his agent, from the *24* day of *Feby* 1866,

---

* Contract between Thomas P. Barter and Isaac and wife, February 24, 1866, enclosed in Christian Raushenberg to Lt. Eugene Pickett, September 4, 1867, box 14, Letters Received, Subassistant Commissioner, Columbus, Ga., Records of the Field Officers for the State of Georgia, Bureau of Refugees, Freedmen, and Abandoned Lands, Record Group 15, National Archives Building, Washington, D.C.

until the close of the year; during all which time the said *Isaac & Wife* doth promise and agree to be faithful, industrious and honest, to obey all reasonable commands of the said *Thos P Bartie* or his agent, and conduct *Themselves* in all things, in a proper manner.

For neglect of duty or other misdemeanor, or any question of doubt arising, the same to be referred to the nearest officer or agent of the Bureau or Justice of the Peace.

And for and in consideration of the service, well and faithfully rendered by the said *Isaac and wife* the said *Thomas P. Bartie* is to allow *them* per [blank] as follows: Good and sufficient food, houseroom and fuel sufficient clothing and medical attendance when sick; besides $16.00 (Sixteen Dollars) per month for both, without any deduction whatever.

This contract to commence with this date, and close with the year.

Given in duplicate at *Columbus Ga.* this *24ᵗʰ* day of *Feby* 1866

Registered at *Columbus Ga* 1866

Thomas P. Bartie
for W. B. Henry

Book [blank] Page [blank]   *his*
Approved: Isaac X and wife
Fred. Mosebach   *mark*
      Capt. & A. S. A. Com'r, Bureau R. F. & A. L.

DOCUMENT NO. 18

A LOWNDES COUNTY MISSISSIPPI LABOR CONTRACT APPROVED BY THE BUREAU, FEBRUARY 26, 1866*

The majority of white Southerners complained about the new contract system. Nevertheless, many planters accepted the documents and the Bureau's supervision of them when they came to understand that they could use

* Contract between Joseph G. Lockhart and freedpeople, [February 1866], reel 50, Records of the Assistant Commissioner for the State of Mississippi, Bureau of Refugees, Freedmen, and Abandoned Lands, 1865–1869, National Archives Microfilm Publication, M826.

them to their own advantage. In the following case, the area subassistant com-missioner Brevet Major George S. Smith found no reason to object to the disciplinary strictures included in the contract. One clause that many assistant commissioners required their men to remove from contracts—the forfeiture clause—remained in this document. The forfeiture clause often led to serious abuses. When the intensive cultivation period for cotton passed and the "lay by" season made plantation routines less taxing during the late summer prior to harvest, planters often took the opportunity to drive off their workers, claiming they broke their agreement. Such fraud rendered the clause operative and the employer free from paying those workers, unless the Bureau investigated and intervened on behalf of the freedpeople. The complaint of being "run off" was a common one brought by freedpeople to Bureau men. Thirty-eight freedpeople between the ages of 51 and 13 signed this contract.

γ   γ   γ

Agreement with Freedmen
    by
J. G. Lockhart
Approved Feb 26th/66

      Agreement With Freedmen

This contract made and entered into the days and date annexed by and between Jos. G. Lockhart party of the first part and the undersigned Freedmen & Freedwomen parties of the second part.

    Witnesseth,

        That for the purpose of cultivating the plantation known as Lockhart's plantation in the county of Lowndes and State of Mississippi, Joseph G. Lockhart party of the first part agrees to give in pay to said parties of the second part for the present year beginning the 1st day of Jany 1866 and ending the 31st of December 1866 for their labor and services one third (1/3) of all the cotton raised on said plantation for said specified time and in addition thereto good and sufficient food and quarters. And it is agreed on the part of the parties of the second part that they will and faithfully perform any and all labor required of them by the party of the first part or his Agent for said specified time and that if they become idle or feign sickness, or refuse to work when able to do or leave the plantation without permission then and in that case this contract is [—] be at an end and all Laborers so defaulting shall forfeit all wages due them to be decided by agents of Freedmen's Bureau or Magistrate. Dependents are to be under the same Rules and Regulations as the Laborers punished when they do wrong and the expense of keeping them to be taken out of the wages of those on whom they are dependent. The parties of the second part also agree to pay out of their one third (1/3) of cotton to be raised one third (1/3) of the current expenses of said plantation. It is further agreed that the following Rules be made part of this contract.

Rules

1 The Laborer will be required to rise at the blowing of the horn at daybreak and begin work at or before sunrise, the beginning and leaving off of work and the mode and manner of doing work will be entirely under the control of the employer or manager. For all time lost and bad work deductions will be made and time lost from any cause deductions will be made sufficient to cover value of rations. Two hours rest will be allowed at noon in summer and one in other months of the year.

2 No visiting allowed except by consent of employer or manager.

3 All abuse and improper use of stocks and negligence in breaking tools &c will be charged for.

4 Every Laborer must attend to stock whenever required Sundays included.

5 Police regulations at discretion of employer

6 For impudence, fighting, stealing and like offences time lost by Laborers in going to the proper officer will be charged against the ones offending.

7 Difficulties between Laborers to be adjudicated by employer or manager

Names	Ages	Dependents	Ages	Remarks
Mary x Anne	50			
[and 37 other freedpeople]				

DOCUMENT NO. 19

COLLECTING THE FREEDPEOPLE'S PAY IN SOUTHWEST GEORGIA, MARCH 21–JUNE 18, 1868*

During Military Reconstruction Bureau men could not take serious action in helping the freedpeople claim their just wages without first receiving permission from the commanders of the military districts. The trail of endorsements (most of which are not reproduced here) that wend their way up to the headquarters of the Third Military District and down again to the local agent in this particular instance is an indication of the Bureau's subordination to the Army. In this case, the agent Christian Raushenberg obtained the proper authority and actually accomplished something. Also not reproduced here are enclosures that accompanied Agent Raushenberg's final report of the rendering of payments. These include receipts for the money paid as well as a listing of the debt owed and paid to the freedpeople. In the end, Raushenberg secured almost all of the original debt of $840.83 for the petitioning freedpeople. Mention of a "fifa," probably a variation of enfeoff or infeffe, refers to a legal encumbrance on the property in question.

γ   γ   γ

> Bureau Refugees, Freedmen & Abandoned Lands.
> Office Agent Division of Albany,
> ALBANY, GA., *March 21,* 1868.

Lieut M. F. Gallagher
A. A. A. Genl
Atlanta, Ga.

Sir,

I have the honor to report that Abner Harrison, Granville Adams & other freedmen applied to me in January last to collect their last years wages from Sam Linton of Augusta for work done on his plantation in

---

* Ch. Raushenberg to Lt. M. F. Gallagher, March 21, 1868 (and enclosures), reel 20, Records of the Assistant Commissioner for the State of Georgia, Bureau of Refugees, Freedmen, and Abandoned Lands, 1865–1869, National Archives Microfilm Publication M798.

Worth County. It appears that Sam Linton is utterly insolvent, that he has disposed of all his cotton except ten bales, that he has given two mortgage liens on his last years crop, of which the older one has been bought up by his brother Dr. John S. Linton of Athens, Ga., that the younger one has been foreclosed by the mortgages of J. Sibley & Son of Augusta Ga. and that the above mentioned ten Bales of Cotton have been levied on by the Sheriff of Worth County under a fifa from Richmond Superior Court obtained under said mortgage and even advertised to be sold on Tuesday of February last.

In consideration of these circumstances an order was issued to the Sheriff of Worth county to retain in his hands the full amount of the proceeds of the ten Bales of cotton and to seize all corn, cotton or other produce belonging to said Linton etc and hold the same subject to the orders of the Bureau etc (see Enclosure A 1 & A 2)

On the 10th of February P. J. Strosier Esq, an attorney of this place, and John Wright, the agent of John L. Linton of Athens Ga. represented at this Office that said John L. Linton, the brother of Samuel Linton, had undertaken to settle the pecuniary difficulties of his brother and that, if the Bureau would release the ten Bales of cotton and the corn seized on Linton's plantation which was much needed to carry on the same, that John S. Linton would pledge himself through them to sell the ten Bales of cotton, place the proceeds in the hands of the Bureau for the payment of the freedmen's wages and pay or secure the early payment of the balance due his brothers freedmen. On this promise the obligation of which a copy, marked "B" is enclosed was taken from the attorney and the Agent of John L. Linton and the order of which a copy marked "C" is enclosed was issued to the Sheriff of Worth county.

A few days ago, P. J. Strosier the attorney and representative of John L. Linton Stated to me that the Sheriff of Worth county would not release the cotton and turn it over to him but retained it under the mortgage fifa of John Sibley & Son of Augusta and *that it would be sold under the same without the interference of the Bureau.*

In consideration of the fact (1st) that John L. Linton holds the oldest mortgage which gives him a prior claim to the ten bales of cotton, if the statements of his attorney, who has been questioned very close on this point, can be relied on, (2nd) that he has pledged himself to become responsible for the whole indebtedness of his brother to his freedmen on release of the ten Bales of cotton, his attorney P. J. Strosier considers his client John L. Linton entitled to the protection of the Bureau to enable him to pay his brothers laborers the balance due them last year.

As these laborers need their wages for the sustainance [*sic*] of life and to enable them to produce a crop this year and as Messrs Sibley & Son of Augusta has undoubtedly better chances to inform themselves of the pecuniary condition and the proceedings of Mr[.] Sam Linton during the last year then the colored laborers and are undoubtedly better able to wait for their claims then the latter[,] I respectfully ask for authority to seize and sell the ten bales of the Linton cotton, now in the hands of the Sheriff of Worth county and to use the proceeds of the same for the payment of such amounts, as may, *on personal investigation* be found *justly due* the laborers of Sam Linton for last years wages.

> I have the honor to remain
> Very respectfully
> Your ob'd't Serv't
> Ch. Raushenberg
> Agent etc—

[enclosure]

> Bureau Refugees, Freedmen & Abandoned Lands.
> Office Agent Division of Albany,
> ALBANY, GA., *Feb 10th* 1868.

We the undersigned, the Attorney of Dr. John L. Linton of Athens Ga. and manager for the same on his place in Worth County Ga. do hereby pledge our words and honor, that upon the release of Ten Bales of Cotton, which the Sheriff of Worth County is ordered to hold untill [*sic*] certain freedmen who have made complaint before this Bureau are settled with, that we will sell said cotton and render a correct and just account of its Sale to the Agent Bureau R.F.&A.L. at Albany Ga. and place the full amount of the money it brings at his disposal for the use of the freedmen and that we pledge ourselves further in the name of the said Dr. John S. Linton of Athens, that whatever balance may be due said freedmen shall be paid to them out of his own means immediately, or fully well secured to them before the Agent Bureau R.F.&A.L.

> (Signed) John Wright
> (Signed) P. J. Strozer Atty for
> John L. Linton

[enclosure, labeled *"A" 1.*]

> Bureau Refugees, Freedmen & Abandoned Lands.
> Office Agent Division of Albany,
> ALBANY, GA. *January 15th* 1868.

Wm. Keen Esqr.
Sheriff Worth County Ca.
Sir

   You are hereby ordered to retain in your hands subject to my order, the whole amount of money which the cotton belonging to Samuel D. Linton levied on under a Mortgage fifa in favor of J. Sibley and Sons and to be sold the first Tuesday in February may bring, or else you and your securities will be held responsible for the same.

> Very Respectfully
> Your Obt. Servt.
> (Signed) Ch. Raushenberg
> Agent

[enclosure labeled *"A" 2*]

> Bureau of Refugees, Freedmen & Abandoned Lands.
> Office Agent Division of Albany,
> ALBANY, GA. *Jany 25th* 1868.

William Keen Esqr.
Sheriff Worth County Ga.

Sir

   You are hereby ordered to proceed to the plantation of Samuel D. Linton, on receipt of this order, and seize all the cotton and corn or other products, or the proceeds of the same, and take possession of all of it, and hold the same safely, unless the said Samuel D. Linton gives security to double the amount of Six hundred dollars, in payment of the wages of Abner Harrison, Granville Adams cold. & others. You will if necessary for safekeeping, remove all the produce you find.

   Your expense and cost will be paid out of the products seized. You will as soon as this is accomplished report to this office the amount of corn, cotton &c. seized under this order.

> Very Repsectfully
> Your Obt. Servt.
> (Signed) Ch. Raushenberg

[enclosure labeled *"B"*]

> Bureau Refugees, Freedmen & Abandoned Lands.
> Office Agent Division of Albany,
> ALBANY, GA. *February 10th* 1868.

Sheriff of Worth County Ga.
Sir

You are hereby ordered to release the ten Bales of cotton, and corn seized under my order for use of freedpeople on the Linton Plantation, so far as the claim of the freedmen or the same is concerned, as Mr. John Wright has made satisfactory arrangements with this office. You will however make a written statement to me of the amount of Corn, Cotton and other produce you have seized.

> I am Sir
> Very Respectfully
> Your Obt. Servt.
> (Signed) Ch. Raushenberg
> Agent

[endorsement]

> Headquars [sic], Third Military District
> Judge Advocates Office
> Atlanta, Ga, April 10/68.

Respectfully returned to the A.A.Genl 3 Mil. Dist. It seems to be just and proper that every mortgage taken on a crop should be subject to the claims for wages of those whose labor a crop is produced, and therefore that the agent of the B.R.F.and A.L. should, in this case, be allowed to proceed, in such manner as he may deem most advisable, to collect, by sale of the cotton, or otherwise, the amount due to the laborers.

> W. W. Dunn
> Asst Judge Advocate General U.S.A.
> Judge Advocate

[endorsement]

> Office ACom'r, Bureau R.F.&c
> Atlanta, Ga., April 15, 1868

Respectfully returned to *C. Raushenberg* Agent thro Lt. *O. H. Howard* S.A.C. Albany, Ga. who is authorized to seize the ten bales of cotton referred to, & sell so much as may be necessary, to satisfy the just claims of the laborers by whose labor it was produced. Making full report of his action & distribution with return of these papers.

> By order of
> Bt Brig Genl Sibley
> M. Frank Gallagher
> Lt. & A.A.A.G.

[enclosure]

> Bur. R. F. & A. Lds
> Office Agent Worth & Dougherty Co.
> Albany, Ga. June 18, 1868

Lieut M. Frank Gallagher
A. A. A. Genl.
Atlanta, Ga.
Sir,

In compliance with instructions contained in endorsement from Office Asst. Comm'r Atlanta Ga April 15, '68 I have the honor to report the result of my investigation of the complaints of Abner Harrison cold & others against Sam. D. Linton of Augusta Ga. and my final action & distribution of the money.

When my original communication, relating to these cases, was received back at this Office the Linton Cotton had already been sold by the Sheriff of Worth Co on the April Sale day and therefore it became necessary to secure the proceeds of that sale. The Sheriff of Worth County was sent for and caused to render in an account of the Sales of the cotton and to turn over the proceeds amounting to $819.79 for the payment of the claims of the freedmen. . . .

. . . The first payments were made to such freedmen on April 24, '68, who had notes on Linton . . .

> I am Sir,
> Very respectfully
> Your ob'd't Servt.
> Ch. Raushenberg
> Agent, etc.

DOCUMENT NO. 20

INSTRUCTIONS FROM THE ASSISTANT COMMISSIONER OF LOUISIANA TO HIS AGENTS, DECEMBER 9, 1867*

Lieutenant Colonel William H. Wood served briefly as the Louisiana assistant commissioner during December 1867. This order, however, gives a good indication of the Bureau's policy at this time to encourage the civil authorities to accept their responsibilities to the freedpeople. While Bureau agents observed the civil authorities' actions, they had little real power to intervene without following bureaucratic procedures. The Civil Rights Act of 1866 mentioned in the circular, however, did give Bureau men the authority to bring suits dealing with violations and allowed the pertinent cases to be heard in federal courts. This law could have been an important tool if properly implemented in the face of public, not private, violations of the freedpeople's rights. Still, the trend was clear. The Bureau, even in the wake of the Military Reconstruction laws passed earlier in the year, was becoming more of an observer and advisor in the freedpeople's efforts to secure their rights.

γ   γ   γ

Headquarters[,] Bureau [of] Refugees[,] Freedmen[,] and
Abandoned Lands
District of Louisiana[,] 191 Julia Street[,] New Orleans[,] La[.,]
Dec[.] 9[,] 1867

Circular}
No. 18 }

The following instructions, relative to the duties and powers of Agents of the Bureau in this State, are promulgated for the information and guidance of all concerned.

I. All cases of difficulty or disagreement between whites and freed-

---

* Circular No. 18, Headquarters, Bureau of Refugees, Freedmen, and Abandoned Lands, Louisiana, December 9, 1867, reel 26, Records of the Assistant Commissioner for the State of Louisiana, Bureau of Refugees, Freedmen, and Abandoned Lands, 1865–1869, National Archives Microfilm Publication M1027.

men, or between freedmen themselves, will be referred, in the first instance, to the Civil Courts for adjudication.

It is the duty of the Bureau Agents, in all minor cases of complaint where freedmen are concerned, to effect, if possible, an amicable and satisfactory settlement between the parties, without referring the same to the Civil Authorities; but in those cases involving legal questions, and which from their nature are properly cognizable before Civil Tribunals, Bureau Agents are not empowered to make final disposition of the same, nor interfere in any way whatever with the action of the Civil Authorities in such cases. It is their duty to advise freedmen, when necessary, in bringing suits before the Civil Courts; and should the exigencies of the case demand it, they will appear as the freedmen's friend, or attorney.

In all cases where planters or other employers, refuse or neglect to pay wages due freedmen, the Bureau Agents will, if necessary make proper application to the Civil Authorities, for the protection of the laborers in their just rights, as provided by law.

If necessary, to ensure payment to the laborers according to the terms of the contract with employers, the Agent will call upon the Civil Authorities to make such seizures of crops and property, as may be requisite to secure the freedmen their just dues.

In no case will the Bureau Agent proceed to make such seizures, unless the Civil Authorities fail or refuse to give that protection to laborers, which is authorized by existing laws, entitling them to a lien on the crops and movable property for labor performed.

The evidence that the Civil Courts have failed or refused to take action must be clear and positive. The Bureau Agent will then seize and hold a sufficient portion of the crop or property to cover the amount justly due the freedmen, reporting immediately to these Headquarters the action taken by him, together with all other information necessary for a full understanding of the case.

The officers and Agents of the Freedmen's Bureau will in all respects, conform their actions to the provisions of the "Civil Rights Bill" which secures to citizens, of every race and color the right to make and enforce contracts, to sue, be parties, and give evidence, to inherit, purchase, lease, sell, hold and convey real and personal property; and which subjects colored citizens to like punishment pains and penalties as white citizens and to none other any law statute, ordinance, regulation or custom to the contrary notwithstanding, and which further makes it their special duty at the expense of the United States to institute proceedings against all and every person who shall violate the provisions of the act, and to cause him, or them, to be arrested and imprisoned or bailed, as the case may be, for trial before such court of the United States, as by the act, has cognizance of the same.

II. Where outrages are perpetrated on freedmen and the Civil Authorities fail, or refuse, on proper application by the Bureau Agent, to take action to ensure the arrest and trial of the party or parties so offending, it will then be the duty of the Agent to call upon the nearest military commander for sufficient force to arrest the party or parties committing the outrage, but this course will not be taken unless the Civil Authorities have failed, or have refuse to perform their duties as the law directs.

Evidence of such failure, or refusal, will be forwarded to these Headquarters, together with a full and comprehensive report of all the circumstance attending the case.

> By order of
> Lieut. Col. W. H. Wood, 1st U.S. Infantry
> Assistant Commissioner
> J. M. Lee
> 1st Lieut[.] 39th U.S. Infantry
> Actg. Asst. Adjt. Genl.

DOCUMENT 21

A REPORT ON EDUCATION IN NORTH CAROLINA AND A RADICAL SUGGESTION FOR FUNDING FREEDMEN'S SCHOOLS, OCTOBER 31, 1866*

F. A. Fiske, the North Carolina Bureau's Superintendent of Education, was coordinator of educational efforts in the state, bringing together the ef-

* F. A. Fiske to Capt. Jacob F. Chur, October 31, 1866, reel 22, Records of the Assistant Commissioner for the State of North Carolina, Bureau of Refugees, Freedmen, and Abandoned Lands, National Archives Microcopy M843.

forts of the northern benevolent societies, the needs of the freedpeople, and the limited resources of the agency. In this report he outlines the work of his department. In the process, he revealed his views concerning the purpose of education, but he also offered a radical proposal for funding freedmen's schools. The more perceptive Bureau men who had to deal with the problems of Reconstruction on a daily basis recognized the flaws inherent in the Yankee ideological parameters of action and broke with old notions of self-help and the proper role of government. Nevertheless, even among these men it was rare for individuals to argue for action that was extraordinary even for the demands of Reconstruction.

γ   γ   γ

Office of Supt. of Education, B.R.F.& A-L.
Raleigh, N.C. Oct. 21. 1866.

Capt. Jacob F. Chur
A.A.A. Genl. B.R.F.&A-L.
Captain,

In compliance with the order of the Asst. Commiss[ione]r dated 13[th] inst. I have the honor to make the following report of the operations of Freedmen's schools in this State for the year ending Oct. 31, 1866. . . .

It is pleasant to note the constant, rapid progress of the educational work among the Freedmen during the most favorable months for our schools, Nov. Dec. Jan. & Feb., when it reached its height for the year. At the close of Feb., we had 115 schools, 151 teachers & 11,314 pupils. There have, probably, not been less in the State, than 20,000 colored persons under the instruction of from 250 to 300 teachers [totals since the beginning of Reconstruction]. The ages of the former have varied from 5 to 75 years. In one of our schools representatives of four generations in a direct line were to be found—a child of six years, her mother, grand-mother, and great grand-mother, the latter being more than seventy-five years of age. They commenced the alphabet together and, in few months, all learned to read the Bible quite fluently. The middle-aged and some fare advanced in years, as well as the young, might have been found in some of our schools. To meet the wants of a large class of adults, who were unable, on account of their business-avocations, to attend school in the day-time,

Night-Schools

have been established. The pupils in these have been generally of a different class from those attending in the day-time. It has been very cheering to witness the eagerness and youthful enthusiasm with which these adults, after the labors of the day, have engaged in the exercises of the school-room, several of them so far advanced in years as to be compelled to study their lessons by the aid of spectacles. . . . The importance of these schools can hardly be over-estimated inasmuch as a large class of the colored people have not the time at their command to attend any other. Such must be taught in these schools, or remain in the most deplorable ignorance.

Day-Schools

These embrace, of course, by far the greater part of our scholars. Most of the pupils are under twenty years of age, though adults and even aged persons are sometimes found in them—one schools in Raleigh having had a class of adults last year in Geography, (some of whom were parents), who attended in the P.M. after having completed their domestic duties in the morning. The progress of the pupils in these schools has, on the whole, been very encouraging. Attainments have sometimes been made, that would have been commendable in any school of white children of the same age and opportunities in any part of the land. Some public examinations, that I have attended, would have been creditable to any school of the same grade in the North.

Generally the scholars have manifested an unexpected thirst for knowledge and enthusiasm in their studies, and the continuance of this, without essential abatement, indicates that its cause has deeper than a mere love of novelty, and, if properly nourished, will continue to inspire them to higher progress in the future. In view of the sustained interest manifested by them, and the attainment made, it is arguing against the logic of stubborn facts to say that the colored race are not susceptible to intellectual improvement and culture, and that it is an idle and useless experiment to attempt it.

Some of the schools have been partially graded, but it has been impracticable to grade them extensively and thoroughly. As the enterprise is comparatively new, sufficient progress has not yet been made for a perfect system. I have no doubt, however, of the expediency and importance of grading the schools as fast as circumstances will permit. . . .

Teachers

Most of those employed in our schools are sent from the North by various Benevolent Societies. The majority of them are ladies. Only a few gentlemen are enlisted in this work. As a class they seem to have labored faithfully, though of course with different degrees of success, according to their different capacities, tact and fitness for the work. . . . As a general thing a desire for usefulness, in elevating the character and condition of the colored people to a higher and fuller christian manhood, seems to have been their great inspiring motive. . . .

Results

. . . One of these results is that several thousands of colored persons have been brought out of a state of utter ignorance of books and taught to read, so that the Bible is now an open volume to them, and in other books, a new world, intellectually is spread out before them. When taught to read, they are intellectually regenerated and are prepared to enter upon a new career of life. . . . Besides the inspiration imparted to so many minds, and the large amount of valuable instruction given to quicken and expand the intellect and promote its development, the whole drift of the instructions in the school-room has been strongly on the side of good habits, good order and good conduct generally. So that the personal character of the pupils has been in the process of moulding and taking the right direction. They are thus in training to become good and useful citizens and members of society . . .

Means of Support

The means of carrying on most of our schools are chiefly derived from various Benevolent Societies at the North, who hitherto have sent teachers and paid their board, salaries and other expenses. In some places all the expenses have been met by these Societies—in others, the Freedmen have aided to some extent. The Bureau also has aided, as it still does, by furnishing the teachers with rations at officers prices. In some few instances, the Freedmen have met all the expenses of their schools, without aid. A few such schools are now in operation, but none of them have continued long, as the burden is too great for their limited means. . . .

In conclusion I have but one suggestion to make in regard to the work for the future. And that I make with great hesitation and distrust, lest it may seem too radical and impracticable. It has reference to the removal of two grand obstacles to much future progress in this work. The obstacles referred to are the pressing need of proper school buildings and a sufficient supply of well qualified teachers, supported without expense to the Freedmen. With the necessary buildings and teachers, it were [*sic*] comparatively easy fully to supply the great mass of the Freedmen throughout the State, with schools in a single year—but without largely increased facilities for securing these tow indispensable means of success, little further progress can be made, and the masses of the people must remain unreached. The Freedmen have not the ability to provide them, and will not have, for at least two or three years, and then but partially. The Benevolent Societies are compelled, for want of sufficient funds, to curtail their operations, at a time when the cause demands large expansion. In view, therefore, of the discrepancy between the inadequate and declining resources of these Societies, (on whom we have thus far depended), and the growing demands of this work, the only adequate source of help I can see is the national Government. And my suggestion is that application be made to Congress to provide, at the expense of the Government, a sufficient number of buildings and teachers to establish at once a full supply of schools and teachers to meet the educational wants of the ignorant and needy Freedmen. As time advances the latter will require, in large numbers, either school-houses of jails, and the more the former, provided for them with good schools, the less the latter. And the Government can infinitely better afford to educate the race than to support vices and crimes that must grow from their ignorance.

Perhaps the plan suggested may be considered impracticable, but I see at present, no other hope of urging onward the work of educating the Freedmen with sufficient rapidity to meet the pressing wants of an enterprise of such surpassing magnitude and importance.

I take pleasure in acknowledging my indebtedness to various Asst. Supts. And other officers of the Bureau, and especially to the present Supt. of the Central Dist. For valuable assistance often rendered to me in the discharge of my official duties.

> I have the honor, Captain, to be
> Your obedt. Servant
> F. A. Fiske
> Supt. of Education, B.R.F.&A-L.

DOCUMENT NO. 22

WILLIAM J. WHITE ORGANIZES SCHOOLS IN GEORGIA, MARCH 29, 1867–JUNE 4, 1867*

The Freedmen's Bureau's primary role in establishing an educational system for the ex-slaves was that of coordinator of the efforts of others, particularly northern aid societies and the freedpeople themselves. In Georgia, William Jefferson White contributed to this purpose by traveling through the state to organize school associations that he expected would establish and sustain the schools needed to serve their communities. White was one of the rare African Americans on the agency's payroll. He served in the Georgia Bureau from early 1867 through the end of 1868 solely as a promoter of freedmen's education. His work ended with a mixed record. Some of the associations he founded never bore fruit because of white opposition or black poverty.

γ   γ   γ

Bureau of Refugees, Freedmen, and Abandoned Lands
Office Assistant Commissioner, State of Georgia
Macon, Ga., March 29th 1867.

Mr. G. L. Eberhart, State Supt Ed Ga
    Sir,
          I have the honor to report, that I have visited Walthourville, Midway, & Newport, in Liberty county, Thomasville, Bainbridge, Albany, Georgetown, Cuthbert, Dawson, and Americus. In Liberty county, there is but one school for Freedmen that I could learn of. This school is taught by Mr. Maxwell, near Riceboro. I do not think that any thing can be done in this county before next fall. The people are very destitute, and ignorant. They have no school house of their own, but, will have one next fall. In Thomasville, I found one large school, taught by Mr. H. A. Pyne, Assisted by Mrs. Norwood. This school is doing remarkably well. I organized a large Educational Association: of which Rev Jacob Wade, is president. I think, another school can be established at this place.

* William J. White to G. L. Eberhart, March 29, May 27, June 4, 1867, Records of the Superintendent of Education for the State of Georgia, Bureau of Refugees, Freedmen, and Abandoned Lands, 1865–1870, National Archive Microfilm Publication M799.

At Bainbridge, I found a small school, taught by Mr. Castleberry. I organized an association, in that place, with Adam Bruton, as president. They want at this place a competent teacher. A large school can be opened there. I think a considerable sum of money can be raised through the association say 25 or 30 dollars per month. They have a house of their own for a school house. At Newton, I could do nothing at present. At Albany, I found three schools taught by Peter Hines, Miss Betty Outlaw, & Mr. Early. I organized a large association, there of which Brown London is president. They have two good churches, which can be used for school houses. They want, at this place, two competent teachers.

At Georgetown, I found no school, but, the people are very anxious to have one, and are willing to do what they can for its support. They have no school house. I organized an Association, and advised them to purchase at once a piece of ground; which I think they will do very soon—if they are assured of having a teacher, sent them. I found at Cuthbert, one large school, taught by Rev. W. H. Nobles, who, was absent while I was there. I organized an association at that place. I am under the impression that a considerable amount per month, will be raised by the association. They need at this place two competent teachers.

At Dawson, I found a small school taught by Mr. Brim. The people in this section, have been so much oppressed by the whites, that they have done very little for themselves educationally; they are building a house which will be used as a church, and a school house. I do not think that much can be done there before next fall. I could not organize an association, at that place. I next visited Americus, where I found two schools, taught respectively by Mr. Christian, & two daughters, and Mr. Su[lli]van[.] The first, is a very prosperous condition; the other is much smaller, though a very good school. I organized a large association, at that place: They will raise in that place a considerable sum for educational purposes. Everywhere I have visited I spoke to the people upon the subject of Education, Economy, the importance of building up Sabbath schools, of procuring homes for themselves &c—and urge them, to do all they can to support their own schools.

> I have the honor to be
> very respectfully
> your obt servant
> Wm. J. White
> Agt Bureau RF&AL

Bureau of Refugees, Freedmen & Abandoned Lands,
Office Sub. Ass't Commissioner,
Columbus, Ga., May 27th 1867

Mr. Eberhart.
        Dear Sir,
                        I gave Lieut Wagner a statement this morning of the way
I was treated at Talbotton Ga. He will forward it to Headquarters for
further instructions. There is one thing certain. The Rebels, in this section of the States, must be taught a lesson. On my arrival there I was
informed by the colored people that threats had been made by the whites
that our meeting should not be held. I called on the local Bureau Agent.
—and showed him my orders, and explained the object of my visit to
him; I also called on Judge Forbes, of the County court. But they were
determined that the meeting should not be held, and failing in that, they
came to the meeting to get into a row with me by making hostile demonstrations. They also failed in that but frightened the colored so, that
they were afraid to organize an association. They snapped a pistol in the
church where we had our meeting, but I could not see who done it[.]
They cursed just as though they had been in a gambling saloon. It does
really seem to me that something ought to be done, or we might just as
well give it up. I shall remain here until we here from H. Qrs.—as I am
anxious to know what protection I can depend on; before I go any farther, in to this mean country. I had not made the least allusion to politics
or political questions. I will write tomorrow and give account of my operations to this point.

                        I have the honor to be
                        very respectfully
                        your obt servnt
                        Wm J. White

Bureau of Refugees, Freedmen & Abandoned lands,
Office Sub. Ass't Commissioner
Columbus, Ga., June 4th 1867

Mr. G. L. Eberhart, Supt Ed Ga B.R.F[.] and A.L.
                        D[ea]r Sir
                                        Since leaving Headquarters I have
visited Fort Valley and Perry, in Houston Co. Knoxville in Crawford Co.
Butler, in Taylor Co. and Talbotton, in Talbot Co. At Fort Valley, there

are two small schools, taught by G. W. Greene, and Miss Freeman, both colored. The colored people, have a church which can be used for a school house. I organized an Educational Association, numbering one hundred members with officers as follows President Richard Hollinshead, Vice P[resident] John Mathews, Secy C. H. Cupid, and Treasurer Scott Wiggins. Mr. J. R. Griffin, a white citizen offers to give one acre of ground to build a school-house upon. Other whites citizens offer to assist but are opposed to Yankee school teachers[.] At Perry, they have no regular schools—they have a church which can be used for a school house. I organized an Educational Association, there, numbering two hundred members with the following officers Tobey James, President, Alfred Patterson, V[ice] president and S. A. Cobb, Secy & Treas. Mr. George Singleton, a white citizen of the place, offers to give one acre of ground for a school house and Fifty dollars, toward building a school house. It is supposed that a school of 75 or 80 scholars can be raised at his place. Mr. Hase, a white citizen of this county, will give 5 acres of ground for a school house on his plantation, where it is thought a large school could be raised. At Knoxville, they have no school and no church or school house. I could not organize an Association there, but appointed a committee to organize an Association as soon as practicable. Mr. Allen a white citizen of the place proposed to give whatever ground is necessary for school buildings. The people in this county are exceedingly poor, but very anxious to have schools and are willing to do what they can. Wm. Dent, Robert Castleberry & Mr. Mathews are the committee.

At Butler, they have one school, taught by Mrs. Pinckard. They have no church, and no school house of their own. The population in this county is very sparse. The whites are not favorable to colored schools I could not get a meeting to organize an Educational Association.

At Talbotton, they have one school of about one hundred scholars. They have no school house. Colored people have a church, but are not allowed by whites to have school in it. I found the whites, so much opposed to our educational movement that it was impossible to organize an Educational Association.—having made two trials. The colored people being very anxious to do so but very afraid.

> I have the honor to be
> very respectfully
> your obt servt
> Wm J. White
> Agent B.R.F. and [A.]L[.]

DOCUMENT NO. 23

THE BUREAU'S CONTINUED EDUCATIONAL ENDEAVORS IN KENTUCKY, JULY 17, 1868*

On December 11, 1867, Commissioner Howard ordered the discharge of Freedmen's Bureau officers and agents in the border states of Maryland, West Virginia, Kentucky and Tennessee. The agency, however, was to maintain a greatly reduced staff in these states to continue its educational efforts within their borders. The educational activities of the Bureau in this region presaged the work it would do after the federal government restricted its duties throughout the South.

γ   γ   γ

Bureau of Refugees, Freedmen & Abandoned Lands,
Assistant Commissioner's Office, State of Kentucky
Louisville, KY., July 17th, 1868

Hiram H. Hunter
Supt. Schools Central Dist
Louisville, Ky.

Dear Sir;

Under the new organization of the Bureau in this State, you have been assigned to duty in the Educational Department. I wish therefore to call your attention to the following suggestions.

First[:] Your District should be thoroughly inspected and the places where new schools can be started reported to this office. Of the 37,000 colored children in the state only 8000 have yet been gathered into schools. Whenever a score of children can be gotten together a school should be organized. Call a meeting of the freedmen, show them the necessity of education, appoint a board of trustees whose duty it shall be to provide a boarding place for the teacher, to collect the monthly tuition from the pupils, to decide who of the parents are too poor to pay this tuition, and to perform such other duties as you may direct.

Second[:] The freedmen should be urged to secure for themselves

* T. K. Noble to Hiram H. Hunter, July 17, 1868, Registers and Letters Received by the Commissioner of the Bureau of Refugees, Freedmen, and Abandoned Lands, 1865–1872, reel 74, National Archives Microfilm Publication, M752.

school houses during the continuance of the Bureau. Whenever there is no building suitable for school purposes encourage them to buy a lot of ground, and raise what they can in money and labor. Report the result to this office with application for such assistance as in your judgement they may need. More than thirty school houses have been built in this way in Ky during the past year.

Third: The school year under the Bureau system of education commences on the first of October and continues till the 30th of June. In this state however the climate will not prevent the schools from opening at an earlier date. Arrangements for the ensuing year should be entered upon at once. Inspections should be made, educational meetings held, teachers engaged during the coming two months, that as many schools as possible may open in September.

Fourth: Whenever competent teachers cannot be obtained within the limits of your district application for such should be made to this office. Special care should be taken that no teacher be put in charge of a school who is not fitted for the work.

	Very respectfully
	Your obdt Servt
A True Copy	Signed T. K. Noble
H. Weindell	Chief Supt Schools
Clerk	State of Ky

Similar letter sent to

S. C. Hale Supt[erintendent of] Schools Eastern Dist[rict] July 20 /68

V. H. Echorn [Supterintendent Schools] Western [District July] 29/68

[enclosure]

Articles of Agreement

We the undersigned Freedmen Citizens of _____ and vicinity being desirous to have and perpetuate a School in the above named place do agree and hereby bind ourselves by the following articles of agreement.

I. Three persons shall be elected trustees of the School from among the Subscribers themselves. Their duties shall be to provide a suitable boarding place for the teacher, to collect the monthly tuition and pay the same to the teacher, to fix the amount to be paid by each Subscriber for the pupils he may send, to decide who of the parents are too poor to pay the prescribed tuition and to perform such other duties as the Supt. of Schools may direct.

II. The teacher shall be punctual in attendance at School and faithful in imparting instruction to the pupils (who shall obey the lawful commands of the teacher) and shall report monthly to the Bureau as required.

III. The Subscribers shall pay to the Trustees the amount they may require monthly for the support of the School and shall abide the decision of the Trustees as to their ability to pay tuition and no child shall be denied the benefit of the School because the parent of guardian is too poor to pay the required tuition.

Names of Subscribers   *No. of Pupils*

DOCUMENT NO. 24

AN OFFICER STANDS UP FOR THE FREEDPEOPLE'S CIVIL RIGHTS IN TYLER, TEXAS, JUNE 8, 1868*

By the summer of 1868, the Freedmen's Bureau had lost much of its power to protect ex-slaves in the face of white injustice. Since March 1868, Lieutenant Gregory Barrett, Jr., an officer of the 26th United States Infantry, was the Bureau officer for the Texas agency's 30th Subdistrict with headquarters in Tyler in east Texas. He and other Bureau agents throughout the South frequently acted as the freedpeople's attorneys or as their "next friends" or advisors when the ex-slaves ended up in local courts.

γ   γ   γ

Office Sub Asst Com. B. R. F. & A. L.
30 Sub Dist Tyler, Texas, June 8th 1868.

Lieut George A. Vernon
A.A.A. Genl. B.R.F.&A.L.
Austin[,] Texas

    Sir,

        I have the honor to state that the civil officials here whose duty is to select from the voters of the county persons to compose a jury have

* Lt. Gregory Barrett, Jr. to Lt. George A. Vernou, June 8, 1868, reel 10, Records of the Assistant Commissioner for the State of Texas, Bureau of Refugees, Freedmen, and Abandoned Lands, 1865–1869, National Archives Microfilm Publication M821.

failed to put into the jury box the names of any freedman, and as a consequence none but whites, and the great majority of those whites disloyal, compose the juries at this place. The result is that the freedpeople do not get justice before the civil courts.

This morning I was solicited by some freedmen who are charged with killing a stray steer, to attend to their cases in Court as they had no money to pay a lawyer: Before the trial commenced I objected to the array of jurors for the reason that the Officers selecting the jurors had acted corruptly, and had wil[l]fully selected persons as jurors known to be prejudiced against the defendants, with a view to cause them to be convicted, this contrary to the Statutes of the State and the Civil Rights Bill, Section I., that section in my opinion having been violated by the persons selecting the jurors; in this that they did exclude freedmen from ["]full and equal benefit of all laws and proceedings for the security of person and property as it is enjoyed by white citizens.["]

My objection was overruled by the Judge Samuel L. Earle, on the ground that he had no control over the parties selecting jurors: the fallacy of such a decision will readily be perceived by referring to Pashcals Digest: Article 2831, where reasons for an objection to the array is shown, and will be found substantially as I made them to the Court: If the Judge has no control over the matter why provide for challenge of an array of jurors! Who is to decide if a jury has been selected corruptly, if not the Judge?

I have always believed that the civil rights bill intended that freedpeople should have the same rights to sit on juries in rebellious states as white men, and that any action on the part of civil officers to prevent them from so doing was a violation of that law, and I now hold that the officials here have violated that law in discriminating against freedpeople, by not placing their names in the box to be drawn for, and that the judge has decided wrong in denying his jurisdiction over officers who have so acted.

If the freedpeople have not the protection which that law gives them, they had far better be returned to slavery, subject as they are to conviction on the oath of people little given to respect oaths, and to trial before rebel juries.

It may seem strange when I charge that the juries here are disloyal, but such is the fact: They do not believe that the reconstruction laws are legal, that they were enacted by legal authority, nor that they should be obeyed: They will resort to any scheme to defraud a freedman of his wages, and prominent among their schemes is to trump up some charge against them, have them brought to Court for trial, and having them convicted by the ever ready witness who does not believe that a black man has any rights which a white one is bound to respect.

If my view of the decision of the Judge is correct I respectfully request instructions as to what course I shall pursue in the future: If not correct please inform me.

> Very respectfully
> Your obedient Servant
> Gregory Barrett Jr.
> 1st Lieut 26 US. Infantry
> Sub Asst Com'r

DOCUMENT NO. 25

BUREAU INTERVENTION IN AN ILLEGAL APPRENTICESHIP IN KENTUCKY, MARCH 9–13, 1867*

The labor of black children in the former slave states was a valuable commodity and thus an important asset to parents and employers alike. The apprenticeship system, which was supposed to regulate the labor of minors separated from their parents by fate or consent while protecting them from exploitation, provided white labor-hungry employers with opportunities to abuse the system and the rights of black parents. In this particular case, Colonel Charles Johnson reveals the frustration experienced by Bureau agents and officers who lacked the power to correct wrongs as soon as they were discovered. One assumes that military force finally settled the dispute, although it is not known whether or not Eliza Berger filed a civil rights case in federal court against her assailant.

γ   γ   γ

* Col. Charles F. Johnson to Bvt. Brig. Gen. John Ely, March 9, 1867, box 42, Unentered Letters Received, Chief Subassistant Commissioner, Bowling Green, Records of the Subordinate Field Offices, State of Kentucky, Bureau of Refugees, Freedmen, and Abandoned Lands, Record Group 105, National Archives Building, Washington, D.C.

Bureau Refugees, Freedmen & Abandoned Lands,
Head-Quarters Southern Sub-District
Bowling Green, Ky., March 9th 1867.

Bvt Brig Genl Jno Ely
Chief Supt &c
        Louisville Ky
General

I have the honor to transmit the enclosed affidavits in reference to the case of Coffer Berger.

Two attempts have been made by the Bureau to obtain possession of the children without incurring any expense. [B]oth failed, the first by Lieut Lawrence whom they treated with "silent contempt" and the last by myself the result of which is stated in the affidavits of Eliza Berger corroborated by Benjamin Kirkendolph and Reuben Castle.

The Gray family claim that the children are indentured to them. [I]f so the indenture must be illegal as the boy is twelve years of age and the girl between 9 and 10 years old and the parents have not given their consent.

Coffer Berger and his wife are able to support and educate their children and under the circumstances I respectfully ask that I may be authorized to hire a waggon [sic] to convey a squad of the troops stationed at this place, to obtain possession of said children.

                        I am
                    Very Respectfully
                        Your Obt Servt
                            Chas. F. Johnson
                            Col. & Chief Supt.
                            S. Sub Dist

[enclosure]

Coffer Burger (colored) being duly sworn says that his two children Isaac Gallaway Burger and Cynthia Bell Burger are now living at widow Jane Gray[']s who refuses to permit the mother to see the children and will not give them up. Also that Mrs. Gray has in her possession Bedding &c belonging to said Burger. [S]he also refuses to give the bedding up and will not permit the parents to come near the house requests the Bureau to assist him. Mrs. Gray lives in Richland school district about

10 miles from Morgantown on the state road between Russellville &
Morgantown[.]
Bowling Green Ky
Nov 28 1866

his
Coffer X Burger
mark

Witness
L A Reynolds

Sworn and subscribed to before me this 28th day of Nov. 1866.

> Charles F. Johnson
> Col. & Chief Supt
> S. Sub Dist

[endorsement]

Bureau R F & A Lands
Head Qrs S. Sub Dist
Bowling Green Ky
Dec 6th 1866

Respectfully referred to *N. C. Lawrence* Supdt for investigation & report.

   If the within statement is found to be correct Supdt *Lawrence* will
forward the children to this place

   These papers to be returned with report of action.

> Chas. F. Johnson
> Col & Chief Supdt
> S. Sub Dist

[endorsement]

> Bureau Ref F. & A. L.
> Russellville Ky
> March 6th 67.

Respectfully returned as directed with information that no indenture of the within mentioned children has been recorded in the court proceedings of this county.

> Nelson C. Lawrence
> Supt &c

[enclosure]

Eliza Berger (Colored) being duly sworn says that I visited Mrs. Jane Gray at her house in Richland school District, Butler Co Ky, on the 28th day of February, 1867, to obtain my two children. When I arrived and stated my business Mrs. Gray blowed a horn and cried here are niggers come and kill them and her three sons ran towards the house one with a pistol in each hand, another with one pistol and the other with a gun. The one with a gun struck me twice, once on the head and once on the arm as I tried to throw off the blow[.]

I told then that I "did not come for a fuss but only to get my children" and handed them the order for my children from the Bureau they then hit me twelve or more times three of them knocked the order out of my hand into the mud and said "God damn you and Col. Johnson to tell him to go to hell!"

I got in the waggon [*sic*] and drove off.

This was my third attempt to get possession of my children. [T]he first time they threatened to shoot my husband if he ever came for them.

> her
> Eliza X Berger
> mark

Witness

L. A. Reynolds

Wm. E. W. Johnson

The undersigned Benjamin Kirkendolph (colored) and Reuben Castle (cold) were with Eliza Berger at the time of the above states affair occurred and witnessed the transaction and know the above to be true in every particular.

> his
> Benjamin X Kirkendolph
> mark
> his
> Reuben X Castle
> mark

Witnesses
L. A. Reynolds
Wm. E. W. Johnson

Sworn and subscribed to before me this ninth day of March, 1867.

> Charles F. Johnson
> Col. & Chief Supt
> S. Sub Dist

[endorsement]
[—] affidavit of Elisa [*sic*] Berger does not mention name of the man
who struck here with a gun— and ought to have been sworn to before
a civil magistrate, so this if necessary could be used in the U.S. Dist.
Court.

Re[c']d A. C. O. Ky March 11—1867

[endorsement]
Bureau Refugees F and A. Lands,
Asst Coms Office, State of Ky,
Louisville March 12—1867,

Respectfully returned to *Col. C. F. Johnson* Chief Supt &c Bowling
Green Ky, who is hereby authorized to hire a waggon [*sic*] for the purpose of transporting a detachment of soldiers to obtain possession of
the children of *Coffer* and *Elisa* [*sic*] *Berger* (col'd)

By Order of Bvt Brig Gen S. Burbank
Asst Comr State of Ky

> John Ely
> Bvt Brig Genl U.S.V.
> Chief Supt.

DOCUMENT NO. 26

REPORTING OUTRAGES IN TEXAS, MARCH 22, 1867*

During 1867 and 1868, Bureau headquarters in Washington collected information from the various assistant commissioners concerning violence directed against the freedpeople. The assistant commissioners based their reports on information provided by their own subordinates. The following document from Subassistant Commissioner Charles F. Rand is a fairly short report of violent activities, but still gives a good example of how limited the Bureau's power was when it came to protecting the freedpeople even as Military Reconstruction commenced. Marshall, Rand's headquarters town, was in Harrison County in northeast Texas.

γ   γ   γ

Office Sub. Asst. Comr.
Bu. of R. F. and A. L.
Marshall, Texas
March 22nd, 1867

Lieut. J. S. Kickman, U.S.A
A. A. A. Genl Bu. of R. F. and A. L.
State of Texas

Lieutenant,

I have the honor to report in obedience too letter dated March 7th, 1867 just received with names, dates and particulars as far as possible of outrages &c since Jan. 1st, 1867.

1st Jan. 7th Scarborough shot twice at a freedman named Toby Hawkins in Harrison Co. at the residence of Judge Patillo 12 miles from Marshall. I sent a Deputy Sheriff named John Sloan for him but he did not arrest him only told him to come when he got ready and both debuty and prisoner have escaped.

* Bvt. Capt. Charles F. Rand to Lieut. J. S. Kickman, March 22, 1867, reel 32, Records of the Assistant Commissioner for the State of Texas, Bureau of Refugees, Freedmen, and Abandoned Lands, 1865–1869, National Archives Microfilm Publication M821.

2nd Jan.10th James Oliver, Rusk Co., shot a freedman named Sam Knowles through the head because he would not contract with him. I sent the U.S. Deputy Marshal after him forty miles but he escaped to the woods and cannot be captured. [N]o action on the part of civil authorities.

3rd Jan. 12th Freedman name unknown robbed and shot near Depot in Marshall by person in disguise. I could get no clue to the party. If the civil authorities took any action I have never heard of it.

4th Jan. 13th Bill Hall, a freedman, was robbed and shot within a mile of Marshall. [He] was cutting wood near the road. Strangers shot six times only one ball taking effect and that struck him in the elbow ruining his arm forever.

5th Jan. 13th Bob Gell freedman was robbed but not shot as he has some money which satisfied the highwayman. Bob was chopping near Bill Hall robbed by the same man same time and place.

6th Jan. 20th Case reported by freedmen named Ned and James Waterhouse that three freedmen were hanging to a limb near Grand Bluff, Panola Co. and one apparently struck dead by a single blow. The case was reported six days after they were discovered and I did not deem it necessary to make any investigation as it would only be a waste of time.

7th Jan. 30th I arrested Thomas Stackey today who shot a freedman named John Brewer during Christmas tried him and fined him $200 and the cost of the Marshal who arrested him.

8th Feb 14th Try Slaughter near Jefferson, Marion Co. shot at two freedmen named Cornelius and Albert Roseborough. I searched several days for him he kept in the woods and several days after he reported in person and had in his possession a bond for $500 to appear at the next term of the court at Jefferson Marion Co. which will be the end of the case in my opinion.

9th March 3rd Freedboy named John Grimes complained that two men *Wade Anderson* and *Phil Simpson* killed his mother last July that they were now within the gang at Elysian fields Harrison Co and that he wanted [my] assistance to get his sister who was at that place but feared his life would be taken and did not go I could not assist him.

10ᵗʰ March 7ᵗʰ A. S. Rutherford shot and killed instantly a freedman named martin Little at Pink [Tutle] place 14 miles from Marshall because the freedman had reported that he could do more work in a day than Rutherford. I sent the deputy Sheriff for him but he escaped.

11ᵗʰ Feb. 27ᵗʰ Mr. George M. Reeves shot and killed Mr. W. Yumlin at Jefferson, Marion Co. and wounded Mr. M. Summers. Civil Action. Reeves under bond.

> Very Respectfully
> Your Obdt. Servt
> Charles F. Rand
> Bvt Capt V.R.C. and Asst. Comr

DOCUMENT NO. 27

ASSISTANT COMMISSIONER NELSON A. MILES URGES THE FREEDPEOPLE'S PARTICIPATION IN THE FREEDMEN'S SAVINGS BANK, MAY 18, 1868*

The Freedman's Savings and Trust Company, chartered by an act of Congress on March 3, 1865, was a bank designed to encourage the newly freed slaves in the habits of thrift. The bank was not officially a part of the Freedmen's Bureau. However, it was an institution that suited the Bureau's purpose of encouraging the middle class values of free-labor ideology among the ex-slaves. Nelson A. Miles, a Massachusetts native, was the assistant commissioner of the Bureau in North Carolina from April 1867 into mid-October 1868.

* Circular No. 4, Assistant Commissioner, North Carolina, May 18, 1868, reel 20, Records of the Assistant Commissioner for the State of North Carolina, Bureau of Refugees, Freedmen, and Abandoned Lands, 1865–1870, National Archives Microfilm Publication M843.

γ   γ   γ

Bureau of Refugees, Freedmen & Abandoned Lands.
Hd. Qrs. Asst. Commissioner, State of N. C.
Raleigh, N. C. May 18, 1868

Circular No. 4

The Asst. Comr. is desirous of drawing the attention of the colored people of this State to the importance & benefit of the "Freedmen[']s Savings Bank"—branches of which are already in operation in Raleigh,
New Berne, and Wilmington, and in a few days others will be established in Charlotte and Salisbury. This institution was incorporated under an Act of Congress—for the special benefit of those whose earnings
will allow them to lay aside small sums of money; providing a deposi-
tory perfectly safe, & at the same time accumulating interest. "A penny
saved is a penny earned", was the maxim of a wise & great man and one
worthy of being followed.

The Banks will receive monies in small or large amounts, and at the
end of every six months, interest is added to the principal; and thus
every deposit earns something and by this system of compounding interest, the original amount doubles itself every few years.

The colored people of this community are to all intents and purposes
free and independent, but in some respects they are still in bondage or
dependent upon others. So long as they are houseless, without shelter
for their families and without proper apparel and food, so long will their
condition be one of extreme want and dependence; and, the present condition of those who are slaves to habits of idleness, prodigality or intem-
perance, is far worse than their former bondage. A full appreciation of
the liberty, advantages of citizenship, and opportunities for education
granted the race, has been manifested, and the benefits arising therefore
fully realized. *Now* is the time to lay the foundation of future wealth,
prosperity & happiness.

Everything has been done for you that was possible; you must now
carve out your own fortunes. Your future career and success in life must
be determined by your actions. There are but two paths before you: in
one you will find idleness, prodigality, vice, crime, slavery—either mor-
ally or physically—the other presents industry, economy, sobriety, pros-

perity and happiness. One great & important lesson for you to learn, is the value & power of money.

The wealthiest men of our land were, a few years since, among the poorest boys of the country. The[y] acquired wealth & independence by industry, honesty and economy. To save the *first* ten, the *first* hundred, or the *first* thousand dollars is the almost insuperable difficulty one experiences in the task of economy. But the *first ten* dollars *saved*, to save the hundred and thousand becomes easier and accumulating money, instead of a task, gradually, but surely, grows to be a satisfaction & pleasure. Unless the commencement is made, and the foundation laid, you will remain in poverty & want. Let every cent now wasted in purchasing tobacco, liqurs [*sic*], jewelry or fancy clothing, be saved, placed in the Savings Bank, and when enough has been accumulated, but a homestead and thus place yourselves in circumstances both comfortable & independent.

Bear in mind that every dollar deposited is earning interest every day; and while sickness & other causes suspend daily employment, the little sum in the Bank grows larger every hour.

The particular attention of all colored people is called to this opportunity afforded by the Government for their benefit. Soldiers especially should take advantage of this offer, and thus provide for future interests, by depositing each pay-day a portion of their monthly pay, thereby providing something to aid them when their term of service expires.

Let the children be taught to lay aside every penny they get, & when it amounts to ten cents put it in the Savings Bank, and when they arrive at the age of twenty one, they will have sufficient funds to materially aid them in business pursuits. It is not only a matter of economy but a wise policy, to provide against contingencies common to all men, such as sickness, misfortune and their attendants. Put every cent you can spare into the Bank and coming years will show the wisdom of such a course.

> Nelson A. Miles
> Bt. Maj. Gen. U.S.A.
> Assistant Commissioner

DOCUMENT NO. 28

REPORT OF THE SOUTH CAROLINA BUREAU'S INSPECTOR IN THE AGENCY'S LAST ACTIVE MONTHS, OCTOBER 17, 1868*

Erastus Everson served for a time as the South Carolina Bureau's Inspector, which gave him a statewide view of the agency's work there as the agency prepared to limit its role in Reconstruction. He reviewed the progress of the freedpeople with great optimism and claimed for the Bureau a good bit of the credit.

γ   γ   γ

Head Quarters Assistant Commr Bu R F. & A. L.
District of South Carolina Inspector[']s Office
Columbia, S.C. October 17th, 1868

Major Horace Neide USA
Acting Asst. Adjutant General

Major,

I have the honor to submit, for the information of the Assistant Commissioner, the following report of affairs relating to the workings of the Bureau R. F. and A. L., pertaining to this office.

There have been received and acted upon two hundred and seventy six communications since the commencement of the present year. The greater portion of these papers were statements of matters in dispute between freedpeople and planters, from different sections of the state, referred from the office of the Acting Asst. Adjutant General for investigation and final settlement; the most of them containing claims of freedpeople, for the produce of their last year[']s labor, much of which had been shipped to factors undivided, and in several instance entirely appropriated for the payment of the debts of the planter. Such cases, with one exception, have been satisfactorily adjusted. Other papers have

* E. W. Everson to Maj. Horace Neide, October 17, 1868, reel 60, Registers and Letters Received by the Commissioner of the Bureau of Refugees, Freedmen, and Abandoned Lands, 1865–1872, National Archives Microfilm Publication M752.

been received,—and endorsements from superior officers complied with,—regarding titles to land now held by Government, loyalty and previous record certain men holding office, frauds in bounty collection, and examination into cases of murder, and the action of the civil authorities therein, have been investigated and the results of the investigation forwarded.

From inspections made at proper intervals, during the past year, it is gratifying to submit as the result of observation made at such times, the apparent great improvement in the condition of the freedpeople, and their prospects of future success. The improvement made in their habits of industry, frugality, education, and understanding of their situation is all that,—and under the circumstances in many localities more than— could have been expected. Where they have had an equal chance to labor, untrammelled [sic] by prejudices, and combinations of owners of land to bring them to an absolute state of dependency, and submission to any terms they might propose, the freedpeople have done as well, with the means they could control, as have most of the planters, under the difficulties which have embarrassed all, caused by the loss of crops if the two preceeding years.

In the upper counties of the state, although the loss of crops has not so much retarded and lessened the chances for improvement, there have been influences equally as severe: murders of colored men, and of white men [advising] them, or sympathizing with them, and assaults for trivial offences, and for no offence at all excepting difference [of] opinion on the question of the day, have been frequent. For this, until recently redress has been tardy, and in some cases none at all has been had. These differences of opinion in some localities have deprived the freedpeople of the benefit of ordinary claims upon humanity. Compacts for neglecting them have been entered into and physicians even have gone so far forgotten their proffession [sic] and calling as to mutually bind themselves under an agreement not to aid those of the colored people who do not conform to their political opinions. Owners of land have refused to employ them for like reasons: yet under all these adverse circumstances, there has been a spirit of forbearance, and a desire to progress, creditable to any race of people.

In closing, I would respectfully remark, that, having been connected with the Bureau in South Carolina, since the first of January 1866, it is natural to compare the condition of the freedpeople as it was at that time, with the present.

Until recently they have had very little protection, except through the offices of the Bureau.

At that time they were in a state of abject poverty. On the Sea Islands with hardly an exception they were living upon oysters and acorns. Many had no shelter and scarcely clothing to cover their nakedness: no bedding, a third of them sick with small pox, and all suffering form exposure and neglect, and some dying of starvation.

Under the provisions of General Sherman[']s Field Order No[.] 15, the freedpeople were led to believe that the Sea Islands were to be allotted to them, for their exclusive use and were of a disposition to repulse any attempt made by the owners to take possession, or return to their lands, held as they were by rights of certificates given in accordance with the provisions of the order before mentioned.

There were but few schools; there was meagre [*sic*] provision for the sick: many died from neglect and exposure, having sold all they possessed in the country, to enable them to reach the islands.

Today they have the conveniences of life, are prosperous. There has been no realization of the prediction made so often by the people in these localities, that they would retrograde:

Much of this success has been brought about by the work of the Bureau R. F. and A. L.

The lands have been restored to their original owners, without the trouble anticipated. Schools are numerous. The freedpeople are now in a condition (generally) to look after their own necessities, and to provide for them and capable of doing it, if not prevented by outside causes and influences: if they receive the protection given in other communities to free and law abiding citizens. There has been a gradual and satisfactory progression: some have been in too great a hurry: have looked for favorable results too early: some have been without hope, but the present condition of the freedpeople compared with that at the time their necessities demanded the aid, such has been afforded by the services of the Bureau R. F. and A. L. is gratifying and promising of a success, such as should attend the efforts of a civilized and Christian nation in such a cause.

> I am Major,
> Very respectfully,
> Your Obedient Servant
> E. W. Everson
> Inspector

DOCUMENT NO. 29

THE FREEDPEOPLE OF FORT BEND COUNTY, TEXAS, PETITION TO KEEP THE BUREAU, OCTOBER 1868*

The following undated petition, received by the Bureau on October 19, 1868, indicates the freedpeople's concern about their loss of protection once the agency ended most of its operations at the close of the year. It also suggests that the freedpeople believed that the Bureau made a difference. Fort Bend County is to the southwest of Houston and Harris County, but freedpeople throughout the South petitioned the Bureau to continue its activities.

γ   γ   γ

To Major General O. O. Howard

Chief of Bureau of Refugees, Freedmen and Abandoned Lands
Washington D.C.

In view of the coming discontinuance of the Bureau. We the following subscribed citizens of Fort Bend County, Texas, have determined to address ourselves to you, and knowing your influence, hope that having gained your co-operation, we will have this, our petition, granted.

We, not only of this county, but as a people throughout the State[,] cannot do without the Bureau. If deprived of its assistance and protection, we will be left at the mercy of unprincipled men, who will find in us objects upon which to vent the accumulated malice of years. These men anxiously await the withdrawal of the Bureau, and do not hesitate to proclaim openly how they intend acting upon its discontinuance.

The Courts can afford us little or no protection. We cannot, when miles distant from a County-Seat, lay our complaints, even if we dared to do so, we have no money to pay lawyers with, and in any case, judgement is almost sure to be against us.

With very few exceptions, those who legislate for us, know nothing of our real condition. Were it but possible that those who can afford us

* Andrew Smith et al. to Maj. Gen. O. O. Howard, [October 1868?], reel 60, Registers and Letters Received by the Commissioner of the Bureau of Refugees, Freedmen, and Abandoned Lands, 1865–1872, National Archives Microfilm Publication M752.

protection could see us as we really do exist, as we drag through life, met by curses and blows, we know that they would give us what we ask— protection. The intentions of the Emancipator will have been miscarried the moment Congress leaves us to ourselves. We are men and can fight, but our Liberator intended that plowing not killing, should be our business.

In the cities and towns of Texas, the Freedman *has* to suffer inumerable [*sic*] wrongs, but on plantations, our lives are spent in fear and misery; and when the Bureau is withdrawn, and our last friend gone, we can only pray for strength to bear up in the darkness of such an hour.

Placing our trust in Heaven, and praying for the continued friendship and interest of you our friend in the past.

We Subscribe ourselves

With deepest gratitude and Respect

Andrew Smith [and 67 other signatories]

CONCLUSION

Bureau agents and officers began Reconstruction with the belief that the laws of the nation had to be enforced in the erstwhile Confederacy and that the Union could never be restored until white and black Southerners respected those laws. Respect for these laws would promote the orderly society in which the new free-labor system would flourish, which would be beneficial to both ex-masters and ex-slaves. As Reconstruction progressed, however, white intransigence convinced the majority of Bureau men that ex-Confederates were the real challenge to preserving the fruits of victory, not "ignorant" freedpeople. Bureau men assumed that the freedpeople, because of the damage done by slavery, required careful monitoring and education, but they came to see the ex-slaves as the federal government's true allies. Officers and agents had hoped that by serving as the freedpeople's guardian they would leave them better off and fit for enjoying their new status. That they failed was not so much for want of effort on their part.

White Southerners, for the most part, acted as if the government had buried the Bureau even before the agency had breathed its last breath. Not all Northerners had accepted the Bureau as a positive extension of the federal government's authority. However, there were Northerners who recognized the positive role the agency had played during the years of Reconstruction and lamented the agency's demise. Bureau officials and, more importantly, the freedpeople understood that the agency had had a positive influence on the course of Reconstruction and feared for the future.

During 1868, Bureau men continued to perform their duties (*See Document No. 28.*) knowing very well that when they soon closed their offices they would be leaving their work unfinished. In January 1868 Rockingham, North Carolina, agent William MacFarland warned, "to discontinue the Bureau will retard reconstruction and plunge the Government into deeper trouble." Other agents in their reports to their superiors expressed their fears that the freedpeople were going to have difficult times without the Bureau.

Throughout 1868, the last year that the Bureau acted broadly in the arena of Reconstruction, freedpeople petitioned the government to keep the agency alive. (*See Document No. 29.*) They continued to flock to the offices of agents indicating by their actions that they still believed the agency had some worth. In January 1870, John W. Alvord in his last education report recounted a meeting in Augusta, Georgia, at which the freedpeople learned that the Bureau was abolished. When asked to raise their hands if they opposed such a course of action, "their came up a whole forest of *arms* from all parts of the house." Indeed, even as the agency shuttered its operations in Alabama, Huntsville agent John H. Wager reported, freedpeople and white Unionists were "not yet able to understand that its agents have not the authority or power to protect, defend and secure them their rights, as in the past." Freedpeople, despite their disappointments, still considered the Bureau to be a useful ally because it had made a difference, even if a fleeting one, in how they defined their new status.

White and black Southerners would continue to negotiate labor arrangements, personal relationships, legal claims, and relative rights without the Bureau's intervention and the freedpeople would have to wait until the next century to begin to claim what the Yankees had promised them. Still, the Bureau had done its best to secure the promise made by emancipation and the various laws and amendments that made up the positive side of the nation's Reconstruction efforts. The Bureau made it clear that freedpeople would never again be slaves and its officials reinforced the freedpeople's understanding that they had rights white men had to respect.

SELECT BIBLIOGRAPHY

Abbott, Martin. *The Freedmen's Bureau in South Carolina, 1865–1872.* Chapel Hill: University of North Carolina Press, 1967.

Abbott, Richard H. *The Republican Party and the South, 1855–1877.* Chapel Hill: University of North Carolina Press, 1986.

Alderson, William T. "The Influence of Military Rule and the Freedmen's Bureau on Reconstruction in Virginia, 1865–1870." Ph.D. diss., Vanderbilt University, 1952.

Alexander, Robert Sue. *North Carolina Faces the Freedmen: Race Relations during Presidential Reconstruciton, 1865–1867.* Durham, NC: Duke University Press, 1985.

Belz, Herman. *A New Birth of Freedom: The Republican Party and Freedmen's Rights, 1861–1865.* Westport, CT: Greenwood Press, 1976.

Bentley, George R. *A History of the Freedmen's Bureau.* Philadelphia: University of Pennsylvania Press, 1954; New York: Octagon Books, 1974.

Berlin, Ira, et al. *Freedom: A Documentary History of Emancipation, 1861–1867.* Cambridge, Eng.: Cambridge University Press, 1982–.

———. *Slaves No More: Three Essays on Emancipation and the Civil War.* Cambridge, Eng.: Cambridge University Press, 1992.

Bowen, David Warren. *Andrew Johnson and the Negro.* Knoxville: University of Tennessee Press, 1989.

Butchart, Ronald E. *Northern Schools, Southern Blacks, and Reconstruction: Freedmen's Education, 1862–1875.* Westport, CT: Greenwood Press, 1980.

Campbell, Randolph B. *Grass-Roots Reconstruction in Texas, 1865–1880.* Baton Rouge: Louisiana State University Press, 1997.

Carpenter, John A. *Sword and Olive Branch: Oliver Otis Howard.* Pittsburgh: University of Pittsburgh Press, 1964; New York: Fordham University Press, 1999.

Carter, Dan T. *When the War Was Over: The Failure of Self-Reconstruction in the South, 1865–1867.* Baton Rouge: Louisiana State University Press, 1985.

Cimbala, Paul A. *Under the Guardianship of the Nation: The Freedmen's Bureau and the Reconstruction of Georgia, 1865–1870.* Athens: University of Georgia Press, 1997.

———. "Lining Up to Serve: Wounded and Sick Union Officers Join Veteran Reserve Corps During Civil War, Reconstruction." *Prologue* 35 (Spring 2003): 38–49.

——— and Randall M. Miller, eds., *The Freedmen's Bureau and Reconstruction: Reconsiderations.* New York: Fordham University Press, 1999.

Click, Patricia C. *Time Full of Trial: The Roanake Island Freedmen's Colony, 1862–1867* Chapel Hill: University of North Carolina Press, 2001.

Cohen, William. *At Freedom's Edge: Black Mobility and the Southern White Quest for Racial Control, 1861–1915*. Baton Rouge: Louisiana State University Press, 1991.

Cox, LaWanda. "From Emancipation to Segregation: National Policy and Southern Blacks." In *Interpreting Southern History: Historiographical Essays in Honor of Sanford W. Higginbothom*, eds. John B. Boles and Evelyn Thomas Nolan, 199–253. Baton Rouge: Louisiana State University Press, 1987.

———. *Lincoln and Black Freedom: A Study in Presidential Leadership*. Columbia: University of South Carolina Press, 1981.

Crouch, Barry. *The Freedmen's Bureau and Black Texans*. Austin: University of Texas Press, 1992.

Currie-McDaniel, Ruth. *Carpetbagger of Conscience: A Biography of John Emory Bryant*. Athens: University of Georgia Press, 1987; New York: Fordham University Press, 1999.

Dawson, Joseph G. III. *Army Generals and Reconstruction, Louisiana, 1862–1877*. Baton Rouge: Louisiana State University Press, 1982.

Duncan, Russell. *Freedom's Shore: Tunis Campbell and the Georgia Freedmen*. Athens: University of Georgia Press, 1994.

Engs, Robert Francis. *Freedom's First Generation: Black Hampton, Virginia, 1861–1890*. Philadelphia: University of Pennsylvania Press, 1979.

Everly, Elaine Cutler. "The Freedmen's Bureau in the National Capital." Ph.D. diss., George Washington University, 1972.

Farmer, Mary J. "Freed*women* and the Freed*men*'s Bureau: Race, Gender, and Public Policy in the Age of Emancipation." Ph.D. diss., Bowling Green State University, 2000.

Finley, Randy. *From Slavery to Uncertain Freedom: The Freedmen's Bureau in Arkansas, 1865–1869*. Fayetteville: University of Arkansas Press, 1996.

Fitzgerald, Michael W. *The Union League Movement in the Deep South: Politics and Agricultural Change during Reconstruction*. Baton Rouge: Louisiana State University Press, 1989.

Foner, Eric. *Reconstruction: America's Unfinished Revolution, 1863–1877*. New York: Harper and Row, 1988.

Foster, Gaines M. "The Limitations of Federal Health Care for the Freedmen, 1862–1868." *Journal of Southern History* 48 (August 1982): 349–72.

Frankel, Noralee. *Freedom's Women: Black Women and Families in Civil War Era Mississippi*. Bloomington: Indiana University Press, 1999.

Fuke, Richard Paul. *Imperfect Equality: African Americans and the Confines of White Racial Attitudes in Post-Emancipation Maryland*. New York: Fordham University Press, 1999.

Ganus, Clifton L., Jr., "The Freedmen's Bureau in Mississippi." Ph.D. diss., Tulane University, 1953.

Gerteis, Louis. *From Contraband to Freedmen: Federal Policy Toward Southern Blacks, 1861–1865.* Westport, CT: Greenwood Press, 1973.

Holbrook, Stephen P. *Freedmen, the Fourteenth Amendment, and the Right to Bear Arms, 1866–1876* (Westport, CT: Praeger, 1998)

Holt, Sharon Ann. *Making Freedom Pay: North Carolina Freedpeople Working for Themselves, 1865–1900.* Athens: University of Georgia Press, 2000.

Hope, W. Martin, and Jason H. Silverman. *Relief and Recovery in Post-Civil War South Carolina: A Death by Inches.* Lewiston, NY: Edwin Mellen Press, 1997.

Jackson, LaVonne Roberts. "'Freedom and Family': The Freedmen's Bureau and African-American Women in Texas in the Reconstruction Era, 1865–1872." Ph.D. diss., Howard University, 1996.

Kaestle, Carl F. *Pillars of the Republic: Common Schools and American Society, 1780–1860.* New York: Hill and Wang, 1983.

Lanza, Michael L. *Agrarianism and Reconstruction Politics: The Southern Homestead Act.* Baton Rouge: Louisiana State University Press, 1990.

Litwack, Leon F. *Been in the Storm So Long: The Aftermath of Slavery.* New York: Alfred A. Knopf, 1979.

Lowe, Richard. "The Freedmen's Bureau and Local Black Leadership." *Journal of American History* 80 (December 1993): 989–98.

———. "The Freedmen's Bureau and Local White Leaders in Virginia." *Journal of Southern History* 64 (August 1998): 455–72.

McFeely, William S. *Yankee Stepfather: General O. O. Howard and the Freedmen.* New Haven, CT: Yale University Press, 1968.

McPherson, James M. *The Struggle for Equality: Abolitionists and the Negro in the Civil War and Reconstruction.* Princeton, NJ: Princeton University Press, 1964.

Morris, Robert C. *Reading, 'Riting, and Reconstruction: The Education of Freedmen in the South, 1861–1870.* Chicago: University of Chicago Press, 1981.

Osthaus, Carl. R. *Freedmen, Philanthropy, and Fraud: A History of the Freedmen's Savings Bank.* Urbana: University of Illinois Press, 1976.

Oubre, Claude F. *Forty Acres and a Mule: The Freedmen's Bureau and Black Land Ownership.* Baton Rouge: Louisiana State University Press, 1978.

Pearson, Reggie L. "'There Are Many Sick, Feeble, and Suffering Freedmen': The Freedmen's Bureau's Health-Care Activities during Reconstruction in North Carolina, 1865–1868." *North Carolina Historical Review,* 79 (April 2002): 141–81.

Peirce, Paul S. *The Freedmen's Bureau: A Chapter in the History of Reconstruction.* Iowa City: State University of Iowa, 1904.

Phillips, Paul David. "A History of the Freedmen's Bureau in Tennessee." Ph.D. diss., Vanderbilt University, 1964.

Richardson, Heather Cox. *The Death of Reconstruction: Race, Labor, and Politics in the Post-Civil War North, 1865-1901*. Cambridge, MA: Harvard University Press, 2001.

Richardson, Joe M. *Christian Reconstruction: The American Missionary Association and Southern Blacks, 1861-1890*. Athens: University of Georgia Press, 1986.

Richter, William L. *Overreached on All Sides: The Freedmen's Bureau Administrators in Texas, 1865-1868*. College Station: Texas A & M University Press, 1991.

Rodrigue, John C. *Reconstruction in the Cane Fields: From Slavery to Freedom in Louisiana's Sugar Parishes, 1862-1880*. Baton Rouge: Louisiana State University Press, 2001.

Rose, Willie Lee. *Rehearsal for Reconstruction: The Port Royal Experiment*. Indianapolis: Bobbs-Merrill, 1964.

Royce, Edward. *The Origins of Southern Sharecropping*. Philadelphia: Temple University Press, 1993.

Saville, Julie. *The Work of Reconstruction: From Slave to Wage Laborer in South Carolina, 1860-1870*. Cambridge, Eng.: Cambridge University Press, 1994.

Savitt, Todd L. "The Politics of Medicine: The Georgia Freedmen's Bureau and the Organization of Health Care, 1865-1866." *Civil War History* 28 (March 1982): 45-64.

Sefton, James E. *The United States Army and Reconstruction, 1865-1877*. Baton Rouge: Lousiana State University Press, 1967.

Stanley, Amy Dru. *From Bondage to Contract: Wage Labor, Marriage, and the Market in the Age of Slave Emancipation*. Cambridge, Eng.: Cambridge University Press, 1998.

Trefousse, Hans L. *Andrew Johnson: A Biography*. New York: W. W. Norton, 1989.

Tunnell, Ted. *Edge of the Sword: The Ordeal of Carpetbagger Marshall H. Twitchell in the Civil War and Reconstruction*. Baton Rouge: Louisiana State University Press, 2001.

Vorenberg, Michael. *Final Freedom: The Civil War, the Abolition of Slavery, and the Thirteenth Amendment*. Cambridge, Eng.: Cambridge University Press, 2001.

Washington, Reginald. "The Freedmen's Bureau Preservation Project," 34 *Prologue* (summer 2002): 144-48.

White, Howard A. *The Freedmen's Bureau in Louisiana*. Baton Rouge: Louisiana State University Press, 1970.

Williams, Lou Falkner. *The Great South Carolina Ku Klux Klan Trials, 1871-1872*. Athens: University of Georgia Press, 1996.

Zipf, Karin L. "'The WHITES shall rule the land or die': Gender, Race, and Class in North Carolina Reconstruction Politics." *Journal of Southern History* 65 (August 1999): 499-534.

INDEX

Ahrens, Louis, 30

aid societies, 5–6, 45, 80, 82–83, 85, 88, 112, 170, 171

Alvord, John W., 78, 80, 81, 82, 83, 87, 88, 196

American Freedmen's Inquiry Commission, 7–8

American Missionary, The, 82

American Missionary Association, 6, 81, 84, 85, 88

apprenticeship, 93, 98, 180–85

Armstrong, Samuel C., 28

Army (United States), 20–21, 29, 30–31, 128, 132, 152

and contraband policy, 4

and Freedmen's Bureau, 19, 28, 31, 98–99, 102

and civil authorities, 103

Army Appropriations Act (1866): and school buildings, 87

Baird, Absalom, 14, 15, 45, 61, 85

Barney, J. W., 130–34

Barrett, Gregory, Jr., 178–80

Barry Farm, 58

Bentley, George R., ix, 14, 88

Black, J. D., 37

black codes, 71

Blanding, Jabez, 38

bounties, 106–8

Brown, De Witt C., 34, 37

Brown, Orlando, 17, 19, 30, 35, 41, 42, 54, 62, 64, 67, 70, 95, 96, 125, 126

Bruton, Adam, 173

Bryant, John Emory, 28, 29, 66, 103, 149–52

Buckley, C. W., 26–27, 84

Burbank, Sidney, 50

Bureau of Refugees, Freedmen, and Abandoned Lands. *See* Freedmen's Bureau

Butler, Benjamin, 4

Butler, John H., 82

Campbell, Tunis G., 26

Carse, George B., 32

charity. *See* poor relief.

civil rights, 91–106, 178–80

Civil Rights Act (1866), 24, 99–101, 165, 166, 179

Clapp, Dexter E., 127–30

confiscation acts, 3, 53

contrabands: blacks as, 4

and aid societies, 5–6

contracts. *See* free-labor system

Conway, Thomas, 14, 15

courts: black testimony in, 91

Freedmen's Bureau tribunals, 94–95, 96–97, 99

civilian, 95, 96, 97–98, 100–1, 147, 165–67, 178

military tribunals, 99

federal, 100

Craig, Samuel, 33, 36

Curtis, George William, 6

Daily Advertiser and Union (Auburn, N.Y.): and freedpeople, 7

Dalton, George, 48

Davis Bend, 65

Dean, E. L., 89

De Forest, John William, 32, 34

De Hanne, J. V., 49

de la Mesa, C. A., 33

Democratic party, 104, 105

Douglass, Frederick, 6

Duvell, E. V., 136–38